Pro SQL Database for Windows Azure

SQL Server in the Cloud
Second Edition

Scott Klein
Herve Roggero

Pro SQL Database for Windows Azure: SQL Server in the Cloud

ISBN-13 (pbk): 978-1-4302-4395-3

ISBN-13 (electronic): 978-1-4302-4396-0

President and Publisher: Paul Manning
Lead Editor: Jonathan Gennick
Technical Reviewer: Thomas LaRock
Editorial Board: Steve Anglin, Ewan Buckingham, Gary Cornell, Louise Corrigan, Morgan Ertel, Jonathan Gennick, Jonathan Hassell, Robert Hutchinson, Michelle Lowman, James Markham, Matthew Moodie, Jeff Olson, Jeffrey Pepper, Douglas Pundick, Ben Renow-Clarke, Dominic Shakeshaft, Gwenan Spearing, Matt Wade, Tom Welsh
Coordinating Editor: Kevin Shea
Copy Editor: James Compton
Compositor: SPi Global
Indexer: SPi Global
Artist: SPi Global
Cover Designer: Anna Ishchenko

Distributed to the book trade worldwide by Springer Science+Business Media New York, 233 Spring Street, 6th Floor, New York, NY 10013. Phone 1-800-SPRINGER, fax (201) 348-4505, e-mail orders-ny@springer-sbm.com, or visit www.springeronline.com.

For information on translations, please e-mail rights@apress.com, or visit www.apress.com.

Apress and friends of ED books may be purchased in bulk for academic, corporate, or promotional use. eBook versions and licenses are also available for most titles. For more information, reference our Special Bulk Sales–eBook Licensing web page at www.apress.com/bulk-sales.

Any source code or other supplementary materials referenced by the author in this text is available to readers at www.apress.com/9781430246831. For detailed information about how to locate your book's source code, go to www.apress.com/source-code.

To my wonderful wife, children, and family. Without them,
I'd be nothing.-Scott To my dear wife, Frederique.

—Herve

Contents at a Glance

Foreword xvii

About the Authors.. xix

About the Technical Reviewer xxi

Acknowledgments.. xxiii

Introduction xxv

■Chapter 1: Getting Started with SQL Database 1

■Chapter 2: Design Considerations 23

■Chapter 3: Security..45

■Chapter 4: Data Migration and Backup Strategies 67

■Chapter 5: Programming with SQL Database 99

■Chapter 6: SQL Reporting 125

■Chapter 7: SQL Data Sync..143

■Chapter 8: Windows Azure and ASP.NET 165

■Chapter 9: Designing for High Performance 183

■Chapter 10: Federations 207

■Chapter 11: Performance Tuning 219

■Chapter 12: Windows Azure Mobile Services..241

■Appendix A: SQL Database Management Portal 257

■Appendix B: Windows Azure SQL Database Quick Reference........................275

Index..283

Contents

Foreword xvii

About the Authors.. xix

About the Technical Reviewer xxi

Acknowledgments... xxiii

Introduction xxv

■Chapter 1: Getting Started with SQL Database 1

Introduction to Cloud Computing...1

    Who Is Doing What in the Cloud?...2

    Typical Cloud Services...2

Discovering the Microsoft Azure Platform 3

    Why Microsoft Azure?..3

    About Geographic Locations..4

    Storing Data in Azure..5

SQL Database Primer 6

    Registering for Azure..6

    Creating a SQL Database Instance 7

    Configuring the Firewall 10

    Connecting with SQL Server Management Studio..11

    Creating Logins and Users..15

    Assigning Access Rights..18

    Understanding Billing for SQL Database..18

Limitations in SQL Database 19

    Security 20

    Backups 20

    Objects 21

    Miscellaneous 21

    Drivers and Protocols 22

Summary 22

■Chapter 2: Design Considerations 23

Design Factors 23

    Offsite Storage 23

    High Availability 23

    Performance 24

    Data Synchronization 27

    Direct vs. Serviced Connections 27

    Pricing 28

    Security 29

    Review of Design Factors 29

Design Patterns 29

    Direct Connection 29

    Smart Branching 30

    Transparent Branching 31

    Sharding 31

    Offloading 35

    Aggregation 36

    Mirroring 37

Combining Patterns 37

    Transparent Branching + RWS 37

    Cascading Aggregation 38

Sample Design: Application SLA Monitoring 39

    Pre-Azure Application Architecture 39

    Azure Implementation 40

Other Considerations 41

    Blob Data Stores 42

    Edge Data Caching 42

    Data Encryption 43

    SaaS Applications and Federations 43

Summary 43

■Chapter 3: Security 45

Overview 45

    Confidentiality 45

    Integrity 46

    Availability 46

Securing Your Data 48

    Encryption 48

    Hashing 50

    Certificates 55

Access Control 59

    Authentication (AUTHN) 59

    Authorization (AUTHZ) 60

    SQL Database Firewall 65

    Internal Firewalls 65

Compliance 65

Summary 66

■Chapter 4: Data Migration and Backup Strategies 67

Migrating Databases and Data to SQL Azure 67

    The Import/Export Service 68

    Generate and Publish Scripts Wizard 83

    The bcp Utility 92

SQL Azure Backup Strategies 95

    Copying a Database 95

    Backing Up Using the Import/Export Features 97

    Third-Party Backup Products 97

Summary 98

■ **Chapter 5: Programming with SQL Database** **99**

Application Deployment Factors 99

    On-Premises Application 100

    Azure-Hosted Application 100

    Which to Choose? 101

Connecting to SQL Database 101

    ADO.NET 102

    ODBC 107

    sqlcmd 109

WCF Data Services 114

    Creating a Data Service 114

    Connecting the Service to the Model 115

    Creating the Client Application 117

Best Practices 119

    Transient Fault Handling Application Block 120

    Using the Transient Fault Handling Application Block 121

Summary 123

■ **Chapter 6: SQL Reporting** **125**

SQL Reporting Overview 125

    Architecture 126

    Feature Comparison 127

Provisioning Your SQL Reporting Server 128

Creating a Report 130

    Creating the SQL Database Data Source 131

    Creating the Report Design 136

Deploying the Report...137

Security 139

    Roles...139

Using the Management Portal 141

Pricing 142

Summary..142

■**Chapter 7: SQL Data Sync**..**143**

Understanding SQL Data Sync 143

    Why the Need? 143

    The Basic Scenario...144

    Common Data Sync Scenarios 145

    Architecture...145

Configuring Synchronization 147

    Provision a SQL Data Sync Server 147

    Creating a Sync Group 149

    Defining the Hub and Member Databases 150

    Selecting Tables to be Synchronized 156

    Deploying the Sync Group 159

    Debugging and the Log Viewer 160

    Looking at the Synchronized Data 161

    Editing Data and Resynchronizing 162

Data Sync Limitations 163

Data Sync Best Practices 163

    Design Considerations..163

    Initial Synchronization 164

    Security 164

    Sync Schedule 164

Summary..164

Chapter 8: Windows Azure and ASP.NET 165

Creating a Cloud Service 165

Creating a Windows Azure Project 168

Configuring Your Development Environment 168

Creating Your First Visual Studio Cloud Project 169

Connecting a GridView to SQL Database 173

Deployment and Configuration Files...176

Deploying an ASP.NET Application in Windows Azure...179

Summary 181

Chapter 9: Designing for High Performance 183

General Performance Concepts...183

Chatty vs. Chunky 183

Lazy Loading..183

Caching..184

Asynchronous User Interface..184

Parallel Processing 185

Shards 185

Coding Strategies Summary 185

Building a Shard..186

Designing the Shard Library Object...187

Managing Database Connections 188

Reading Using the Shard 190

Caching..193

Updating and Deleting Records in the Shard...194

Adding Records to the Shard...196

Managing a Shard 198

Managing Exceptions 198

Managing Performance 199

Working with Partial Shards 202

Managing Transaction Consistency 203

Managing Foreign Key Constraints..203

Designing a Multitenant System 204

Creating Vertical Partition Shards 206

Big Data with Hadoop for Windows Azure 206

Summary 206

Chapter 10: Federations 207

Introducing Federations 207

Federations versus Sharding 207

Why Use Federations? 208

Federations Overview 208

Creating More Federations 213

Managing Federations 214

Advanced Considerations 216

Limitations 216

Sharding Library 217

Summary 218

Chapter 11: Performance Tuning 219

What's Different with SQL Database 219

Methods and Tools 219

Coding Implications 220

Tuning Techniques 220

Dynamic Management Views 220

Connection Pooling 223

Execution Plans with SSMS 224

Execution Plans with the Management Portal 228

Query Performance with the Management Portal 230

Indexing 231

Indexed Views 235

Stored Procedures 236

Provider Statistics 238

Application Design 239

Summary 240

■ **Chapter 12: Windows Azure Mobile Services** **241**

Getting Started 241

Data 248

Browse 248

Columns 249

Permissions 249

Script 251

Advanced Settings 251

Push 251

Identity 252

Scale 253

Summary 255

■ **Appendix A: SQL Database Management Portal** **257**

Launching the Management Portal 257

Administration Features 259

Run T-SQL Statements 259

View Execution Plans 261

Monitor Current Query Performance 262

Design Features 263

Designing Tables 263

Designing Views 270

Designing Stored Procedures 271

Summary 273

▓**Appendix B: Windows Azure SQL Database Quick Reference**................................**275**

Supported T-SQL Statements 275

Partially Supported T-SQL Statements 276

Unsupported T-SQL Statements 280

Supported Data Types 280

Index...**283**

Foreword

My journey from box software engineer to cloud service engineer began over four years ago when I moved into the SQL cloud team at Microsoft. I would like to say it was my brilliant foresight that led me to make the jump, but the truth is it was a fortuitous accident resulting from a group reorganization. I couldn't be more thankful for the opportunity, as working on Windows SQL Azure has been the most interesting and exciting project of my career. The journey to build a relational database as a service was not a straightforward one. We tried several different incarnations and had to back out from a couple of dead ends before we landed on the service you see today.

We also went through several iterations on the value proposition. What are we building? What is it good for? How does it help customers? There were a lot of naysayers who said a SQL relational database had no place in the cloud. Some thought cloud was just a fad and not really any different from what people already did. We believed differently. We knew you could have the benefits of a relational database system (a well understood model and programming APIs, and an existing rich tooling ecosystem) and combine them with the best of a cloud service (high availability, easy and fast provisioning, drastically reduced management, and a pay as you go model).

Clearly it is resonating with customers. We are seeing adoption from all sorts of usage scenarios. Some are well known scenarios of simple web sites, departmental enterprise applications. Others are net new scenarios like the one we call *data hub*, which is about sharing between islands of data, such as a company and its outlet sites, a company and its vendors/suppliers or between multiple companies that are collaborating. Our most common scenario is a mixture of old and new, the SaaS Line of Business application. This includes cloud-only companies as well as existing box software vendors who are moving their software to the cloud. Moving to an SaaS is a huge advantage for these companies. It allows them to streamline the sales cycle, focus their resources on their core competency, and easily extend their global market reach.

However, running a cloud service is not the same as building box software. While the business logic of the applications is pretty straightforward to get up and running, especially if you have existing code from an on-prem application; keeping it running well in the cloud is not easy. Security is something that goes beyond compliant algorithms and best practices for your customer. You are on the hook to prevent, or least identify and stop, malicious attacks on your system. You have to make sure you isolate one tenant from another. Availability and performance are things customers take for granted and they are your responsibility. Where there is a problem, you get the call at that wakes you out of bed. Troubleshooting is much harder. Root-causing an issue on a single SQL database can be difficult. How do you do it when you have 1000 SQL databases? There are also model shifts to absorb, like embracing failure and building compensation into your system. One of the hardest ones SQL Database customers struggle with is the notion that they have to scale out instead of scaling up. This is hard because scale up was the preferred pattern in the box world and scaling out is a lot harder. There is also a lot of new stuff to deal with, like multi-tenancy. How do I host 1000 customers? Which parts say isolated and which parts are shared? How do I do billing? How do I measure COGS (and make sure they are low enough!).

These are not trivial problems. In order to tackle them efficiently you need to understand the capabilities of the platform you are running on. Which of the problems can it can help you to solve and for which ones are you on your own? Authors Scott Klein and Herve Roggero have done a great job walking you through the ins and outs of Windows Azure SQL Database. From Programming Model to Migration Strategies, Security to Scale out. Whether you are focused on using the latest high-level interfaces like WCF and OData or diving into the details of performance, tuning the book covers everything you need to know about SQL Database.

Rick Negrin
Lead Program Manager
Windows Azure SQL Database

About the Authors

Scott Klein is a Windows Azure Technical Evangelist for Microsoft focusing on Windows Azure SQL Database (formally known as SQL Azure) and related cloud-ready data services. He started his career in SQL Server with version 4.2 and has worked with every version since then during his 20+ year career. Prior to joining Microsoft he was a SQL Server MVP and then became one of the first four SQL Azure MVPs. Scott is the author or coauthor of several books for both Wrox and Apress, including this one. Scott can be found talking about Windows Azure SQL Database wherever he can get people to listen to him. You can reach Scott at SQLScott@live.com and read some of his musings at http://www.scottlklein.com.

Herve Roggero, Windows Azure MVP, is the founder of Blue Syntax Consulting, a company specializing in cloud computing products and services. Herve's experience includes software development, architecture, database administration and senior management with both global corporations and startup companies. Herve holds multiple certifications, including MCDBA, MCSE, and MCSD. He also holds a Master's degree in Business Administration from Indiana University. Herve is the co-author of *Pro SQL Database for Windows Azure* from Apress. For more information, visit www.bluesyntax.net.

About the Technical Reviewer

Thomas LaRock is a seasoned IT professional with over a decade of technical and management experience. Currently serving as a Technical Evangelist for Confio Software, Thomas has progressed through several roles in his career, including programmer, analyst, and DBA. Thomas holds an MS degree in Mathematics from Washington State University and is a member of the Usability Professionals' Association. Thomas currently serves on the Board of Directors for the Professional Association for SQL Server (PASS), and is also a SQL Server MVP. Thomas can also be found blogging at http://thomaslarock.com and is the author of *DBA Survivor: Become a Rock Star DBA* (http://dbasurvivor.com).

Acknowledgments

This book exists because of the diligence and patience of a handful of individuals to whom we are extremely grateful. First, to Jonathan Gennick at Apress for letting us do a second edition and being a wonderful sounding board for ideas and thoughts regarding this book. Second, to Kevin Shea of Apress and Chris Nelson for keeping us on track, reviewing our work, correcting our grammar, and making the writing of this book quite a delightful process.

A very special thanks to Tom LaRock, the technical editor, for his meticulous and detailed work ensuring that the our examples actually work and that the message we are sharing is clear and thorough for the readers. If you ever have an opportunity to meet Tom LaRock, be sure to thank him, and take the opportunity to talk SQL Server with him. You will be glad you did.

We can't thank the fine individuals at Microsoft enough for their insight and feedback on many of these chapters. So, a huge thank you to Rick Negin, Mike Morrison, Ariel Netz, and Barclay Hill. It is a pleasure to associate with individuals who have a passion in what they do. We also thank Rick Negrin again for contributing the Foreword for this book.

Nothing in this life is worth doing without the love and support of family. Thus, Scott would like to profoundly express thanks to his wife, Lynelle, and his children for their endless love, support, understanding, and LOADS of patience. Professionally, Scott would also like to thank a few of his co-workers for their thoughts, insight, and advice. Cory Fowler, Brady Gaster, and Wenming Yi, thank you!

Introduction

Windows Azure SQL Database, formally known as SQL Azure, appeared on the scene about five years ago. At the time, little was known about it, but Microsoft was beginning to talk quite a bit about the Azure platform. Most people thought that SQL Azure was another NoSQL offering, while in reality it was, and is, nothing of the sort. At that time, the largest database it could handle was 1GB, and no one was really taking it seriously. Since that time, Windows Azure SQL Database has grown into an enterprise-ready PaaS (Platform as a Service) offering based on the proven SQL Server technology.

Cloud computing is not hype anymore. Today, cloud-based solutions are becoming the norm rather than an afterthought or sitting on the fringe. The benefits of the Windows Azure cloud platform, including Windows Azure SQL Database, allow businesses to rapidly create and scale solutions with low acquisition costs, yet provide high availability and interoperability. SQL developers and DBAs can use existing skills and knowledge to extend their on-premises solutions and quicken cloud development time. This book covers the fundamental Windows Azure SQL Database concepts, practices, and approaches your valuable data needs as it prepares for the journey to the cloud and Windows Azure SQL Database.

Because of the rapid pace at which Windows Azure SQL Database is updated, some of the services discussed in this book are in Preview as we write and may change somewhat by the time you read this. However, we have tried our best to bring you the most up-to-date information. Updated information can be found at our blogs, the Windows Azure blog (http://blogs.msdn.com/b/windowsazure/), and the all-important Windows Azure home page (http://www.windowsazure.com/) where you can find features, pricing, developer information, and much more.

Our hope is that after reading this book you have a better understanding of, and appreciation for, Windows Azure SQL Database. Whether you are just getting started with it or are a "seasoned veteran," each chapter contains scenarios and information that we hope you will find helpful and beneficial as you design and build Windows Azure projects. There also is a plethora of source code that is used in chapters where examples are given.

Who This Book Is For

Pro SQL Database for Windows Azure, 2nd Edition is aimed at developers and database administrators who want instant access to a fully-capable SQL Server database environment without the pain of sorting out and managing the physical infrastructure.

How This Book Is Structured

Pro SQL Database for Windows Azure is designed to take you from knowing almost nothing at all about SQL Database to being able to configure and deploy it for use by production applications. The book does assume a knowledge of databases in general, and of SQL in general. From that base, the book takes you from the point of getting started through performance tuning and the use of other Azure Data Services.

Chapters in the book are as follows:

Chapter 1, *Getting Started with SQL Database,* helps you create your first database in the cloud.

Chapter 2, *Design Considerations,* discusses design issues you should think about when creating an application to run against a database that is cloud-based instead of one hosted in your own data center.

Chapter 3, *Security,* covers the all-important issue of securing your data in a scenario in which it is accessed across the public Internet.

Chapter 4, *Data Migration and Backup Strategies,* helps you move data efficiently into and out of SQL Database. It also covers backup strategies to protect yourself in the event of your database being lost or damaged.

Chapter 5, *Programming with SQL Database,* covers the differences between using SQL Database from on-premises applications and from Azure-hosted applications.

Chapter 6, *SQL Reporting,* shows how to create cloud-based reports.

Chapter 7, *SQL Data Sync,* Covers replication between multiple SQL Database instances, and between SQL Database in the cloud and SQL Server within your data center.

Chapter 8, *Windows Azure and ASP.NET,* provides an example and guidance for building ASP.NET applications backed by Windows Azure and SQL Database.

Chapter 9, *Designing for High Performance,* covers topics and features such as sharding, lazy loading, caching, and others that are important in building highly performant applications.

Chapter 10, *Federations,* discusses how to achieve greater scalability and performance from the database tier through the horizontal partitioning of data.

Chapter 11, *Performance Tuning,* provides techniques to use in troubleshooting applications when they aren't executing fast enough to meet business requirements.

Chapter 12, *Windows Azure Mobile Services,* covers how to easily connect a scalable cloud-based data backend to your client and mobile applications.

Also in the book are two appendixes. Appendix A provides a walk-through of the SQL Database Management Portal. Appendix B is a quick-reference to T-SQL syntax supported by SQL Database.

Conventions

Throughout the book, we've kept a consistent style for presenting SQL and results. Where a piece of code, a SQL reserved word or fragment of SQL is presented in the text, it is presented in fixed-width Courier font, such as this (working) example:

```
select * from dual;
```

Where we discuss the syntax and options of SQL commands, we've used a conversational style so you can quickly reach an understanding of a command or technique. This means we haven't duplicated large syntax diagrams that better suit a reference manual.

Downloading the Code

The code for the examples shown in this book is available on the Apress web site, `www.apress.com`. A link can be found on the book's information page under the Source Code/Downloads tab, located below the Related Titles section of the page.

Contacting the Authors

Should you have any questions or comments—or even spot a mistake you think we should know about—you can contact the authors at the following addresses: `scottkl@microsoft.com` (Scott Klein), and `hroggero@BlueSyntax.onmicrosoft.com` (Herve Roggero).

CHAPTER 1

■ ■ ■

Getting Started with SQL Database

Born only a few years ago, cloud computing is capturing the imagination of startups and large corporations alike. In its simplest form, cloud computing is an evolution of traditional hosting models; as such, it isn't necessarily a new technology. Rather, it's a new concept that offers new opportunities and challenges not found in existing business models. Much as agile programming provided a new software development paradigm, cloud computing provides a new delivery model for Internet-based solutions. And when it comes to relational data, Microsoft delivers the only cloud database available today: Windows Azure SQL Database.

Introduction to Cloud Computing

Let's begin with what cloud computing has to offer compared to traditional hosting services. The following capabilities are generally expected from large cloud-computing providers:

- **Automatic and unlimited scalability.** The promise that if your service needs more resources, more resources will be provisioned automatically or with limited effort. For example, if you deploy a web service, and you experience a sudden surge in processing needs, your services will automatically expand to additional servers to handle the temporary surge and contract to fewer servers during off-peak activity.

- **Unassisted deployment.** The promise that if you need to deploy additional services or databases, you don't have to call anyone or open a service ticket. The cloud service provider will give you the necessary tools to perform self-service.

- **Built-in failover.** The promise that if one of your servers fails, no one will ever notice. For example, if the server on which your service is installed crashes, a new server immediately takes over.

- **Grow as you need; pay for what you use.** The promise that you only pay for the resources you use. For example, if your service experiences a sudden surge in processing needs for a day, but it scales down to its usual usage for the rest of the month, you're only charged marginally more than usual for the temporary surge.

Cloud providers deliver on those promises in different ways. For example, the promise for automated and unlimited scalability comes in different flavors depending on the service being considered. A Web Service layer will be easier to scale than a database layer. And scaling a Web Service layer with Amazon will be different than with Microsoft. As a result, understanding how cloud providers implement these capabilities can be important in your application design choices and support operations.

The fact that each cloud provider implements its services differently has another, more subtle implication. Switching cloud providers can be very difficult. If you design your application in a way that takes advantage of Amazon-specific services, adapting your application for the Azure platform may be very difficult. As a result, you should choose your cloud service provider carefully before adopting a cloud strategy to avoid costly application rewrites in the future.

Who Is Doing What in the Cloud?

Smaller companies, including startups, are building services that can run in the cloud, whereas larger companies are investing in building cloud-enabled infrastructure. Some corporations are building consulting services and offering to assist customers implement cloud-enabled solutions; others, like Microsoft, are investing in the core infrastructure and services that make the cloud a reality.

Microsoft has traditionally been a software provider, but the company has slowly moved closer to hardware solutions over the years. In the late 1990s, Microsoft engaged with Unisys, HP, Dell, and other hardware manufacturers to provide highly available Windows-based platforms (Windows Data Center Edition). At the same time, Microsoft invested significant resources to build its Microsoft Systems Architecture (MSA). This program was designed to help corporations plan, deploy, and manage Microsoft-based IT architecture. These initiatives, along with many others, helped Microsoft develop strong knowledge capital around highly available and scalable architectures, which is a prerequisite for building cloud computing platforms.

Amazon entered the cloud computing space with its Elastic Compute Cloud (EC2) services in 2005. A few years later, Google and IBM joined forces to enter this market, and Microsoft announced many of its cloud computing plans during 2009, including the Azure platform. As part of its Azure platform, Microsoft delivered a very unique component in its cloud computing offering: a transactional database called Windows Azure SQL Database (also called SQL Database for simplicity, and previously called SQL Azure).

Typical Cloud Services

Generally speaking, cloud computing comes in one of three flavors:

- **SaaS: software as a service.** This delivery platform is usually in the form of web applications that are made available on the Internet for a fee. This model has been around for a few years. Microsoft Office 365 and Google Apps are examples of SaaS offerings.

- **PaaS: platform as a service.** This service offers a computing platform that facilitates the use and deployment of other services and meets the general expectations of cloud computing, such as scalability and pay-as-you-go. Windows Azure SQL Database and Amazon S3 (Simple Storage Service) are examples of PaaS offerings.

- **IaaS: infrastructure as a service.** This offering provides the necessary infrastructure that offers the scalability typically associated with cloud computing, such as Windows Azure and Amazon EC2 (Elastic Compute), but falls short of delivering cloud services that applications can use directly.

SaaS, PaaS, and IaaS are considered the fundamental building blocks of cloud computing. Other acronyms are being manufactured to depict new flavors of cloud computing, such as desktop as a service (DaaS), hardware as a service (HaaS), and even research as a service (RaaS). Pretty soon, the entire alphabet will be consumed in describing the many flavors of services that can be created in the cloud.

More recently private cloud offerings are starting to emerge. A private cloud offers a key advantage over public cloud offerings because it allows corporations to keep their data onsite. This allows certain companies to take advantage of cloud computing without the risk associated with storing data on the Internet. However, private cloud offerings offer fewer benefits than public cloud hosting in other areas. For example, the promise to pay for only what you use no longer applies to private cloud offerings.

Discovering the Microsoft Azure Platform

Let's discover three major components of the Microsoft Azure platform: Windows Azure, Cloud Services, and Windows Azure SQL Database. All three offer unique capabilities that provide a complete array of services needed to build highly scalable and secure solutions:

- **Windows Azure.** A collection of virtual Microsoft operating systems that can run your web applications and services in the cloud. For example, you can create a web service that converts US dollars to Euros; then, you can deploy the service on Windows Azure Web Site and allow it to scale as needed. Note that Windows Azure can run. NET applications and other platforms, as well, including PHP.

- **Cloud Services.** A set of services that provide core capabilities such as federated identity for access control, and a service bus for a messaging-based subscriber/publisher topology.

- **SQL Database.** Microsoft's transactional database offering for cloud computing based on Microsoft SQL Server 2012. For example, you can store your customer database in the cloud using SQL Database and consume customer data using services deployed in Windows Azure.

Microsoft also released, or will be releasing, additional services worth noting, including a Caching Service, High Performance Computing (HPC) and Apache Hadoop for Azure. Additional services are likely to be released over time, offering additional ways to leverage the promises of cloud computing.

Figure 1-1 shows a simplified corporate environment connecting to the Microsoft Azure platform and consuming various Azure services. This diagram is overly simplified, but it conveys an important message: Microsoft Azure is designed to extend a corporate environment securely for web applications, services, messaging, and data stores.

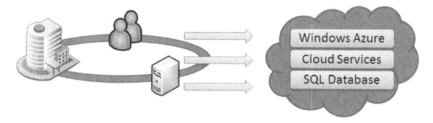

Figure 1-1. *Microsoft Azure platform overview*

Why Microsoft Azure?

One fundamental question that's frequently asked is, "Why?" Who's interested in developing applications in Windows Azure in the first place? To answer this question, let's look at the evolution of web platforms.

About 20 years ago, when the public Internet was all about bulletin board systems (BBBs), Gopher services, and $500 9600-baud modems, the question was, "Will the Internet stick as a technology?" That question has been answered, but many new concepts have grown since then, including web sites, hosting centers, and SaaS.

This evolution relies on a common theme: *decoupling*. BBSs decoupled public information from libraries; web sites decoupled user interfaces from computers; hosting centers decoupled hardware from a company's own infrastructure; and SaaS decoupled complex applications from corporate computers.

Cloud computing on Microsoft Azure is a natural evolution of computing flexibility in which the actual physical storage and implementation details are decoupled from the software solution. For example, deploying services in Windows Azure doesn't require any knowledge of the machine running the service or any of the core services (IIS version, operating system patches, and so on). You may never know which machine is running your software. You connect to a Windows Azure server through logical names, and connecting to a SQL Database instance requires an Internet address instead of an actual server name.

The ability to disassociate machines from data and services is very powerful in itself. Microsoft's Azure environment allows multiple business scenarios to flourish, including these:

- **Seasonal applications.** Developing web sites or services that have a tendency to grow and contract over time provides potential savings opportunities because cloud computing uses a pay-as-you-use model.

- **Short life span.** Development of prototypes or applications with short lifespans is also attractive, such as event-registration sites. You can also build development and test environments for remote teams.

- **Split storage.** Certain applications need to keep storage in a safe location but may not require frequent access, or may require high availability. Designing or modifying an application so that the data is stored locally and in SQL Database (or other data-storage formats) may make sense.

- **Small companies and ISVs.** Smaller companies that can't afford large and complex infrastructure to start their business can take advantage of the financial and inherent infrastructure benefits of Microsoft Azure. Independent software vendors (ISVs) can also benefit from cloud computing. For example, an ISV can use SQL Database to store application logs or centralize reporting features from multiple disconnected locations.

See Chapter 2 for more information about design patterns and application scenarios that use the Azure platform.

About Geographic Locations

In order to provide high availability, Microsoft established regional data-center operations that allow customers to select geographically dispersed services. When you create your Azure servers, you need to specify which geographic location the servers should be provisioned in. This feature is called *Windows Azure geolocation*.

Initially, it may be tempting to choose your company's geographic location for improved performance. However, if the availability of your Azure services is more important than response time, you may need to pick another location. When selecting a geographic location, make sure to consider the following:

- **Performance.** When your data is closer to your users, network latency may be noticeably lower, improving customer experience.

- **Disaster recovery.** If ensuring the availability of your cloud platform is important, you may want to disperse your services and data across multiple regions.

- **Legal factors.** Consider the type of information that will be stored in the cloud, and ensure that you aren't bound by specific regulations and mandates that may prevent you from selecting remote geographic locations.

At the time of this writing, you can select from one of the following geographic locations, each of which is supported by a regional data center:

- East Asia

- East US

- North Central US

- North Europe

- South Central US

- Southeast Asia
- West Europe
- West US

In addition, you can create an *affinity group* that lets you keep certain Azure services together. Such a group creates a geographic dependency between Windows and data services deployed in the Microsoft Azure platform. If Microsoft is required to move a service to another geolocation for regulatory reasons, the related services are likely to move along. For example, if you develop an Azure service that depends on a SQL Database instance, you may want to ensure that they both reside in the same geolocation and that they belong to the same affinity group.

Additional locations will be added over time. As a result, you may need to reevaluate on a regular basis whether a service is deployed in the most appropriate geographic location. Keep in mind that moving services to other geographic locations can be time consuming.

Storing Data in Azure

As you can imagine, cloud computing is all about storing data in a simple yet scalable manner. The Microsoft Azure platform offers a variety of storage models that you can choose from. This section summarizes the four ways you can store your data in Azure; three of these approaches are considered part of the Azure services.

Figure 1-2 provides an overview of the storage options and the available access methods. The set of storage options provided by Windows Azure is referred to as *Windows Azure storage*, which includes blobs, tables, and queues. Windows Azure storage can be accessed directly from a corporate environment using HTTP/S calls, providing a simple hook into the Microsoft Azure platform. In addition to using Windows Azure storage, consumers can make requests directly to a SQL Database instance using ADO.NET or ODBC, because SQL Database supports the Tabular Data Stream (TDS) protocol that SQL Server uses. As a result, applications and services connecting to a SQL Server database can just as easily connect to SQL Database.

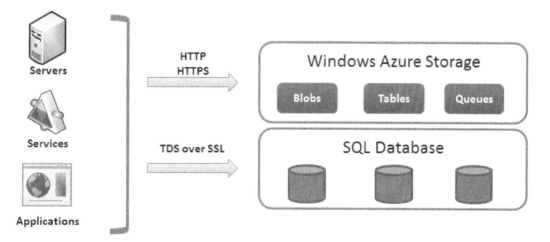

Figure 1-2. *Microsoft Azure data storage access*

Following are further details of the four storage types:

- **Windows Azure Storage.** The Windows Azure Storage offers three distinct storage models that are tailored to specific needs:

  - **Table.** A named value-pair storage that allows you to store very large amounts of data. This storage model includes automatic load balancing and fail-over. It's called a table because you can store multiple values in each row. However, this isn't a transactional storage mechanism; no indexing or table joins are possible. Also, the columns defined in a table have storage limitations. For example, a string data type is limited to 64KB.

  - **Blobs.** An interface to store files, with a maximum limit of 200GB or 1TB of storage depending on the type of blob you create. You can easily access blobs using a straight HTTP request through a Representational State Transfer (REST) call.

  - **Queue.** A highly available mechanism for storing messages for consumption by other applications or services. A typical usage of queues is to send XML messages. Certain limitations apply to queues, but you can access queues through REST, as well.

- **SQL Database.** SQL Database is a transactional database that provides familiar data access through ADO.NET or other providers and gives you the ability to manipulate the data using standard T-SQL statements. Database instances in SQL Database come in two editions: Web and Business. The Web edition offers two maximum database sizes: 1GB and 5GB. The Business edition offers the following maximum database sizes: 10, 20, 30, 40, 50, 100 and 150GB.

Table 1-1 summarizes the current characteristics of these data-storage options available in the Azure platform.

Table 1-1. *Storage Summary in Azure*

Storage Mode	Maximum Size	Access	Format	Relational
Table	N/A	ADO.NETREST	Rows and columns	No
Page Blob	1TB	REST	File	No
Block Blob	200GB	REST	File	No
Queue	64KB*	REST	String	No
SQL Database	150GB	ADO.NET	Rows and columns	Yes

* Recommended limit

SQL Database Primer

As you've seen, SQL Database is a relational database engine based on SQL Server technology. It supports many of the features of SQL Server including tables, primary keys, stored procedures, views, and much more. This section gives a brief primer to get you started using SQL Database. You'll see how to register for Azure, how to create a database and then an account, and how to log in.

Registering for Azure

To register for Windows Azure, visit the Pricing page on the Windows Azure web site: http://www.windowsazure.com/en-us/pricing/purchase-options/. Figure 1-3 shows some of the available options available at the time of this writing.

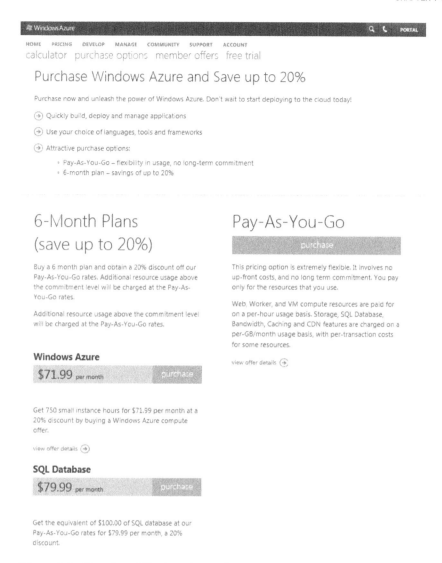

Figure 1-3. *Choosing a Windows Azure plan*

From this page, you can pick the offer that best fits your profile and needs. After you've chosen your preferred plan, click Purchase, and follow the onscreen instructions. When this is complete, you'll receive an e-mail with instructions for configuring your Windows Azure platform.

To access the Azure portal, open your web browser and enter the following URL: http://windows.azure.com. The Azure portal allows you to deploy, manage and view the health status of your services.

Creating a SQL Database Instance

This first thing you need to do is to create a new SQL Database server. The name of the SQL Database server becomes a fully qualified Internet address, and a logical name under which database instances are created. When the SQL Database server is created, the master database is provisioned automatically. This database is read-only and contains configuration and security information for your databases. You can then create your user databases. You can either use the Windows Azure Management Portal or issue a T-SQL statement against the master database using SQL Server Management Studio.

Using the Windows Azure Management Portal

One way to create a database is to do so from the Windows Azure Management Portal. Selecting the SQL Databases tab in the Navigation pane (left side of the page) will list all of your existing SQL Database instances and the server they are associated with. Creating a database can be accomplished in the portal in either of two ways. First, with the list of database instances displayed, click the New button in the lower-left corner of the portal page in the lower menu bar, and then select SQL Database ➤ Quick Create. Second, you can optionally select the Servers tab on the top of the portal page (next to the Databases tab), select the appropriate server name from the list of servers, select the Databases tab, and then click Add on the lower menu bar. Figure 1-4 shows the management portal with a few subscriptions and SQL Database instances created.

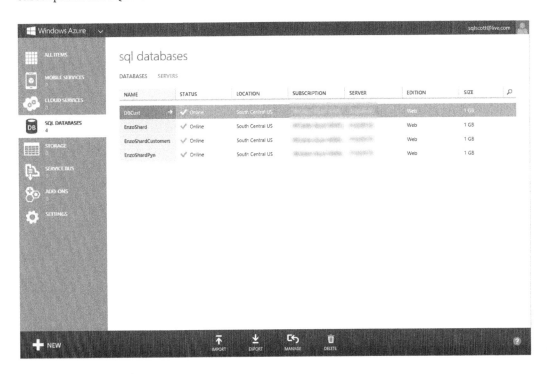

Figure 1-4. *SQL Database instances*

Creating a SQL Database instance via the Quick Create option lets you quickly create a database by specifying the database name, and the subscription and server in which to create the new database instance. If you are creating a new database in a subscription in which no server has been created, you will also be asked to provide an administrator user name and password for the new server that will be provisioned. Creating a database through the Quick Create option creates a 1GB Web Edition database instance.

Creating a database through the Servers tab is a bit different, in that it brings up the New SQL Database-Custom Create dialog box, as shown in Figure 1-5. In the Custom Create dialog, in addition to entering a database name, you also have the option of selecting a database edition (Web or Business) and specifying the size of your database and its database collation. Once you have entered the appropriate information in the Custom Create dialog, click OK.

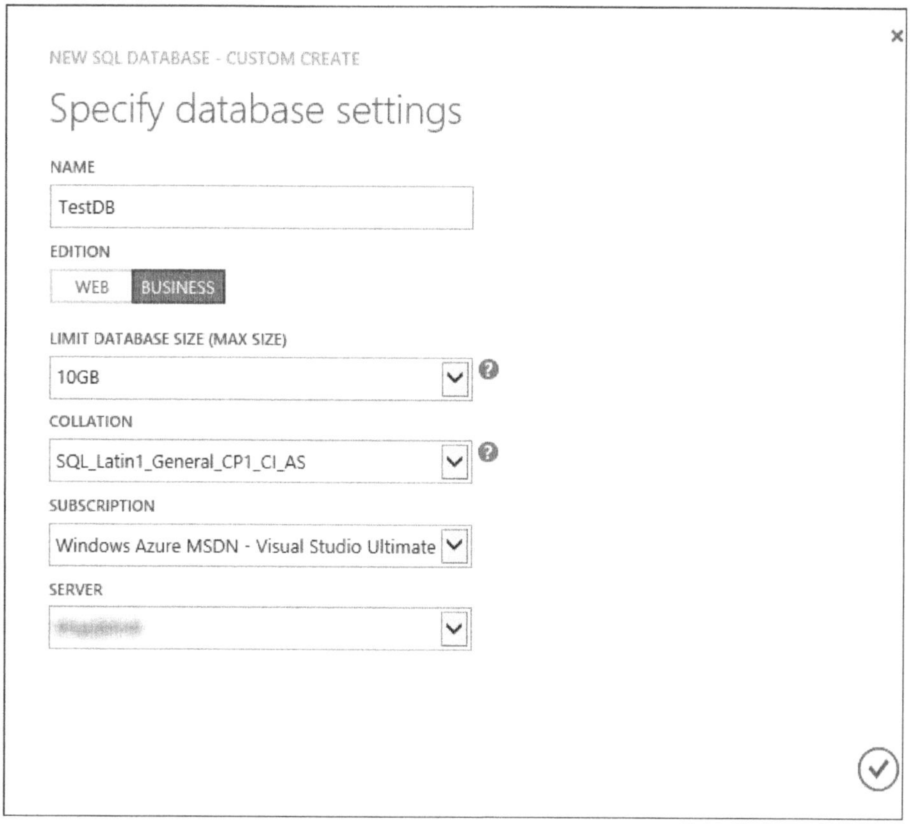

Figure 1-5. *Creating a SQL Database instance*

For database sizes, you can choose the Web edition if 1GB or a 5GB is sufficient for you. If you need to create larger databases, choose the Business edition, which lets you select a size between 10GB and 150GB.

■ **Note** The monthly fee varies, depending on the size of the database. See the additional information later in this chapter and the complete pricing information on Microsoft's web site: www.microsoft.com/azure.

Using a T-SQL Command

Creating a new database using a T-SQL command is straightforward. Because a database instance in SQL Database is managed by Microsoft, only a few options are available to you. In addition, you must be connected to the master database to create new databases.

To create a new database using SQL Server Management Studio, log in using the administrator account (or any user with the dbmanager role), and run the following T-SQL command:

```
CREATE DATABASE TextDB (MAXSIZE = 10 GB)
```

As previously discussed, the size of the database can be 1GB or 5GB for Web edition, or 10GB–150GB for Business. If the MAXSIZE parameter isn't defined, the size of the database is set to 1 GB.

Configuring the Firewall

SQL Database implements a firewall on your behalf. That's a benefit that helps protect your database. Indeed, the default firewall rule is that *no one* can connect to a newly created SQL Database server. You can use the management portal to configure your firewall rules at any time and create databases even if no firewall rules are defined. Allowing no connections by default is a good security practice, because it forces you to think through what IP addresses you wish to allow in.

Follow these steps to add an IP address (or IP range) for a computer that needs access to the SQL Database server:

1. In the Windows Azure Management Portal, select the SQL Databases tab in the left navigation bar.

2. Select the Servers tab above the List Items section.

3. Select the server name you want to add the firewall rule to.

4. Select the Configure tab on the top of the List Items section.

5. In the Allowed IP Addresses section, enter a rule name and the Start and End IP addresses as shown in Figure 1-6. Click Save.

Figure 1-6. *Firewall settings*

6. Additionally, if you have Windows Azure services that need access to your SQL Database server, select Yes for the Windows Azure Services option in the in the Allowed Services section.

If for some reason the firewall rules aren't correctly configured, you will see an error message saying so. Figure 1-7 shows the error message you get using SQL Server Management Studio if the firewall rules don't allow you to connect. The error message looks like a login failure, but the description of the error clearly indicates that the client with the given IP address isn't allowed to access the server.

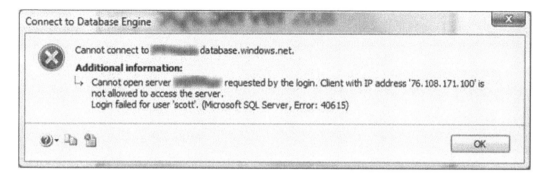

Figure 1-7. *Firewall error*

▓ **Note**   When you're creating a firewall rule, you may need to wait a few minutes for the rule to take effect.

You can also view and edit firewall settings directly using T-SQL, by connecting to the master database with the administrator account and using the following objects:

- sys.firewall_rules
- sp_set_firewall_rule
- sp_delete_firewall_rule

Now that you've configured your SQL Database instance, the fun can begin!

Connecting with SQL Server Management Studio

Follow these steps to connect to your SQL Database instance using SQL Server Management Studio:

1. You need to obtain the fully qualified server name of the SQL Database server. Figure 1-8 shows the server information on the management portal. The fully qualified server name is located in the Properties pane on the right.

Figure 1-8. *Obtaining the server name of your SQL Database server*

▪ **Note** This example uses SQL Server 2008 SP1 Management Studio. Although you can connect to and manage SQL Database instances using this release, additional features are available using the SQL Server 2008 R2 and SQL Server 2012 releases, such as the ability to view database objects using the Object Browser.

---

2. Start SQL Server Management Studio. Click the Cancel button in the Login screen.

▪ **Note** If you're using SQL Server Management Studio for SQL Server 2008 R2 or higher, you can log in using the first Login window. However, if you're using a previous version of SQL Server Management Studio, you need to click Cancel in the first Login window. The instructions provided in this section work for all editions.

---

3. Click the New Query button, or press Ctrl + N. A new Login screen opens (see Figure 1-9). In this window, enter the following information:

Figure 1-9. *Logging in to a SQL Database server*

- **Server name.** Enter the fully qualified server name.

- **Authentication.** Select SQL Server Authentication.

- **Login.** Type the administrator username (created previously).

- **Password.** Type the password of the administrator account.

4. By default, clicking Connect authenticates you against the master database. If you want to connect to another database instance, click Options and type the desired database name in the "Connect to database" field, as shown in Figure 1-10. Note that you can't select the database name; the database name must be typed. For added security you can also check the Encrypt connection option; although all connections are encrypted with SQL Database, this option will force an encrypted connection immediately and bypass the negotiation phase with SQL Database that could be exploited by a man-in-the-middle attack.

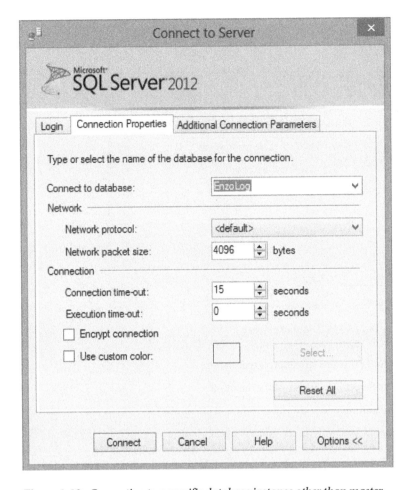

Figure 1-10. *Connecting to a specific database instance other than master*

5. When you're ready, click Connect. A new query window opens, and you can execute T-SQL commands against your SQL Database instance.

■ **Note** The USE command doesn't work against SQL Database to switch database contexts. Because a database can be physically located on any server, the only practical way to switch databases is to reconnect.

Figure 1-11 shows the query window connected to master in SQL Database, on which a simple command has been executed.

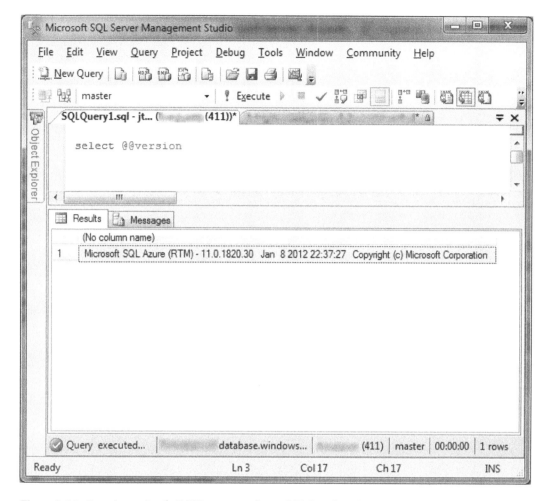

Figure 1-11. Running a simple T-SQL command on a SQL Database instance

Creating Logins and Users

With SQL Database, the process of creating logins and users is mostly identical to that in SQL Server, although certain limitations apply. To create a new login, you must be connected to the master database. When you're connected, you create a login using the CREATE LOGIN command. Then, you need to create a user account in the user database and assign access rights to that account.

Creating a New Login

Connect to the master database using the administrator account (or any account with the loginmanager role granted), and run the following command:

```
CREATE LOGIN test WITH PASSWORD = 'T3stPwd001'
```

At this point, you should have a new login available called test. However, you can't log in until a user has been created. To verify that your login has been created, run the following command, for which the output is shown in Figure 1-12:

```
select * from sys.sql_logins
```

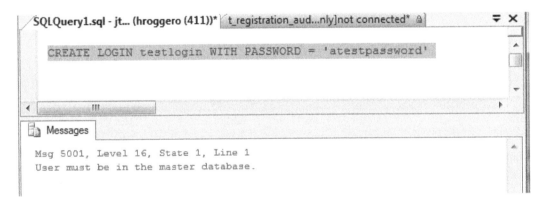

Figure 1-12. *Viewing a SQL login from the master database*

If you attempt to create the login account in a user database, you receive the error shown in Figure 1-13. The login must be created in the master database.

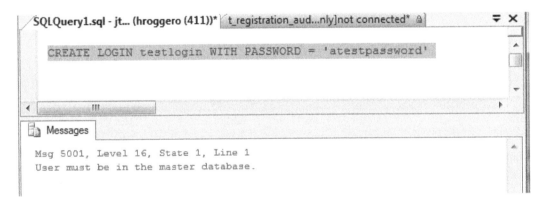

Figure 1-13. *Error when creating a login in a user database*

If your password isn't complex enough, you receive an error message similar to the one shown in Figure 1-14. Password complexity can't be turned off.

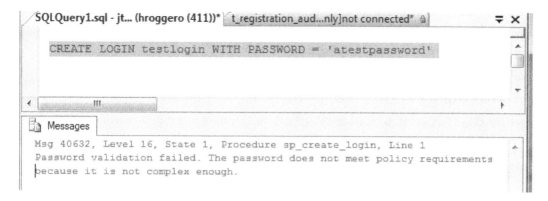

Figure 1-14. *Error when your password isn't complex enough*

> ■ **Note**   Selecting a strong password is critical when you're running in a cloud environment, even if your database is used for development or test purposes. Strong passwords and firewall rules are important security defenses against attacks to your database. Chapter 3 reviews security in depth.

Creating a New User

You can now create a user account for your test login. To do so, connect to a user database using the administrator account (you can also create a user in the master database if this login should be able to connect to it), and run the following command:

```
CREATE USER test FROM LOGIN test
```

If you attempt to create a user without first creating the login account, you receive a message similar to the one shown in Figure 1-15.

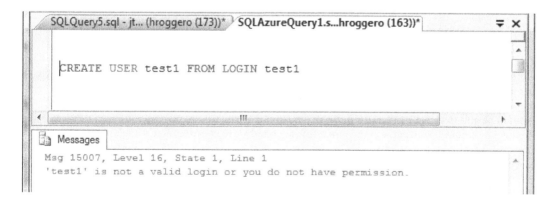

Figure 1-15. *Error when creating a user without creating the login account first*

■ **Note** You cannot create a user with the same name as the administrator login. That's because the administrator login is already mapped to user dbo. You can find the administrator login in the Properties pane in Figure 1-8.

Assigning Access Rights

So far, you've created the login account in the master database and the user account in the user database. But this user account hasn't been assigned any access rights.

To allow the test account to have unlimited access to the selected user database, you need to assign the user to the db_owner group :

```
EXEC sp_addrolemember 'db_owner', 'test'
```

At this point, you're ready to use the test account to create tables, views, stored procedures, and more.

■ **Note** In SQL Server, user accounts are automatically assigned to the public role. However, in SQL Database the public role can't be assigned to user accounts for enhanced security. As a result, specific access rights must be granted in order to use a user account.

Understanding Billing for SQL Database

SQL Database is a pay-as-you-go model, which includes a monthly fee based on the cumulative number and size of your databases consumed daily, and a usage fee based on actual bandwidth usage. With SQL Database you pay for what you use; so a 7GB database instance will be cheaper than an 8GB database instance. And as you might expect, the cost per GB of space used goes down with larger database sizes. So it is cheaper to have one 100GB database instance than two 50GB database instances. Also, as of this writing, when the consuming application of a SQL Database instance is deployed as a Windows Azure application or service, and it belongs to the same geographic region as the database, the bandwidth fee is waived.

To view your current bandwidth consumption and the databases you've provisioned from a billing standpoint, you can run the following commands:

```
SELECT * FROM sys.database_usage     -- databases defined
SELECT * FROM sys.bandwidth_usage    -- bandwidth
```

The first statement returns the number of databases available per day of a specific type: Web or Business edition. This information is used to calculate your monthly fee. The second statement shows a breakdown of hourly consumption per database.

Note that information stored in this database is available for a period of time, but is eventually purged by Microsoft. You should be able to view up to three months of data in this table.

Figure 1-16 shows a sample output of the statement returning bandwidth consumption. This statement returns the following information:

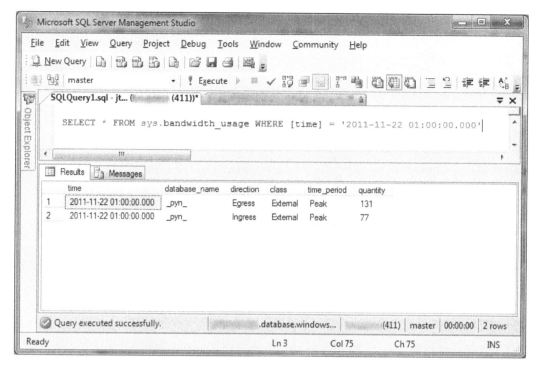

Figure 1-16. *Hourly bandwidth consumption*

- **time.** The hour for which the bandwidth applies. In this case, you're looking at a summary between the hours of 1 AM and 2 AM on December 22, 2011.

- **database_name.** The database for which the summary is available.

- **direction.** The direction of data movement. Egress shows outbound data, and Ingress shows inbound data.

- **class.** External if the data was transferred from an application external to Windows Azure (from a SQL Server Management Studio application, for example). If the data was transferred from Windows Azure, this column contains Internal.

- **time_period.** The time window in which the data was transferred.

- **quantity.** The amount of data transferred, in kilobytes (KB).

  Visit http://www.microsoft.com/windowsazure for up-to-date pricing information.

Limitations in SQL Database

As you've seen so far, creating databases and users requires manual scripting and switching database connections. The fundamental differences between SQL Server and SQL Database lie in the basic design principles of cloud computing, in which performance, ease of use, and scalability must be carefully balanced. The fact that user databases can be located on different physical servers imposes natural limitations. In addition, designing applications and services against SQL Database requires you to have a strong understanding of these limitations.

Security

Chapter 3 covers security in depth, but the following list summarizes important security considerations before you deploy your SQL Database instances. From a security standpoint, you need to consider the following constraints:

- **Encryption.** Although SQL Database uses SSL for data transfers, it doesn't support the data-encryption functions available in SQL Server. However, SQL Database provides support for hashing functions.

- **SSPI authentication.** SQL Database only supports database logins. As a result, network logins using Security Support Provider Interface (SSPI) aren't supported.

- **Connection constraints.** In certain cases, the database connection is closed for one of the following reasons:

  - Excessive resource usage

  - Long-running query

  - Long-running single transaction

  - Idle connection

  - Failover due to server failure

- **Disallowed user names.** Certain user names can't be created, for security reasons:

  - sa

  - admin

  - administrator

  - guest

  - root

- **Login name.** In certain cases, you may need to append the server name to the login name to correctly log in, in this format: [loginName]@[servername]. So, avoid using the arrobas character (@) in login names.

- **TCP port 1433.** Only TCP Port 1433 is allowed. It isn't possible to define another listening port for SQL Database.

Backups

Backing up your SQL Database instance is somewhat different from backing up traditional SQL Server databases. You can't back up a SQL Database instances in the traditional sense, nor can you restore a SQL Server database in SQL Database. You do, however, have the ability to create a transactionally consistent clone of a SQL Database instance before you export/import your data. You can expect the following regarding backups:

- **Backup/Restore operations.** These operations aren't available. In addition, you may not attach or detach a SQL Database instance.

- **Clone operations.** You may create a clone of a SQL Database instance into another one using the CREATE DATABASE statement.

- **Log files.** You can't access the database log files, nor can you create a log backup.

- **Export/Import data.** You can perform these operations using the Import and Export feature.

- **Restore.** You can use the Point in Time Restore feature.

Objects

Certain objects available in SQL Server aren't available in SQL Database. If your applications depend heavily on these features, you may have difficulty using SQL Database, and you may need to rethink your application design to accommodate these limitations. The following are some of the limitations that currently apply to SQL Database:

- **CLR.** The.NET CLR isn't available in SQL Database. As a result, you can't create extended stored procedures or extended functions.

- **System functions.** SQL Database supports many system functions, including Aggregate functions and Ranking functions. However, SQL Database doesn't support RowSet functions, including these:

    - OPENQUERY

    - OPENXML

    - OPENROWSET

    - OPENDATASOURCE

- **System stored procedures.** Only a small subset of system stored procedures are available in SQL Database, in the following categories:

    - Catalog stored procedures

    - Database engine stored procedures

    - Security stored procedures

- **System tables.** None of the system tables are available.

- **System views.** A subset of system views is available; you can access some of them from the master database and others from user databases. The following are some of the system views available (for a complete list, refer to the online MSDN library for SQL Database):

    - sys.sql_logins

    - sys.views

    - sys.databases

    - sys.columns

    - sys.objects

- **Heap tables.** SQL Database doesn't allow the use of heap tables. All tables must have a clustered index.

Miscellaneous

In addition to the limitations outlined so far, additional components and options offered by SQL Server aren't available in SQL Database. For the most part, these limitations shouldn't affect your application designs, but they're good to keep in mind:

- **Maximum number of databases.** You can create no more than one hundred and fifty user databases.

- **Distributed transactions.** Although SQL transactions are supported, distributed transactions aren't supported across SQL Database instances.

- **Collation.** SQL Database supports collation at the column and database levels, or using an expression at execution time. Server- level collations can't be changed and are set to SQL_ LATIN1_GENERAL_CP1_CI_AS. Once set at the database level, the collation cannot be changed using the ALTER DATABASE command.

- **English language.** SQL Database only supports the English language.

- **Database size.** You can only create databases of specific sizes, as outlined previously.

- **Row Versioning-Based Isolation Levels.** READ_COMMITTED_SNAPSHOT and ALLOW_SNAPSHOT_ ISOLATION options are set at the database level, and cannot be changed.

- **Database file placement.** You can't choose how the database files are deployed physically; you can't control filegroups, either. This is handled automatically by the Microsoft data center for optimum performance.

- **Trace flags.** Trace flags aren't available.

- **SQL Server configuration options.** None of the general SQL Server options are available, including CPU and I/O affinity.

- **Service Broker.** The Service Broker isn't available.

- **Global temporary tables.** The global temporary tables aren't available. However, you can use local temporary tables.

- **SQL Server Agent.** The SQL Server Agent isn't available.

Drivers and Protocols

You should also know that accessing SQL Database can only be performed using specific libraries. This may be relevant if you don't use ADO.NET in your programming stack. For example, older versions of Delphi can't connect to SQL Database. Here is a summary of the supported data libraries:

- **TDS version 7.3 or higher.** Any client using a TDS version prior to 7.3 isn't supported.

- **Drivers and libraries.** The following drivers and libraries are allowed:

  - .NET Framework Data Provider for SQL Server from.NET 3.5 SP1

  - SQL Server 2008 Native Client ODBC driver or higher

  - SQL Server 2008 driver for PHP version 1.1 or higher

Summary

This chapter focused on a fast-track overview of SQL Database by providing a high-level introduction to cloud computing and how Microsoft is delivering its cloud offering. You also learned the major steps involved in creating an Azure account and how to get started with SQL Database. You saw some important limitations of the SQL Database platform, but keep in mind that Microsoft is releasing new versions of its cloud database every few months; as a result, some of these limitations will be lifted over time.

CHAPTER 2

Design Considerations

In order to use cloud computing with the Azure platform for more than simple hosting, you must explore the vast array of options available for designing solutions. In addition to understanding the design options presented in this chapter, you need a strong grasp of cloud computing's current shortcomings, which may affect your design choices.

Design Factors

Before reviewing various design patterns, let's start with some opportunities and limitations that impact your design choices. Keep in mind that although this book focuses primarily on SQL Database, many of the concepts in this chapter apply to Azure development in general.

Offsite Storage

As introduced in Chapter 1, the Azure platform offers four distinct storage models: Blob, Table, Queue, and SQL Database. Storing data in SQL Database is similar to storing data in SQL Server. All you need to do is issue T-SQL statements and review some of the limitations of the syntax specific to SQL Database, and off you go!

The ability to store data in SQL Database using T-SQL offers unique opportunities. In many cases, you can easily extend or port certain types of applications in SQL Database with no (or limited) modifications. This portability allows you either to implement solutions that directly depend on SQL Database for storage, or to use a local database while using SQL Database transparently for additional storage requirements (such as reporting).

However, keep in mind that you're limited to the amount of data you can store in a single SQL Database instance. At the moment, SQL Database supports two editions: Web (1GB or 5GB) and Business (from 10GB to 150GB). So, if your application needs to store more than 150GB of data, or if your database can benefit from a multithreaded data access layer, you need to consider splitting your data across multiple databases through a form of partitioning called a *shard*. You'll learn about shards later in this chapter and in more detail throughout this book.

High Availability

When designing applications, software developers and architects are usually concerned about high-availability requirements. SQL Database uses a very elaborate topology that maximizes workload redistribution, transparency, and recovery. Figure 2-1 shows a high-level implementation of SQL Database that gives a hint about how advanced the backend infrastructure must be.

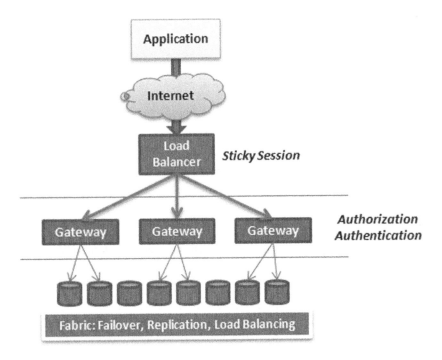

Figure 2-1. *SQL Database topology*

Figure 2-1 illustrates that connections are made through a load balancer that determines which gateway should process the connection request. The gateway acts as a firewall by inspecting the request, performing authentication and authorization services, and forwarding the packets to an actual SQL Database instance. Because databases can be moved dynamically to ensure fair resource allocation, the gateway may alter the destination endpoint. The process is mostly transparent.

In addition, each SQL Database instance is replicated twice on different servers for redundancy. Behind the scenes, a replication topology ensures that a SQL Database instance exists on two other physical servers at all times. These two additional copies are totally transparent to consumers and can't be accessed.

■ **Note**   SQL Database offers 99.9% availability in any given month. For specific terms related to the Service Level Agreement, check the following link: https://www.windowsazure.com/en-us/support/legal/sla/.

Performance

The performance of applications you write can be affected by two things: throttling and how you design the application. Microsoft has put *performance throttling* in place to prevent one client's applications from impacting another. (It's a good feature, not nearly so bad as it may sound.) Application design is something you control.

Throttling

SQL Database runs in a multitenant environment, which implies that your database instances share server resources with databases from other companies. As a result, the SQL Database platform has implemented a throttling algorithm that prevents large queries from affecting performance for other users. If your application issues a large query that could potentially affect other databases, your database connection is terminated.

In addition, to preserve valuable resources and control availability, SQL Database disconnects idle sessions automatically. The session timeout is set to 30 minutes. When you're designing for SQL Database, your application should account for automatic session recovery. This also means that performance testing in your development phase becomes more critical.

Note, however, that high CPU activity is not throttled like other resources. Instead of losing connection to the database when high CPU activity is detected, SQL Database will limit your CPU bandwidth but allow the execution of your T-SQL operation. This means that certain statements may take longer to execute.

Any of the following conditions will terminate your database connection:

- **Lock Consumption.** If your application consumes more than 1 million locks, you will get error code 40550. Monitoring the `sys.dm_tran_locks` management view provides the state of your locks.

- **Uncommitted Transactions.** A transaction locking internal resources for more than 20 seconds will be terminated with error code 40549.

- **Log File Size.** If the log file for a single transaction exceeds 1GB in size, the connection will be terminated with error code 50552.

- **TempDB.** If you run large transactions, or large batches of commands, or a large sorting operation consuming more than 5GB of space, the session will be terminated with error code 40551.

- **Memory.** If your statements consume more than 16MB of memory for over 20 seconds, your session will be terminated with error code 40553.

- **Database Size.** If the database exceeds its configured maximum size, any attempt to update or insert data will fail with error code 40544. You can resolve this error by dropping indexes, purging tables, or increasing the size of the database using the `ALTER DATABASE` statement.

- **Idle Connections.** Any connection staying idle for more than 30 minutes will be terminated. No error is returned in this case.

- **Transactions.** Transactions lasting more than 24 hours will be terminated with error code 40549.

- **Denial-of-Service Attacks.** If many login attempts fail from a specific IP address, any attempt to connect from that IP address will fail for a period of time in order to protect the SQL Database service. No error code is returned.

- **Network Problems.** If a network problem is the source of a terminated session, you will not receive a specific error code from SQL Database; however, you may receive Socket errors.

- **Failover.** When SQL Database is in the midst of failing your database over to another node, your active sessions will be disconnected. You may receive a Socket exception or a generic error indicating that you should retry your operation.

- **High Activity.** If the server hosting your database experiences significant stress or exceeds its operating boundaries, such as too many busy workers, SQL Database might disconnect the sessions with error code 40501.

Additional conditions, called transient errors, may cause your session to be terminated as well. Your code should account for these errors and retry the operation when they occur. Here is a partial list of common errors your code may need to account for:

- **Error 20.** The instance of SQL Server you attempt to connect to does not support encryption.

- **Error 64.** A connection was successfully established with the server, but then an error occurred during the login process:

```
provider: TCP Provider, error: 0 - The specified network name is no longer available.
```

- **Error 233.** The client was unable to establish a connection because of an error during the initialization process before login. Possible causes include the following: the client tried to connect to an unsupported version of SQL Server; the server was too busy to accept new connections; or there was a resource limitation (insufficient memory or maximum allowed connections) on the server:

  ```
  provider: TCP Provider, error: 0 - An existing connection was forcibly closed
  by the remote host.
  ```

- **Error 10053.** A transport-level error has occurred when receiving results from the server. An established connection was aborted by the software in your host machine.

- **Error 10054.** A transport-level error has occurred when sending the request to the server:

  ```
  provider: TCP Provider, error: 0 - An existing connection was forcibly closed
  by the remote host.
  ```

- **Error 10060.** A network-related or instance-specific error occurred while establishing a connection to SQL Server. The server was not found or was not accessible. Verify that the instance name is correct and that SQL Server is configured to allow remote connections:

  ```
  provider: TCP Provider, error: 0 - A connection attempt failed because the connected
  party did not properly respond after a period of time, or established connection
  failed because connected host has failed to respond.
  ```

To account for most of the errors identified previously, Microsoft released the Transient Fault Handling Application Block. This framework is designed to account for transient errors for various cloud services, including SQL Database. The framework also provides different retry strategies, including Incremental, Fixed Interval, and Exponential Back Off options. Visit the Microsoft Enterprise Library Integration Pack for Microsoft Azure for more information: `http://msdn.microsoft.com/en-us/library/hh680934(v=PandP.50).aspx`.

▪ **Note** In the context of SQL Database, *throttling* generally means terminating the database connection. Whatever the reason for throttling is, the outcome is usually the same: the loss of a database connection.

Application Design Considerations

When considering how to design your application to best take advantage of SQL Database, you need to evaluate the following items:

- **Database roundtrips.** How many roundtrips are necessary to perform a specific function in your application? More database roundtrips mean a slower application, especially when the connection is made over an Internet link and is SSL encrypted.

- **Caching.** You can improve response time by caching resources on the client machine or storing temporary data closer to the consumer.

- **Property lazy loading.** In addition to reducing roundtrips, it's critical to load only the data that's absolutely necessary to perform the required functions. Lazy loading can help significantly in this area.

- **Asynchronous user interfaces.** When waiting is unavoidable, providing a responsive user interface can help. Multithreading can assist in providing more responsive applications.

- **Shards.** A *shard* is a way of splitting your data across multiple databases in a manner that is as transparent as possible to your application code, thus improving performance. Federation is the sharding technology available in SQL Database.

Designing an application for performance becomes much more important for cloud computing solutions that depend on remote storage. For more information on these topics and more, see Chapter 9.

Data Synchronization

There are two primary ways to synchronize data with SQL Database: the Microsoft Sync Framework and the SQL Data Sync service. The Microsoft Sync Framework offers bidirectional data-synchronization capabilities between multiple data stores, including databases. SQL Data Sync uses the Microsoft Sync Framework, which isn't limited to database synchronization; you can use the framework to synchronize files over different platforms and networks.

Specifically, as it relates to SQL Database, you can use the Microsoft Sync Framework to provide an offline mode for your applications by keeping a local database synchronized with a SQL Database instance. And because the framework can synchronize data with multiple endpoints, you can design a shard, described in detail later, in which all database instances keep their data in sync transparently.

The SQL Data Sync service provides a simpler synchronization model between on-premise SQL Server databases and SQL Database, or between SQL Database instances. Since this service runs in the cloud, it is ideal for synchronizing cloud databases without having to install and configure a service on-premise.

Direct vs. Serviced Connections

You may also consider developing Azure services to keep the database connection to a local network, and send the data back to the client using SOAP or REST messages. If your Azure services are deployed in the same region as your SQL Database instances, the database connection is made from the same datacenter and performs much faster. However, sending data back to the consumer using SOAP or REST may not necessarily improve performance; you're now sending back XML instead of raw data packets, which implies a larger bandwidth footprint. Finally, you may consider writing stored procedures to keep some of the business logic as close to the data as possible.

Figure 2-2 shows the two different ways an application can retrieve data stored in a SQL Database instance. A direct connection can be established to the database from the application, in which case the application issues T-SQL statements to retrieve data. Alternatively, a serviced connection can be made by creating and deploying custom SOAP or REST services on Windows Azure, which in turn communicate to the database. In this case, the application requests data through web services deployed in Azure.

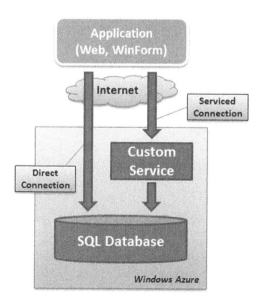

Figure 2-2. *Data connection options*

27

Keep in mind that you can design an application to use both connection methods. You may determine that your application needs to connect directly when archiving data, while using services to perform more complex functions. Generally speaking you should try to use a serviced connection so that you can leverage connection pooling and centralized caching that would be otherwise difficult or impossible to achieve. Connection pooling and caching are performance techniques that help you avoid throttling conditions.

■ **Note**   Most of this chapter provides direct connection diagrams; however, many of the patterns presented would work just as well using a serviced connection to a Windows Azure service first.

Pricing

Pricing of a hosted environment isn't usually considered a factor in standard application design. However, in the case of cloud computing, including Azure, you need to keep in mind that your application's performance and overall design have a direct impact on your monthly costs.

For example, you incur network and processing fees whenever you deploy and use Azure services. Although this is true, at the time of this writing, the data traffic between a Windows Azure application or service and a SQL Database instance is free within the same geographic location.

Pricing may affect your short-term application design choices, but you should keep in mind that Microsoft may change its pricing strategy at any time. As a result, although pricing is an important consideration especially for projects on limited budget, long-term viability of a design should be more important than short-term financial gains.

If you're designing an application to live in the Azure world and you depend on this application to generate revenue, you must ensure that your pricing model covers the resulting operational costs. For example, your application should be designed from the ground up with billing capabilities in mind if you intend to charge for its use.

Another factor related to pricing is that your SQL Database instance cost consists of a monthly fee and a usage fee. The monthly fee is prorated, so if you create a database at 1PM and drop it at 2PM the same day, you're charged a fraction of the monthly fee, plus the usage fee. The usage fee is strictly limited to bandwidth consumption: CPU utilization, I/O consumption, and your database's memory footprint aren't factors in the usage fee (see Figure 2-3). However, your database connection may be throttled if your database activity reaches specific thresholds, as previously discussed.

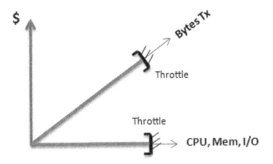

Figure 2-3. *Pricing and resource throttling*

In summary, you can consider moving certain CPU-intensive activities (within reason) onto the SQL Database instance without being charged. You may, for instance, perform complex joins that use large datasets in a stored procedure and return a few summary rows to the consumer as a way to minimize your usage fee.

Security

It goes without saying that security may be a concern for certain types of applications; however, these concerns are similar to those that companies face when using traditional hosting facilities. The question that comes to mind when considering security in cloud computing is related to the lack of control over data privacy. In addition, certain limitations may prevent certain kinds of monitoring, which automatically rules out the use of SQL Database for highly sensitive applications unless the sensitive data is fully encrypted on the client side.

As a result, encryption may become an important part of your design decision. And if you decide to encrypt your data, where will the encryption take place? Although the connection link is encrypted between your application code and SQL Database, and you can use hashing functions with SQL Database, the data itself isn't encrypted when it's stored in SQL Database on disk. You may need to encrypt your data in your application code before sending it over the public Internet so that it's stored encrypted.

Encryption is good for data privacy, but it comes with a couple of downsides: slower performance and difficulty in searching for data. Heavy encryption can slow down an application, and it's notoriously difficult to search for data that is encrypted in a database.

Review of Design Factors

So far, you're seen a few considerations that can impact your design choices. Table 2-1 provides a summary. Some of the considerations are related to opportunities that you may be able to take advantage of; others are limitations imposed by the nature of cloud computing or specifically by the Azure platform.

Table 2-1. *Summary of design factors*

Opportunities	Limitations
Offsite storage	Limited amount of storage
Elastic cost	Performance
Instant provisioning	Backups
SQL Data Sync	Security concerns
High availability	

As you design applications, make sure you evaluate whether specific Azure limitations discussed in this book still apply—the Azure platform is likely to change quickly in order to respond to customer demands.

Design Patterns

Let's review the important design patterns that use SQL Database. Before designing your first cloud application, you should read this section to become familiar with a few design options. Some of the advanced design patterns explained in this chapter can also provide significant business value, although they're more difficult to implement.

Note that for simplicity, the diagrams in this section show only a direct connection to SQL Database. However, almost all the patterns can be implemented using a serviced connection through Azure services.

Direct Connection

The *direct connection pattern*, shown in Figure 2-4, is perhaps the simplest form of connectivity to a SQL Database instance. The consumer can be either an application located in a corporation's network or a Windows Azure service connecting directly to the SQL Database instance.

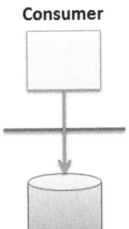

Figure 2-4. *Direct connection pattern*

As simple as it is, this may be one of the most widely used patterns, because it requires no special configuration or advanced integration technique. For example, a Software as a Service (SaaS) application may use this pattern; in this case, the consumer is the web site hosted in Azure (or on any other hosting provider). Alternatively, the consumer may be a smart device or a phone accessing records in SQL Database.

Smart Branching

The *smart branching pattern* (see Figure 2-5) describes an application that contains sufficient logic to determine whether the data it needs to load is located in the cloud or in a local database. The logic to make this determination is either hardcoded in the application or driven from a configuration file. It may also be provided by a data access layer (DAL) engine that contains logic that fetches data from either a local or a cloud database.

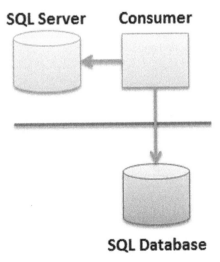

Figure 2-5. *Smart branching pattern*

One of the uses for smart branching is to implement a form of caching in which the consumer caches parts of its data locally or fetches it from a cloud database whenever necessary. You can also use this pattern to implement a disconnected mode to your application, in case Internet connectivity becomes unavailable.

Transparent Branching

Whereas smart branching depends on the consumer (or one of its components) to determine whether data is local or in the cloud, *transparent branching* (see Figure 2-6) removes this concern from the consumer. The consuming application no longer depends on routing logic and becomes oblivious to the ultimate location of the data.

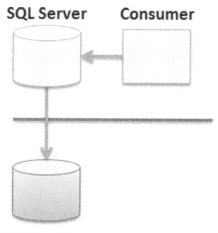

Figure 2-6. *Transparent branching pattern*

This pattern is best implemented by applications that are difficult to modify or for which the cost of implementation is prohibitive. It can effectively be implemented in the form of extended stored procedures that have the knowledge to fetch data from a cloud data source. In essence, this pattern implements a DAL at the database layer.

Sharding

So far, you've seen patterns that implement a single connection at a time. In a *shard* (see Figure 2-7), multiple databases can be accessed simultaneously in a read and/or write fashion and can be located in a mixed environment (local and cloud). However, keep in mind that the total availability of your shard depends partially on the availability of your local databases.

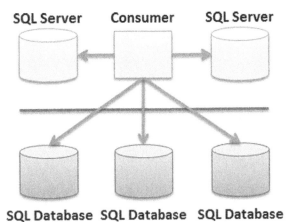

SQL Database   SQL Database   SQL Database

Figure 2-7. *Shard pattern*

Shards are typically implemented when performance requirements are such that data access needs to be spread over multiple databases in a scale-out approach.

Shard Concepts and Methods

Before visiting the shard patterns, let's analyze the various aspects of shard design. Some important concepts are explained here:

- **Decision rules.** Logic that determines without a doubt which database contains the record(s) of interest. For example, *if Country = US, then connect to SQL Database instance #1*. Rules can be static (hardcoded in C#, for example) or dynamic (stored in XML configuration files). Static rules tend to limit the ability to grow the shard easily, because adding a new database is likely to change the rules. Dynamic rules, on the other hand, may require the creation of a rule engine. Not all shard libraries use decision rules.

- **Round-robin.** A method that changes the database endpoint for every new connection (or other condition) in a consistent manner. For example, when accessing a group of five databases in a round-robin manner, the first connection is made to database 1, the second to database 2, and so on. Then, the sixth connection is made to database 1 again, and so forth. Round-robin methods avoid the creation of decision engines and attempt to spread the data and the load evenly across all databases involved in a shard.

- **Horizontal partition.** A collection of tables with similar schemas that represent an entire dataset when concatenated. For example, sales records can be split by country, where each country is stored in a separate table. You can create a horizontal partition by applying decision rules or using a round-robin method. When using a round-robin method, no logic helps identify which database contains the record of interest; so all databases must be searched.

- **Vertical partition.** A table schema split across multiple databases. As a result, a single record's columns are stored on multiple databases. Although this is considered a valid technique, vertical partitioning isn't explored in this book.

- **Mirrors.** An exact replica of a primary database (or a large portion of the primary database that is of interest). Databases in a mirror configuration obtain their data at roughly the same time using a synchronization mechanism like SQL Data Sync. For example, a mirror shard made of two databases, each of which has the Sales table, has the same number of records in each table at all times. Read operations are then simplified (no rules needed) because it doesn't matter which database you connect to; the Sales table contains the data you need in all the databases.

- **Shard definition.** A list of SQL Database instances created in a server in Azure. The consumer application can automatically detect which databases are part of the shard by connecting to the master database. If all databases created are part of the shard, enumerating the records in `sys.databases` give you all the databases in the shard.

- **Breadcrumbs.** A technique that leaves a small trace that can be used downstream for improved decisions. In this context, breadcrumbs can be added to datasets to indicate which database a record came from. This helps in determining which database to connect to in order to update a record and avoids spreading requests to all databases.

When using a shard, a consumer typically issues CRUD (create, read, update, and delete) operations. Each operation has unique properties depending on the approach chosen. Table 2-2 outlines some possible combinations of techniques to help you decide which sharding method is best for you. The left column describes the connection mechanism used by the shard, and the top row identifies the shard's storage mechanism.

Table 2-2. *Shard access techniques*

	Horizontal partitions	Mirror
Decision rules	Rules determine how equally records are spread in the shard. **Create**: Apply rules. **Read**: Connect to all databases with rules included as part of a WHERE clause, or choose a database based on the rules. Add breadcrumbs for update and delete operations. **Update**: Apply rules or use breadcrumbs, and possibly move records to another database if the column updated is part of the rule. **Delete**: Apply rules, or use breadcrumbs when possible.	This combination doesn't seem to provide a benefit. Mirrored databases aren't partitioned, and so no rule exists to find a record.
Round-robin	Records are placed randomly in databases based on the available connection. No logic can be applied to determine which database contains which records. **Create**: Insert a record in the current database. **Read**: Connect to all databases, issue statements, and concatenate result sets. Add breadcrumbs for update and delete operations. **Update**: Connect to all databases (or use breadcrumbs), and apply updates using a primary key. **Delete**: Same as update.	All records are copied to all databases. Use a single database (called the *primary database*) for writes. **Create**: Insert a record in the primary database only. **Read**: Connect to any database in a round-robin fashion. **Update**: Update a record in the primary database only. **Delete**: Delete a record in the primary database only.

Shards can be very difficult to implement. Make sure you test thoroughly when implementing shards. You can also look at some of the shard libraries that have been developed. The shard library found on CodePlex and explained further in this book (in Chapter 9) uses .NET 4.0; you can find it with its source code at http://enzosqlshard.codeplex.com.

It uses round-robin as its access method. You can also look at another implementation of a shard library that uses SQLAzureHelper; this shard library uses decision rules as its access method and is provided by the SQL Database Team (http://blogs.msdn.com/b/windowsazure/). Finally, you can also evaluate SQL Database Federations, a built-in sharding mechanism within SQL Database. SQL Database Federations are explained in Chapter 10 in greater detail.

Read-Only Shards

Shards can be implemented in multiple ways. For example, you can create a read-only shard (ROS). Although the shard is fed from a database that accepts read/write operations, its records are read-only for consumers.

Figure 2-8 shows an example of a shard topology that consists of a local SQL Server to store its data with read and write access. The data is then replicated using the SQL Data Sync Framework (or other method) to the actual shards, which are additional SQL Database instances in the cloud. The consuming application then connects to the shard (in a SQL Database instance) to read the information as needed.

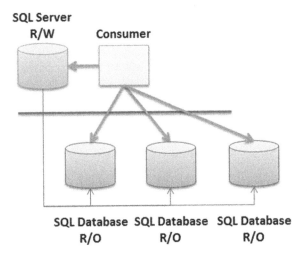

Figure 2-8. *Read-only shard topology*

In one scenario, the SQL Database instances each contain the exact same copy of the data (a mirror shard), so the consumer can connect to one of the SQL Database instances (using a round-robin mechanism to spread the load, for example). This is perhaps the simpler implementation because all the records are copied to all the databases in the shard blindly. However, keep in mind that SQL Database doesn't support distributed transactions; you may need to have a compensating mechanism in case some transactions commit and others don't.

Another implementation of the ROS consists of synchronizing the data using horizontal partitioning. In a horizontal partition, rules are applied to determine which database contains which data. For example, the SQL Data Sync service can be implemented to partition the data for US sales to one SQL Database instance and European sales to another. In this implementation, either the consumer knows about the horizontal partition and knows which database to connect to (by applying decision rules based on customer input), or it connects to all databases in the cloud by applying a WHERE clause on the country if necessary, avoiding the cost of running the decision engine that selects the correct database based on the established rules.

Read-Write Shards

In a read-write shard (RWS), all databases are considered read/write. In this case, you don't need to use a replication topology that uses the SQL Data Sync Framework, because there is a single copy of each record within the shard. Figure 2-9 shows an RWS topology.

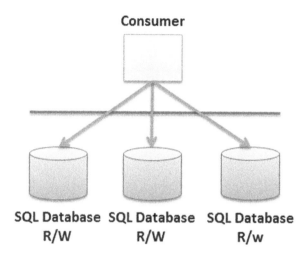

Figure 2-9. *Multimaster shard topology*

Although an RWS removes the complexity of synchronizing data between databases, the consumer is responsible for directing all CRUD operations to the appropriate cloud database. This requires special considerations and advanced development techniques to accomplish, as previously discussed, unless you use SQL Database Federations.

Offloading

In the offloading pattern, the primary consumer represents an existing onsite application with its own database; but a subset of its data (or the entire database) is replicated to a cloud database using SQL Data Sync (or another mechanism). The offloaded data can then be used by secondary consumers even if the primary database isn't accessible.

You can implement the offloading pattern in two ways, as shown in Figure 2-10. The primary database can be either the local SQL Server database or the cloud database. For example, a legacy application can use a local SQL Server database for its core needs. SQL Data Sync is then used to copy relevant or summary data in a cloud database. Finally, secondary consumers such as portable devices and PDAs can display live summary data by connecting to the cloud for their data source. Note that if you use the SQL Data Sync service, you can choose to have bidirectional synchronization of data.

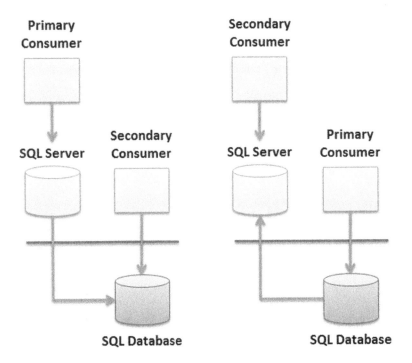

Figure 2-10. *Offloading patterns*

Aggregation

In its simplest form, the aggregation pattern provides a mechanism to collect data from multiple data providers into a SQL Database instance. The data providers can be geographically dispersed and not know about each other, but they must share a common knowledge of the schema so that, when aggregated, the data is still meaningful.

The aggregation patterns shown in Figure 2-11 use the direct connection pattern. You can use an aggregation pattern to provide a common repository of information, such as demographic information or global warming metrics collected from different countries. The key in this pattern is the ability to define a common schema that can be used by all providers and understood by the consumers. Because SQL Database supports XML data types, you can also store certain columns in XML, an option that provides a mechanism to store slightly different information per customer.

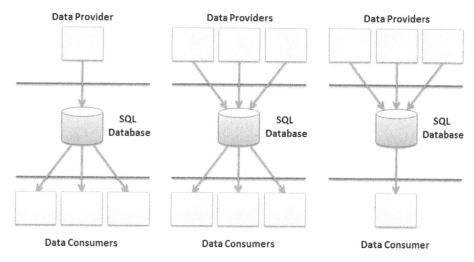

Figure 2-11. *Aggregation patterns*

Mirroring

The mirror pattern, shown in Figure 2-12, is a variation of the offloading pattern where the secondary consumer can be an external entity. In addition, this pattern implies that a two-way replication topology exists, so that changes in either database are replicated back to the other database. This pattern allows a *shared nothing* integration, in which neither consumer has the authority to connect to the other consumer directly.

Figure 2-12. *Mirror pattern*

Combining Patterns

The previous design patterns provide the necessary basis to build systems with SQL Database. Some of these patterns can be used as is, but you're very likely to combine patterns to deliver improved solutions. This section describes some useful combinations.

Transparent Branching + RWS

Figure 2-13 shows the transparent branching and the read-write shard patterns combined. This pattern can be used to offload, into the cloud, storage of historical data that an existing Enterprise Resource Planning (ERP) application generates. In this example, the shard provides a way to ensure high throughput by using asynchronous round-robin calls into SQL Database instances.

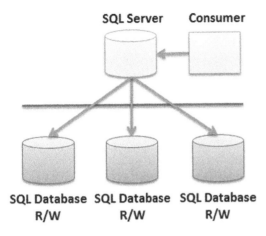

Figure 2-13. *Transparent branching + RWS patterns*

This pattern offers the following advantages:

- **Transparent data transfer.** In this case, the transparent branching pattern copies an existing application's data into cloud databases without changing a single line of code in the existing application.

- **High performance.** To ensure high performance and throughput, the round-robin shard pattern is used along with asynchronous calls into the cloud.

- **Scalable.** When using a shard, it's very simple to expand it by adding a new SQL Database instance into the cloud. If implemented correctly, the shard automatically detects the new database and storage capacity, and throughput automatically increases.

Cascading Aggregation

In cascading aggregation (see Figure 2-14), the aggregation pattern is applied serially to generate a summary database. The mechanism to copy (or move) data from one SQL Database instance to another must be accomplished using a high-level process, such as a worker process in Windows Azure.

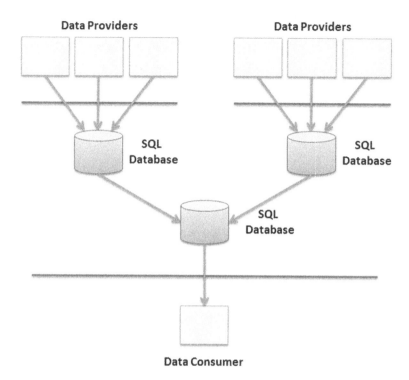

Figure 2-14. *Aggregation + MMS patterns*

For example, this pattern can be used to collect information from multiple SQL Database instances into a single one used by a third party to monitor overall performance. A Windows Azure worker process can run a performance view provided by SQL Database and store the data into another database. Although the SQL Database instances being monitored for performance may have a totally different schema, the output of SQL Database's performance data management view (DMV) is consistent. For example, the monitoring service can call sys.dm_exec_connections to monitor connection activity in various SQL Database instances every 5 minutes and store the result in a separate SQL Database instance.

Sample Design: Application SLA Monitoring

To put a few of the patterns in perspective, let's try an example. We'll create a formal design around a system that monitors application performance service-level agreements (SLAs). In this design, a company already has a monitoring product that can audit activity in existing SQL Server databases at customer sites. Assume that the company that makes this monitoring product wants to extend its services by offering a SQL Database storage mechanism so it can monitor customers' database SLAs centrally.

Pre-Azure Application Architecture

First, let's look at the existing application-monitoring product. It contains a module that monitors one or more SQL Servers in an enterprise and stores its results in another database located on the customer's network.

In this example, Company A has implemented the monitoring service against an existing ERP product to monitor access security and overall SLA. The monitoring application performs the auditing based on live activity on the internal SQL Server storing the ERP data. When certain statements take too long to execute, the monitoring service receives an alert and stores an audit record in the local auditing database, as shown in Figure 2-15.

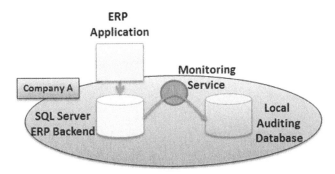

Figure 2-15. *Onsite monitoring implementation*

On a monthly basis, managers run reports to review the SLAs of the ERP system and can determine whether the ERP application is still performing according to predefined thresholds as specified in the ERP vendor contract. So far, the benefits of this implementation include the following:

- **Visibility.** The customer has visibility into its internal database's performance.

- **SLA management.** Measured SLAs can be used to negotiate contract terms with the ERP vendor.

However, the customer needs to store the auditing data internally and manage an extra SQL Server instance; this adds database management overhead, including making sure all security patches (operating system and database) are up to date. In addition, the local auditing database running on SQL Server isn't readily accessible to the ERP vendor, so the ERP vendor can't take proactive actions on any SLA issues and must wait to be informed by the customer about serious performance issues. Finally, the customer doesn't know how its internal SLA measures compare to those of other customers running the same ERP product.

Azure Implementation

The monitoring provider has created an enhanced version of its monitoring system and includes an optional cloud storage option, in which the monitoring service can forward performance events in a centrally located database in the cloud. The monitoring provider has decided to implement an asynchronous smart branching pattern so that events can be stored in a SQL Database instance.

Figure 2-16 shows the implementation architecture that lets the monitoring service store data in a cloud database. Each monitoring service can now store SLA metrics in the cloud in addition to the local auditing database. Finally, the local auditing database is an option that customers may choose not to install. To support this feature, the monitoring provider has decided to implement a queuing mechanism in case the link to SQL Database becomes unavailable.

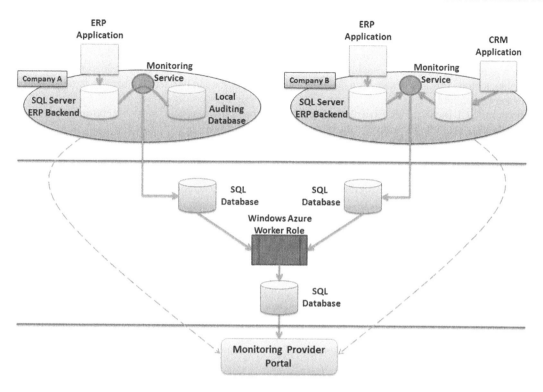

Figure 2-16. *Azure monitoring implementation*

The monitoring provider has also built a portal on which customers can monitor their SLAs. Customer B, for example, can now use the portal to monitor both its CRM and ERP application database SLAs. The customer can prepare reports and make them available to the ERP and CRM vendors for review online, with complete drilldown access to the statements from the same portal.

In this implementation, additional benefits include the following:

- **Improved sharing.** Sharing information with vendors becomes much easier because drilldown access to issues is provided through a cloud-enabled portal.

- **Local storage optional.** With the improved solution, customers may decide to implement the cloud storage only if they're short staffed to handle the necessary internal database-management activities.

- **External monitoring.** Customers A and B also have the ability to use the monitoring provider to monitor their ERP products proactively and remotely with specific escalation procedures when the SLAs aren't met. The monitoring provider can, for example, manage performance issues directly with the ERP provider.

Other Considerations

This chapter has introduced many important design factors to help you design a solution that uses SQL Database. Are few more concepts are worth a glance, such as blob data stores, edge data caching, and data encryption.

Blob Data Stores

Blobs are files that can be stored in Windows Azure. What is interesting about blobs is that they can be easily accessed through REST, there is no limit to the number of blobs that can be created, and each blob can contain as much as 200GB of data for block blobs and 1TB of data for page blobs. As a result, blobs can be used as a backup and transfer mechanism between consumers.

A system can dump SQL Database tables to files using the Bulk Copy Program (BCP), possibly compressing and/or encrypting the files beforehand, and store the blobs in Windows Azure.

Edge Data Caching

The chapter briefly mentioned caching earlier, but you should remember that caching may yield the most important performance gains in your application design. You can cache relatively static tables in memory, save them as blobs (or a form of in-memory storage) so that other caching systems use the same cache, and create a mechanism to refresh your data cache using queues in Azure.

Figure 2-17 shows an example of a design that creates a shared cache updated by two ERP systems. Each ERP system uses the transparent branching pattern to update shared records in a SQL Database instance. At this point, however, the edge caches aren't aware of the change in data. At a specific interval (every 10 minutes, for example), a worker process in Windows Azure picks up the changes and stores them in blobs. The worker may decide to apply logic to the data and resolve conflicts, if any. Blobs are then created (or replaced) with the latest cache information that should be loaded. The edge cache refreshes its internal data by loading the blobs at specific intervals (every 5 minutes, for example) and replaces its internal content with the latest cache. If all edge caches are configured to run against a public atomic clock, all the caches are updated virtually at the same time.

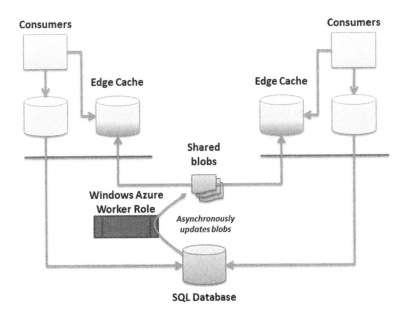

Figure 2-17. *Shared edge data caching*

Data Encryption

You can encrypt your data in two environments: onsite or in Windows Azure using a service. SQL Database, as previously mentioned, doesn't support encryption at this time (although hashing is supported). If you need to encrypt Social Security numbers or phone numbers, you should consider where encryption makes sense.

Generally speaking, unless your application runs in a public environment where your private keys can be at risk, you should consider encrypting onsite before the data goes over the Internet. But if you need a way to decrypt in Windows Azure, or you need to encrypt and decrypt data across consumers that don't share keys, you probably need to encrypt your data in Windows Azure before storing it in SQL Database.

SaaS Applications and Federations

Designing SaaS applications typically requires the use of multiple databases in order to scale both data storage and performance. In order to build a solid SaaS solution, developers typically develop a custom framework that provides the connection routing logic needed by an application to determine which database it should connect to.

If you are building a SaaS application, you should investigate the use of Federations, a feature of SQL Database. Federations help with scalability by distributing data across multiple databases by using administrative SQL commands. I will review Federations in greater detail in Chapter 11, including how the feature works and some of its current limitations.

Summary

This chapter reviewed many design concepts that are unique to distributed computing and for which cloud computing is a natural playground. Remember that designing cloud applications can be as simple as connecting to a SQL Database instance from your onsite applications or as complex as necessary (with distributed edge caches and shards) for enterprise-wide systems.

The chapter provided multiple parameters that you should consider when designing your application, each of which can significantly impact your final design, such as performance, billing, security, storage options, and throttling. You should consider creating two or more cloud-based designs and reviewing them with other designers to discuss pros and cons before making your final selection. And if you have the time, build a proof-of-concept to validate your assumptions and measure how effective the solution will be.

CHAPTER 3

Security

Compared to other systems in most corporations, database environments are probably the weakest point when it comes to security, with a few exceptions such as the banking sector. The reason is that databases are considered well within the boundaries of internal networks, which are considered secured and usually inaccessible directly from the Internet.

With the advent of SQL Database and most Database as a Service solutions, the focus on database security rises all the way to the top for two primary reasons: you're no longer in control of your data, and the data can be directly accessed from the Internet. As a result, it becomes even more important to take advantage of all the capabilities of SQL Database and understand its limitations.

Overview

Before diving into the specifics of SQL Database, let's look at a general security framework to assess how Database as a Service can impact you. The following discussion is based on the basic security principles encapsulated by confidentiality, integrity, and availability (CIA). This is referred to as the *CIA triad* and is one of the most accepted forms of security categorization. SQL Database has different strengths and weaknesses than traditional SQL Server installations, so it is important to review each area of the CIA triad to understand how to deal with its weaknesses and to leverage its strengths.

Confidentiality

Confidentiality is the ability to ensure that data can be accessed only by authorized users. It's about protecting your data from prying eyes or from inadvertent leakage, and it's achieved by using multiple technologies, including the following:

- **Encryption**. Creates a *ciphertext* (encrypted information) that can be decrypted through the use of a shared key or a certificate.

- **Hashing**. Generates a ciphertext that can't be decrypted (typically used for password storage).

- **Access control**. Controls access to data based on contextual information.

- **Authentication**. Controls who can access the database and which objects in the database a user can access.

- **Firewall**. Uses technology to limit network connectivity to a list of known machines.

SQL Database offers new features, such as a firewall (as previously discussed); however, it doesn't yet support data encryption natively (such as Transparent Data Encryption [TDE] and field-level encryption), which places more emphasis on the other confidentiality techniques.

SQL Server, on the other hand, doesn't provide a native firewall (although it's possible to use Windows' native firewall or purchase after-market database firewalls), but it offers strong encryption capabilities. Finally, both SQL Server and SQL Database offer hashing capabilities.

Because SQL Database doesn't provide native encryption, your code needs to do all the hard work. Not to worry! In this chapter, you see how to implement hashing and encryption using C# and how to store the ciphertext in SQL Database (or SQL Server, for that matter).

Integrity

Data *integrity* refers to the objective of ensuring that information is modified only by authorized users, and that damage can be undone if necessary. Integrity of data can be compromised in multiple ways, such as a malicious SQL Injection attack or the unintentional execution of a TRUNCATE statement on a table, wiping out all the records. Generally speaking, you can implement the following integrity measures in a database:

- **Authorization**. Controls who can change what data.

- **Backup**. Creates a transactionally consistent database snapshot from which data can be recovered.

- **Roles-based access**. Provides the minimum access rights to different roles in a company, such as developers and support.

- **Auditing**. Tracks database access and data changes to provide an audit trail for forensic analysis.

From an integrity standpoint, SQL Database doesn't yet provide the same capabilities as SQL Server. SQL Database does deliver strong authorization capabilities and role-based security, similar to SQL Server 2012. However, traditional database backups and activity auditing aren't available as of this writing. Microsoft is building new backup mechanisms for SQL Database, above and beyond the BCP (Bulk Copy Program) operations available now. See Chapter 4 for more information about how to back up your data in SQL Database.

Availability

Availability ensures service uptime so your data can be accessed when it's needed. Designing highly available systems can be very complex and requires advanced knowledge in multiple areas including disk configuration, system administration, disaster-recovery locations, and more. The following are some of the technologies involved in high availability:

- **Redundant disks**. Allows you to recover from the loss of a disk spindle. Usually involves a RAID configuration.

- **Redundant networks**. Allows you to survive the loss of multiple network components, such as a network card or a router.

- **Redundant services**. Allows you to survive the interruption of services such as security and databases. An example is the use of Microsoft Cluster Service.

- **Redundant hardware**. Allows you to survive the loss of machine hardware, such as a CPU or a memory chip.

- **Scalability**. Delivers information at near constant speed under load.

- **DoS prevention**. Prevents successful denial of service (DoS) attacks that would otherwise prevent data availability.

In addition to ensuring redundancy of infrastructure components, you need to understand the recovery objectives of your business to determine how to best implement your availability requirements.

SQL Database offers a unique platform because all the areas just listed are automatically provided for. SQL Database offers a 99.9% monthly availability guarantee through its service-level agreement (SLA). In order to deliver this high availability, SQL Database transparently keeps two additional standby databases for each user database you create. If anything happens to one of your user databases, one of the two standby databases takes over within a few seconds; you may not even notice the failover process. SQL Database also provides automatic handling of DoS attacks.

SQL Database accomplishes failover using the architecture shown in Figure 3-1. You interact with a proxy that directs your request to whichever of your databases is current. The standby databases aren't accessible to you.

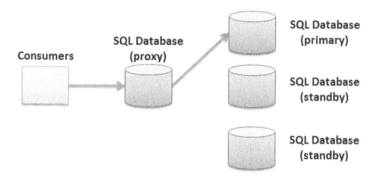

Figure 3-1. *SQL Database's standby database architecture*

■ **Note**   In terms of availability, SQL Database far surpasses SQL Server out of the box; SQL Database is built on a scalable and highly available platform that doesn't require configuration or tuning. None of the typical SQL Server configuration settings are available in SQL Database (such as CPU Affinity, Replication, Log Shipping, and so on).

Let's take an example of a project that needs to deploy a new application with high availability requirements. The following items would need to be planned for in a traditional SQL Server installation but are provided to you automatically with SQL Database:

- **Clustered SQL Server instance**. Install and configure Microsoft Cluster Service and SQL Server instances in an active/active or active/passive configuration.

- **RAID configuration**. Purchase new disks and hardware to install and configure a RAID 10 (or RAID 0+1) disk array (for disk redundancy and performance).

- **Disaster-recovery server**. Purchase similar hardware and configure it at a disaster-recovery site.

- **Replication topology**. Create a mechanism to transfer the data from the primary site to the secondary site using log shipping, replication, disk-level replication, or another technique, depending on your needs.

- **Database tuning**. In larger systems, tuning SQL Server for high performance can be very difficult and involves CPU, memory, I/O affinitization, degree of parallelism, and many other considerations.

- **Testing**. Plan and execute a disaster-recovery plan once a year, to make sure it's working as intended.

And of course, you must consider the costs associated with all these activities, the time it takes to plan and execute such a project, and the specialized resources needed to implement a highly available database environment.

By now, you can see that although SQL Database offers fewer options in certain areas of security, it excels in others, especially its availability model, which is one of the CIA triad components. Deploying a highly available SQL Database database is quick and extremely simple.

Securing Your Data

Let's dive into some specifics and code examples to show how to secure your data in SQL Database. You may need to secure specific columns in your database that contain sensitive information, such as Social Security numbers or credit card numbers. Certain medical applications store patient data, which can fall under compliance review, and as such may need to be encrypted as well. As hinted previously, not all security mechanisms are currently available, so this section focuses on what SQL Database provides and on ways to mitigate the missing features. Regarding data encryption, because SQL Database provides none, you'll see how to implement your own security classes to simplify data encryption in your projects.

■ **Note**   The examples that follow use a database script called `Security.sql` and a Visual Studio 2008 project called `SQLAzureSecurity.sln`. You can run the SQL script on your local SQL Server database if you don't have a Windows Azure account yet.

This chapter uses a few classes and methods to demonstrate how to use encryption, hashing, and other techniques. Figure 3-2 shows the objects being used. The `Encryption` class performs the actual encryption and returns a `CipherText` structure; the `UserProperties` class uses extension methods from the `Extensions` class and a helper method in the `Util` class. The `CDatabase` class returns the database connection string.

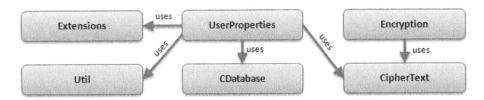

Figure 3-2. *Object model used in the examples*

Encryption

As mentioned previously, data encryption isn't available. Why? Because SQL Database doesn't support X.509 certificates. Certificates are necessary for many encryption-related features, such as Transparent Data Encryption (TDE), column-level encryption, and certain T-SQL commands, such as `FOR ENCRYPTION` and `SIGNBYCERT`.

However, SQL Database requires the use of SSL encryption for its communication. This means your sensitive data is always transmitted safely between your clients and your SQL Database instance. There is nothing you need to do to enable SSL encryption; it's required and automatically enforced by SQL Database. If an application tries to connect to SQL Database and the application doesn't support SSL, the connection request fails.

But SSL doesn't encrypt data at rest; it only encrypts data in transit. How can you protect your data when it's stored in SQL Database? Because SQL Database doesn't support encryption natively, you must encrypt and decrypt your data in the application code.

The Security.sql script contains the following T-SQL statement:

```
1. CREATE TABLE UserProperties
2. (
3.    ID int identity(1,1) PRIMARY KEY,        -- identity of the record
4.    PropertyName nvarchar(255) NOT NULL,      -- name of the property
5.    Value varbinary(max) NOT NULL,            -- encrypted value
6.    Vector binary(16) NOT NULL,               -- vector of encrypted value
7.    LastUpdated datetime NOT NULL,            -- date of last modification
8.    Token binary(32) NOT NULL                 -- record hash
9. )
```

Each record contains a property name (line 4) that can be used as a search key and an encrypted value (line 5). The value itself is a binary data type, which lends itself well to encryption. A vector is used for additional security; this column is explained shortly. The Token and LastUpdated columns are addressed later when discussing hashing.

The following C# code shows how to encrypt a string value using the Advanced Encryption Standard (AES) algorithm; you can easily add support for Triple Data Encryption Standard (3DES) or other algorithms. It uses a shared secret to create the ciphertext and returns a byte array. The byte array is stored later in the Value column in the database:

```
1. /// <summary>
2. /// A result structure that stores the encrypted value
3. /// and its associated vector
4. /// </summary>
5. public struct CipherText
6. {
7.    public byte[] cipher;
8.    public byte[] vector;
9. }
10.
11. /// <summary>
12. /// The encryption class that encapsulates the complexity behind encrypting
13. /// and decrypting values
14. /// </summary>
15. public class Encryption
16. {
17.    private byte[] _SECRET_KEY_ = new byte[] { 160, 225, 229, 3,
18.        148, 219, 67, 89, 247, 133, 213, 26, 129, 160, 235, 41,
19.        42, 177, 202, 251, 38, 56, 232, 90, 54, 88, 158, 169,
20.        200, 24, 19, 27 };
21.
22./// <summary>
23./// Encrypt using AES
24./// </summary>
25./// <param name="value">The string to encrypt</param>
26.public CipherText EncryptAES(string value)
27.{
28.    // Prepare variables...
29.    byte[] buffer = UTF8Encoding.UTF8.GetBytes(value);
30.    CipherText ct = new CipherText();
31.    System.Security.Cryptography.Aes aes = null;
32.    ICryptoTransform transform = null;
33.
```

```
34.    // Create the AES object
35.    aes = System.Security.Cryptography.Aes.Create();
36.    aes.GenerateIV();
37.    aes.Key = _SECRET_KEY_;
38.
39.    // Create the encryption object
40.    transform = aes.CreateEncryptor();
41.
42.    // Encrypt and store the result in the structure
43.    ct.cipher = transform.TransformFinalBlock(buffer, 0, buffer.Length);
44.    // Save the vector used for future use
45.    ct.vector = aes.IV;
46.
47.    return ct;
48.    }
49.}
```

The CipherText structure (line 5) is used as a return value. Each encrypted byte array comes with its initialization vector, which is a security mechanism that prevents dictionary attacks on your database. The Encryption class contains an EncryptAES method that performs the actual encryption of a string value; this method returns CipherText.

Because AES requires a secret key, you created one in the form of a byte array on line 17. The secret key must be 32 bytes in length. You can easily generate your own by using the GenerateKey method provided by the Aes class provided by .NET.

On line 29, you transform the string value to its byte representation using UTF-8 encoding. This encoding scheme is very practical because it automatically chooses between ASCII and Unicode based on the input value.

You declare the AES object on line 31 and instantiate it on line 35 using the static Create() method on the Aes class. This method creates the vector automatically on line 36 and sets the private key discussed earlier.

On line 40, you create a cryptographic object using the CreateEncryptor() method. A call to its TransformFinalBlock() method does the trick and outputs a variable-length byte array that you store in the CipherText structure instance on line 43. You save the previously generated vector as well and return the structure on line 47.

That was simple, right? Now all you have to do is store the CipherText content in the UserProperties table. But before doing this, let's discuss hashing.

■ **Note**   This example uses AES, but other algorithms are available with the .NET Framework. Because you also use an initialization vector, running the same code over and over yields different output, given the same input. That makes the encrypted value harder to crack. The Visual Studio Solution provided includes additional methods to decrypt data.

Hashing

Hashing isn't nearly as complicated as you've seen so far. And although you can store the values you've encrypted so far in the database, in this example you hash all the columns of the rows (except the ID value) to make sure they're unchanged. Why? The answer goes back to the integrity concern of the CIA triad discussed earlier. You want a way to tell whether your data has been modified outside of your code. Encrypting your secret value makes it virtually impossible to break the confidentiality aspect of the triad, but someone can still update the PropertyName column—or, worse, the Value column. Hashing doesn't prevent data from being modified, but you have a way to detect whether it was changed without your authorization.

To simplify the code, start by creating a couple of extension methods. Extension methods are a handy way to extend the methods available to a class (or data type) even if you don't have the original source code. Here you can see how to declare an extension method on the string and DateTime data types:

```
1.  public static class Extensions
2.  {
3.      public static byte[] GetBytes(this string value)
4.      {
5.          byte[] buffer = UTF8Encoding.UTF8.GetBytes(value);
6.          return buffer;
7.      }
8.
9.      public static byte[] GetBytes(this DateTime value)
10.     {
11.         return value.ToString().GetBytes();
12.     }
13. }
```

This code adds a GetBytes() method to the string and DateTime data types. You also create a utility class that allows you to create a hash value based on a collection of byte arrays. The following code shows that class:

```
1.  public class Util
2.  {
3.  /// <summary>
4.  /// Computes a hash value based on an array of byte arrays
5.  /// </summary>
6.  /// <param name="bytes">Array of byte arrays</param>
7.  public static byte[] ComputeHash(params byte[][] bytes)
8.  {
9.      SHA256 sha = SHA256Managed.Create();
10.     MemoryStream ms = new MemoryStream();
11.
12.     for (int i = 0; i < bytes.Length; i++)
13.     ms.Write(bytes[i], 0, bytes[i].Length);
14.
15.     ms.Flush();
16.     ms.Position = 0;
17.
18.     return sha.ComputeHash(ms);
19.     }
20. }
```

This Util class will be very handy shortly. Note on line 7 the declaration of the variable as params byte[][]; this means each parameter passed to this method must be a byte array. You declare a memory stream, loop on each byte-array variable, and append it to the memory stream on line 13. Finally, you return the computed hash of the memory stream on line 18. You will see how to call this method shortly.

The UserProperties class is next, in the following example, and makes the actual call to the SQL Database instance. It takes two input parameters: the property name to save and its encrypted value stored in the CipherText structure. On line 13, you retrieve the connection string from another class and open the database connection on line 15. You then create the command object, specifying a call to a stored procedure. The code for the stored procedure is provided later in this section. The hash value is then created on line 39; as you can see, you call the ComputeHash method just reviewed by passing each stored procedure parameter as a byte array. This is where you use both the extension methods created earlier and the hashing method. After the hash result is calculated, you pass it into the last stored procedure parameter on line 45:

```
1.   using System.Data.SqlDbType;
2.   public class UserProperties
3.   {
4.
5.       /// <summary>
6.       /// Saves a property value in a SQL Azure database
7.       /// </summary>
8.       /// <param name="propertyName">The property name</param>
9.       /// <param name="ct">The CipherText structure to save</param>
10.      public static void Save(string propertyName, CipherText ct)
11.      {
12.          using (SqlConnection sqlConn =
13.                      new SqlConnection(CDatabase.ConnectionString))
14.          {
15.              sqlConn.Open();
16.
17.              using (SqlCommand sqlCmd = new SqlCommand())
18.              {
19.
20.                  DateTime dateUpdated = DateTime.Now;
21.
22.                  sqlCmd.Connection = sqlConn;
23.                  sqlCmd.CommandType = System.Data.CommandType.StoredProcedure;
24.                  sqlCmd.CommandText = "proc_SaveProperty";
25.                  sqlCmd.Parameters.Add("name", NVarChar, 255);
26.                  sqlCmd.Parameters.Add("value", VarBinary, int.MaxValue);
27.                  sqlCmd.Parameters.Add("vector", VarBinary, 16);
28.                  sqlCmd.Parameters.Add("lastUpdated", DateTime);
29.                  sqlCmd.Parameters.Add("hash", VarBinary, 32);
30.                  sqlCmd.Parameters[0].Value = propertyName;
31.                  sqlCmd.Parameters[1].Value = ct.cipher;
32.                  sqlCmd.Parameters[2].Value = ct.vector;
33.                  sqlCmd.Parameters[3].Value = dateUpdated;
34.
35.                  // Calculate the hash of this record...
36.                  // We pass the list of values that should be hashed
37.                  // If any of these values changes in the database,
38.                  // recalculating the hash would yield a different result
39.                  byte[] hash = Util.ComputeHash(
40.                      propertyName.GetBytes(),
41.                      ct.cipher,
42.                      ct.vector,
43.                      dateUpdated.GetBytes());
44.
45.                  sqlCmd.Parameters[4].Value = hash;
46.
47.                  int res = sqlCmd.ExecuteNonQuery();
48.
49.              }
50.
```

```
51.            sqlConn.Close();
52.
53.          }
54.        }
55.
56. }
```

As promised, following is the code for the stored procedure. You create a stored procedure because it allows you to provide additional security from an access-control standpoint. As you see later, you create a schema that contains the tables and a separate schema for the stored procedures that access the tables. This provides greater control over your database security. You'll review schemas later in this chapter.

```
IF (Exists(SELECT * FROM sys.sysobjects WHERE Name = 'proc_SaveProperty' AND Type = 'P'))
   DROP PROC proc_SaveProperty

GO

-- SELECT * FROM UserProperties
CREATE PROC proc_SaveProperty
   @name nvarchar(255),
   @value varbinary(max),
   @vector binary(16),
   @lastUpdated datetime,
   @hash binary(32)
AS

IF (Exists(SELECT * FROM UserProperties WHERE PropertyName = @name))
BEGIN
   UPDATE UserProperties SET
      Value = @value,
      Vector = @vector,
      LastUpdated = @lastUpdated,
      Token = @hash
   WHERE
      PropertyName = @name
END
ELSE
BEGIN
   INSERT INTO UserProperties
       (PropertyName, Value, Vector, LastUpdated, Token)
   VALUES (
      @name,
      @value,
      @vector,
      @lastUpdated,
      @hash )
END
```

This stored procedure performs both updates and inserts depending on the property name. Note the use of varbinary(max); because you don't know how long the encrypted value will be, you allow large but variable binary objects to be stored. However, the vector is always 16 bytes in length and the hash 32.

Running the Save() method on the UserProperties class creates a record in the UserProperties table. The following code shows how to call the Save method:

```
1.    class Program
2.    {
3.        static void Main(string[] args)
4.        {
5.            // Declare the encryption object and encrypt our secret value
6.            Encryption e = new Encryption();
7.            CipherText ct = e.EncryptAES("secret value goes here...");
8.
9.            UserProperties.Save("MySecret", ct);
10.
11.       }
12.   }
```

Figure 3-3 shows the content of the table after you run the program. The Value column is your encrypted value, the Vector is the @vector variable from the stored procedure, and the Token column is the calculated hash passed as the @hash variable.

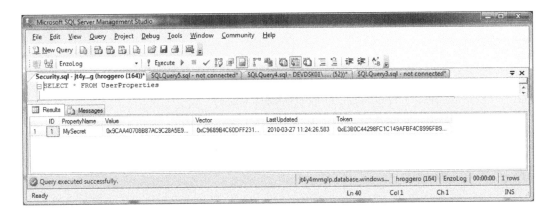

Figure 3-3. *Record with the encrypted value, a hash, and a vector*

Last but not least, you should know that SQL Server and SQL Database both support hashing natively. Support for hashing was until recently limited to the MD5 and SHA-1 algorithms. However SQL Database and SQL Server 2012 now support hashes with 256 and 512 bit strengths. As a result you could use the HASHBYTES command to create the Token value previously created in C#. Here is a quick example of how to compute an SHA-256 hash in SQL:

```
SELECT HASHBYTES('sha2_256', 'MySecret')
```

The output of HASHBYTES() is a byte array as well:

```
0x49562CFC3B17139EA01C480B9C86A2DDACB38FF1B2E9DB1BF66BAB7A4E3F1FB5
```

You could change the stored procedure created previously to perform the hashing function in it, instead of using C# code. However keeping the hashing algorithm in C# may make sense for performance reasons because it is a CPU-intensive operation. If your application calculates hashes constantly you may want to keep hashing in C# to save database CPU cycles for other tasks. If you decide to hash values using T-SQL you may want to first convert your strings to Unicode; this will help you generate comparable hashes if you end up using hash functions in C# (strings in C# are Unicode by default). To hash the MySecret string as Unicode in SQL Database or SQL Server, use the N converter in T-SQL, as such:

```
SELECT HASHBYTES('sha2_256', N'MySecret')
```

So far, you've seen a way to encrypt sensitive information for confidentiality, hashed certain columns of a record for increased integrity, and deployed in Azure for strong availability. As you can see, developing encryption and hashing routines can be very complex and requires a strong command of the programming language. You may find it beneficial to create a generic encryption library, like the one shown in the previous examples, that can be reused across projects.

Certificates

As discussed previously, SQL Database doesn't support X.509 certificates, although you can deploy X.509 certificates in Windows Azure. Your client code (hosted either on your company's network or in Windows Azure) can use certificates to encrypt and decrypt values. The use of certificates implies that you're encrypting using a public/private key pair. The public key is used to encrypt data, and the private key is used to decrypt data.

■ **Note**   For more information on how to deploy X.509 certificates in Windows Azure, visit the MSDN blog `http://blogs.msdn.com/jnak` and look at the January 2010 archive. The blog entry by Jim Nakashima contains detailed instructions.

You can easily create a self-signed certificate using the MakeCert.exe utility which is a utility you can find in the Windows SDK. To create a certificate on your machines, run the following command at a command line. You need to execute this statement as an Administrator or the command will fail:

```
makecert -ss root -pe -r -n "CN=BlueSyntaxTest" -sky Exchange -sr LocalMachine
```

Here is a brief overview of the options used to create this certificate:

- -ss root stores the certificate in the root certificate store.

- -pe marks the private key exportable.

- -r creates a self-signed certificate (meaning that it wasn't issued by a root certificate authority (CA) like Thawte).

- -n "CN=..." specifies the subject's name of the certificate.

- -sky Exchange specifies that the certificate is used for encryption.

- -sr LocalMachine specifies that the certificate store location as LocalMachine.

■ **Note** Make sure you run this statement as an Administrator, or you'll get an error that looks like this: `Error:Save encoded certificate to store failed => 0x5 (5)`.

To verify that your certificate was properly installed, open `mmc.exe`. Select File ➤ Add/Remove Snap In. Then, select Certificates, click Add, choose Computer, and click OK. Expand the tree on the left to view the certificates under Trusted Root Certification Authorities. Figure 3-4 shows the BlueSyntaxTest certificate that was created with the earlier command.

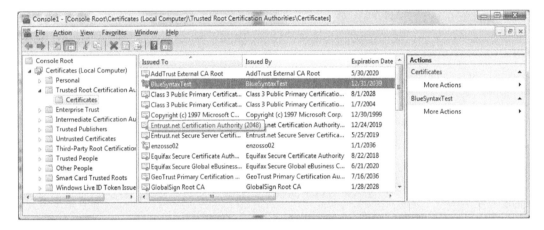

Figure 3-4. *Viewing certificates on your machine*

Now that you have a certificate installed, you can search for and locate it with code. Usually, a certificate is searched for by its unique identifier (*thumbprint*) or by its *common name* (CN). To view the thumbprint of your certificate, double-click the certificate, select the Details tab, and scroll down until you see the `Thumbprint` property, as shown in Figure 3-5.

Figure 3-5. *Obtaining a certificate's thumbprint*

You can select the thumbprint and copy it into a string variable. The following code shows a new private variable and a new method in the Encryption class you saw earlier. Line 1 contains the thumbprint as seen in Figure 3-5, line 13 opens the root certificate store on LocalMachine, and line 17 instantiates an X.509 object by searching the thumbprint. Note that the Find method returns a collection; you're interested in the first certificate because only one will match this thumbprint. On line 24, you create the RSA encryption object and call its Encrypt method on line 27. Because encrypting with RSA automatically incorporates a vector, there is no need to keep track of it, and so the CipherText vector variable is set to 0:

```
1.  private string _THUMBPRINT_ =
2.     "01 71 11 17 0a b4 96 7b ca 1f f3 e5 bc 0f 68 9d c6 c0 3b 7b";
3.
4.          /// <summary>
5.          /// Encrypts a string value using a self-signed certificate
6.          /// </summary>
7.          /// <param name="value">The value to encrypt</param>
```

```
8.          /// <returns></returns>
9.          public CipherText EncryptByCert(string value)
10.         {
11.             byte[] buffer = UTF8Encoding.UTF8.GetBytes(value);
12.
13.             X509Store store = new X509Store(StoreName.Root,
14.                 StoreLocation.LocalMachine);
15.             store.Open(OpenFlags.ReadOnly);
16.
17.             X509Certificate2 x509 =
18.                 store.Certificates.Find(
19.                 X509FindType.FindByThumbprint,
20.                 _THUMBPRINT_, true)[0];
21.
22.             store.Close();
23.
24.             RSACryptoServiceProvider rsaEncrypt = null;
25.             rsaEncrypt = (RSACryptoServiceProvider)x509.PublicKey.Key;
26.
27.             byte[] encryptedBytes = rsaEncrypt.Encrypt(buffer, false);
28.
29.             CipherText ct = new CipherText();
30.             ct.cipher = encryptedBytes;
31.             ct.vector = new byte[] {0, 0, 0, 0, 0, 0, 0, 0, 0,
32.                 0, 0, 0, 0, 0, 0, 0};
33.
34.             return ct;
35.         }
```

The decryption code is shown next and is very similar to the preceding example. You make a call to Decrypt instead of Encrypt on the RSA object:

```
1.          public string DecryptByCert(CipherText ct)
2.          {
3.              X509Store store = new X509Store(StoreName.Root,
4.                  StoreLocation.LocalMachine);
5.              store.Open(OpenFlags.ReadOnly);
6.
7.              X509Certificate2 x509 =
8.                  store.Certificates.Find(
9.                  X509FindType.FindByThumbprint,
10.                 _THUMBPRINT_, true)[0];
11.
12.             store.Close();
13.
14.             RSACryptoServiceProvider rsaEncrypt = null;
15.             rsaEncrypt = (RSACryptoServiceProvider)x509.PrivateKey;
16.
17.             byte[] bytes = rsaEncrypt.Decrypt(ct.cipher, false);
18.
19.             return UTF8Encoding.UTF8.GetString(bytes);
20.         }
```

The following code calls the RSA encryption routine and saves its result to the UserProperties table as previously described. The table now contains two records. Note that the length of the ciphertext is much greater with the certificate encryption approach:

```
1.    class Program
2.    {
3.        static void Main(string[] args)
4.        {
5.            // Declare the encryption object and encrypt our secret value
6.            Encryption e = new Encryption();
7.            CipherText ct = e.EncryptAES("secret value goes here...");
8.            CipherText ct2 = e.EncryptByCert("another secret!!!");
9.
10.           UserProperties.Save("MySecret", ct);
11.           UserProperties.Save("MySecret2", ct2);
12.
13.       }
14.   }
```

Access Control

So far, you've spent a lot of time encrypting and hashing values for increased confidentiality and integrity. However, another important aspect of the CIA triad is access control. This section reviews two subcategories of access control: authentication (also referred to as AUTHN) and authorization (AUTHZ).

Authentication (AUTHN)

AUTHN is a process that verifies you're indeed who you say you are. In SQL Server, the AUTHN process is done through one of two mechanisms: network credentials (which are handled through Kerberos authentication over the Security Support Provider Interface [SSPI]) or SQL Server credentials. Connection strings must specify which AUTHN is being used. And when you use SQL Server AUTHN, a password must be provided before attempting to connect, either by a user at runtime or in a configuration file.

Keep the following items in mind when you're considering AUTHN with SQL Database:

- **No network authentication**. Because SQL Database isn't on your network, network AUTHN isn't available. This further means you must use SQL AUTHN at all times and that you must store passwords in your applications (in configuration files, preferably). You may want to store your passwords encrypted. Although you can encrypt sections of your configuration files in Windows using the aspnet_regiis.exe utility, this option isn't available in Windows Azure using the default providers. However, you can encrypt sections of your web configuration file using a custom configuration provider: PKCS12 (found on the MSDN Code Gallery). For more information on how to use this custom provider, visit http://tinyurl.com/9ta8m5u.

- **Strong passwords**. SQL Database requires the use of strong passwords. This option can't be disabled, which is a good thing. A strong password must be at least eight characters long; must combine letters, numbers, and symbols; and can't be a word found in a dictionary.

- **Login name limitations**. Certain login names aren't available, such as sa, admin, and guest. These logins can't be created. You should also refrain from using the @ symbol in your login names; this symbol is used to separate a user name from a machine name, which may be needed at times.

Authorization (AUTHZ)

Authorization gives you the ability to control who can perform which actions after being authenticated. It's important to define a good AUTHZ model early in your development cycle, because changing access-control strategy can be relatively difficult.

Generally speaking, a strong AUTHZ model defines which users can access which objects in the database. This is typically performed in SQL Database and SQL Server by defining relationships between logins, users, schemas, and rights.

Creating Logins and Users

A login account is used to manage authentication in SQL Database; it is a server-level entity. If you know a login account with its password, you can log in. A user is a database entity and is used for access control. The user determines which objects you can access and what actions you can perform. Each login can map to 0 or 1 user in each database, including master.

In SQL Database, you must be connected to the master database to manage your logins. The CREATE LOGIN T-SQL statement is partially supported. Also, remember that you must use a strong password when creating logins.

SQL Database offers two new roles:

- **LoginManager**. Grants a user the ability to create new logins in the master database.

- **DBManager**. Grants a user the ability to create new databases from the master database.

First let's create a login account in the master database:

```
CREATE LOGIN MyTestLogin WITH PASSWORD='MyT3stLOgin'
GO
```

You can optionally grant this login access to master. The following code shows how to give that login access to the master database and grant the LoginManager role in the master database. If your intention is to only grant this login access to the user database, you can skip this step.

```
CREATE USER MyTestLoginUser FROM LOGIN MyTestLogin
GO
EXEC sp_addrolemember 'loginmanager', MyTestLoginUser
GO
```

In most cases you will want to create the login account in master and the user in the user database. The following code shows how to create the user in a user database with read rights. You must first connect to the user database or the statement below will fail.

```
CREATE USER MyTestLoginUser FROM LOGIN MyTestLogin
GO
EXEC sp_addrolemember 'db_datareader', MyTestLoginUser
GO
```

Now the MyTestLogin account can connect to your user database.

Finally, you should note that the SQL Database admin account is always added as a user in every new SQL Database instance and is the dbo by default. This means that you do not need to create a user for the admin account. If you try to do so, you will receive an error saying the user already exists. For example, if my admin login account is 'hroggero', the following command will fail because the user is already created automatically and mapped to dbo:

```
CREATE USER hroggero WITH LOGIN hroggero

Msg 15007, Level 16, State 1, Line 1
'hroggero' is not a valid login or you do not have permission.
```

Schemas

A *schema* is a container that holds database objects; schemas reside inside a database. Schemas are part of the three-part naming convention of database objects; they're considered namespaces. Each object in a schema must have a unique name.

By default, objects created are owned by the DBO schema when you connect with the dbo login. For example, the CREATE TABLE statement showed previously for the UserProperties table uses DBO as the schema owner (schema_id is always 1 for DBO). See Figure 3-6.

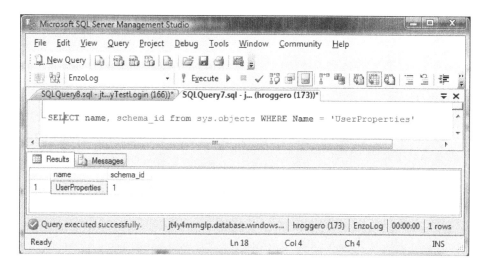

***Figure 3-6.** Viewing an object's schema ownership*

Right now, the new user MyTestLoginUser can't read from this table. Attempting to issue a SELECT statement against UserProperties returns a SELECT permission denied error. So, you have a choice: you can either give that user account SELECT permission on that table, assign the user to the appropriate role, or create a schema for that user and assign the SELECT permission to the schema.

It's usually much easier to manage access rights through roles instead of users directly. However, if you want finer control over access rights, you should consider using schema-driven security. To do this properly, you need to change the ownership of the UserProperties table to a new schema (other than DBO) and then assign access rights to the schema.

To create a new schema, you must be connected to the desired user database where MyTestLoginUser has been created. Then run the following statement:

```
CREATE SCHEMA MyReadOnlySchema AUTHORIZATION DBO
```

At this point, a schema has been created; it's owned by DBO. You now need to change the ownership of the UserProperties table to MyReadOnlySchema:

```
ALTER SCHEMA MyReadOnlySchema TRANSFER DBO.UserProperties
```

The table now belongs to the schema, as shown in Figure 3-7.

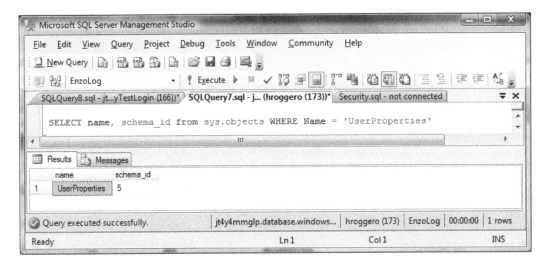

Figure 3-7. *Viewing the new schema owner*

However, you aren't done just yet. MyTestLoginUser can no longer see the table. Issuing a `select` statement on the table returns an `Invalid object` name message, as shown in Figure 3-8.

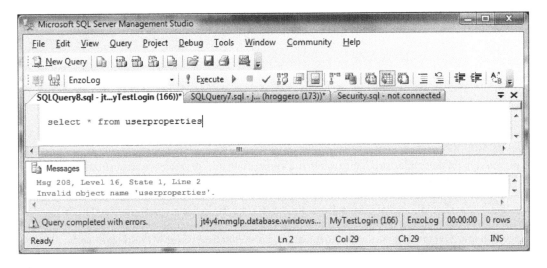

Figure 3-8. *Error when the user can't see an object*

The default schema of MyTestLoginUser is DBO, as shown in Figure 3-9. The default schema of a user is the schema that's used if none is specified in a T-SQL statement. To make it easier on developers, change the default schema to MyReadOnlySchema, so it doesn't have to be specified in T-SQL statements.

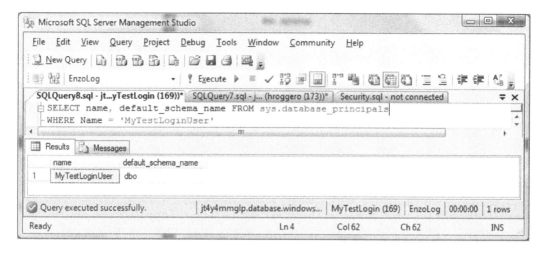

Figure 3-9. *Schema owner of a login*

To change the user's default schema, you need to execute this statement:

```
ALTER USER MyTestLoginUser WITH DEFAULT_SCHEMA = MyReadOnlySchema
```

Now that the user has MyReadOnlySchema as its default schema, it can see the objects owned by that schema directly, without having to specify the object owner. However, you haven't set the access rights yet. Let's grant SELECT rights to MyTestLoginUser:

```
GRANT SELECT ON SCHEMA :: MyReadOnlySchema TO MyTestLoginUser
```

The following statement works again for the MyTestLoginUser account:

```
SELECT * FROM UserProperties
```

Why did you go through all this trouble? Because creating your own schemas is a great way to manage access control by granting rights to schemas instead of objects directly. In a way, schemas can be used as a group, like a Windows Group, on which rights are granted or denied.

Figure 3-10 shows how you've switched the security model around for greater flexibility and control.

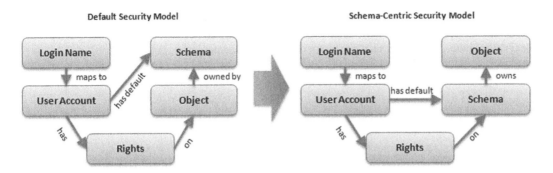

Figure 3-10. *Moving to a security model through schemas*

Schema Separation

The schema security model presented previously is the foundation for implementing a multitenant model using schema separation as a sharding mechanism. From a storage standpoint, a multitenant system is a collection of databases that hosts multiple customers in such a way that each customer is isolated from a security and management standpoint.

Although you can create a multitenant system by creating a database for each customer, you can also create a schema container for each customer and co-locate customers in fewer databases. The schema security model discussed in this chapter allows you to securely co-locate customers in the same database and keep strong security boundaries by using different logins and users for each customer, where each user is only given access to a specific schema.

In Figure 3-11, I am creating a new customer container in an existing database, called DB1. Because the database stores other customers and my objective is to ensure strong security isolation, I first create a new login (L3) for my customer in master (the customer is called C3 in this example).

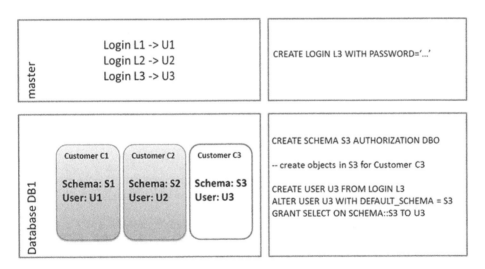

Figure 3-11. *Creating a new schema container for a customer*

Then I connect to DB1 and create the schema container (S3), in which the customer data will be stored. Once the schema container is created I can create all the necessary objects in S3, such as tables, views, and stored procedures.

Next I create a user (U3) for the login account L3. I make sure to change the default schema of U3 from DBO to S3.

Finally I grant U3 all the necessary access rights. At this point I have a newly created schema with strong security isolation from other customers in an existing database.

You can learn more about this sharding model in Chapter 9.

SQL Database Firewall

SQL Database comes with its own firewall, which you can configure directly from the SQL Database portal, as previously covered in Chapter 1. You can also view and change firewall rules in T-SQL. Let's take a quick look at the available SQL statements.

■ **Note**   You need to be connected to the master database to view or change firewall rules. At least one connection rule must be added to the firewall through the SQL Database portal before a connection can be made.

To view the current firewall rules, execute this statement:

```
SELECT * FROM sys.firewall_rules
```

You can see that each rule has a name; the name is used as a unique key. The sp_set_firewall_rule command allows you to add a new rule.

It may take a few minutes for the new rules to take effect. For example, the following statement adds a new rule called NewRule. Notice that the first parameter must be a Unicode string:

```
sp_set_firewall_rule N'NewRule', '192.168.1.1', '192.168.1.10'
```

To delete a rule, run the following statement:

```
sp_delete_firewall_rule N'NewRule'
```

Internal Firewalls

Some organizations control network access with advanced rules for connecting to the Internet using internal firewalls. Because connecting to SQL Database from your internal network requires opening port "TCP 1433 out," if your company uses an internal firewall you may need to request this port to be open. For security reasons your network administrator may request the IP Range of SQL Database so that the port is only open for specific destinations. Unfortunately, restricting the connection to an IP Range may become an issue at a later time because SQL Database IP Ranges may change over time. As a result you should open the port to ANY IP destination.

Compliance

Although cloud computing creates new challenges for organizations from a risk-management standpoint, Microsoft's cloud data centers undergo multiple audits and assessments based on their local regulations. In order to facilitate its compliance audits and assessment, Microsoft created the Operational Compliance team, which designed a common compliance framework for its operations.

According to Microsoft, parts of its cloud computing infrastructure are compliant with multiple regulations including PCI, Health Insurance Portability and Accountability Act (HIPAA), and Sarbanes-Oxley. It also has achieved numerous certifications, including

- ISO/IEC 27001:2005

- SAS 70 Type I and II

Microsoft recently announced a Trust Services framework as a technology preview. Although this service is in its early stage it offers a standard mechanism for securing the exchange of sensitive data across organizations. For more information check the SQL Azure Labs website (`www.sqlazurelabs.com`).

▨ **Note** For more information about Microsoft's compliance initiatives, visit `www.globalfoundationservices.com`.

Summary

Security in the cloud is a complex topic and involves careful analysis of your requirements and design options. This chapter covered the basics of the CIA triad and classified security options in terms of confidentiality, integrity, and availability.

You also reviewed how to plan for strong encryption and hashing in your Visual Studio applications. Finally, keep in mind that schema separation can be very useful and should be implemented early in your development cycles.

By now, you should understand the many options available to you in order to secure you data in SQL Database and be aware of some of the limitations of the SQL Database platform. Keep in mind, however, that some of those limitations are likely to be either removed or mitigated at some point in the future as Microsoft provides additional updates to its SQL Database platform.

CHAPTER 4

■ ■ ■

Data Migration and Backup Strategies

When companies talk about their research into or experiences with the Azure technology—specifically the SQL side of Azure—two of their most frequent concerns (aside from security) are migrating local databases and data into the cloud, and backup strategies. Until Azure came around, databases were housed locally (and they still are): they're contained within the walls of the company or in a data center. Moving to the Azure platform and SQL Azure means moving all or a portion of your data into the cloud and storing it there.

Chapter 3 talked at length about security concerns, considerations, and best practices for storing your precious data in the cloud. Moving data into the cloud is a decision that you shouldn't and can't take lightly. But after you make the decision to utilize SQL Azure, the question becomes, how do you get your data into the cloud? As nice as it would be if moving your local database into SQL Azure was seamless, it isn't as cut-and-dried as you may think. You do have several viable options available; but you must consider things beyond just moving the data, such as costs from data transfers.

After your data is in the cloud, further questions arise regarding the backup strategies that are common with local databases. In SQL Azure, gone are the concepts of backup devices and backing up and restoring databases. As shocking as this may sound, remember that Microsoft is managing the hardware behind the scenes. For now, there are no such things as drives, devices, and so on.

In this chapter we will discuss the different migration tools, strategies, and concepts for moving your database and data into the cloud. You'll see examples illustrating how these tools are used. We'll finish the chapter off by spending a page or two on backup strategies and tools that help provide SQL Database backup capabilities.

Migrating Databases and Data to SQL Azure

So you want to move one or more of your applications and its databases to the cloud. It's a noble idea. More than likely, you're in the same category as countless others who are looking into moving applications into the cloud: you don't want to start from scratch. You'd rather migrate an existing application to the cloud, but you aren't sure about the steps necessary to do so, or the technologies available to help in the process. This section discusses three tools from Microsoft that come as part of SQL Server:

- The Import/Export Service
- The Generate and Publish Scripts Wizard
- The bcp utility

In addition to these three tools, we will also briefly mention a free utility found on CodePlex called the SQL Azure Migration Wizard, which provides a wizard-driven interface to walk you through migrating your database and data to SQL Azure.

The examples in this chapter use SQL Server 2012, which is available from Microsoft's MSDN site. These examples also work with SQL Server 2008, although some the screens may be a bit different.

The database you use in these examples is AWMini, which is a mini version of the AdventureWorks database. This database can be downloaded from the APress site for this book.

The Import/Export Service

In 2012 Microsoft released some great functionality for migrating an on-premises database to SQL Azure in the form of the Import/Export service. To understand what this service is and how it works, you first need to know about the Data-Tier Application Framework, more commonly known as DAC Fx.

Data-Tier Application Framework

DAC Fx was introduced in SQL Server 2008 R2 as part of the Application and Multi-Server Management services, a way to manage your database environments efficiently and proactively. It was designed with scale in mind to provide an effective way to manage the deployment of the database schema between environments, such as from Development to Test, and Test to Production.

DAC Fx is a set of tools, APIs, and services designed to improve the development, deployment and management of SQL Server database schemas. In most environments, the DBA creates and maintains sets of T-SQL scripts that create or alter database objects, such as tables and stored procedures. The issue is that in many instances the DBAs need to maintain multiple sets of scripts; one for the initial creation and another for updates and modifications that update the database from one version to another. Add on top of that multiple versions of those scripts, and you have the makings of a complex maintenance scenario.

This is where DAC Fx comes in. Instead of building and maintaining sets of T-SQL scripts, SQL Server 2008 R2 introduced the concept of a *BACPAC*. A DAC, or Data-Tier Application, is an entity that contains all of the database objects used by an application. Its purpose is to provide a single unit for creating, deploying, and managing objects instead of managing each object individually.

When a DAC is ready to be deployed, it is built into a DAC package, or *DACPAC*. This package is a file that contains the DAC definition, and is simply a zip file containing multiple XML files.

However, these *DACPAC*s only contain schema, not data. This is where the new version of the DAC Fx comes in. Version 2.0 now supports data as well as schema, dumping your table data right alongside your schema in a new file format called .bacpac. Using the DAC Fx, you can now extract a BACPAC from an existing database and deploy it to a different SQL Server environment, including, wait for it . . . SQL Azure.

Now, it should be noted that SQL Server 2012 comes with the DAC Fx version 2.0 and the ability to export to a BACPAC. The next two sections are going to walk you through creating and deploying BACPACs using SQL Server 2012. You will see how the Import/Export service is used in the Windows Azure Management Portal to import and export to and from a SQL Azure database.

Deploying to SQL Azure via a BACPAC using SQL Server 2012

For all those who have not upgraded to SQL Server 2012 the next session will address that, but for now, this section will use SQL Server 2012. First you'll see how to deploy an on-premises database directly to SQL Azure, and then how to use the built-in import and export features to migrate using BACPACs from SQL Server 2012.

Keep in mind that all of the examples in this section assume that your database is *Azure-ready*, meaning that your on-premises SQL Server database is ready to be migrated to SQL Azure. For example, if you were to download the full AdventureWorks database, such as the SQL Server 2008 R2 version, and then try to walk through the examples in this section, the examples in this section will fail due to objects that aren't supported in Windows Azure SQL Database (such as native encryption and Full Text Search). The section "Generate and Publish Scripts Wizard" in this chapter explains how to make your database Azure-ready by taking an on-premise database and applying the appropriate modifications and changes. More importantly, it also explains why those changes need to be made.

The database that these samples use is a database called AWMini, which is a mini version of the AdventureWorks database. This database can be downloaded from the Apress download page for this book. This database is installed Azure-ready so that you can walk though these examples.

Download the `AWMini.zip` file from the APress site for this book and extract the `.sql` file. Open the `.sql` file in SQL Server Management Studio (for SQL Server 2012) and connect to your local SQL instance. Run the `.sql` file, which will create the AWMini database. Once the script has completed, refresh your database list and you'll see the new AWMini database in your list of databases.

Deploying Directly To SQL Azure

SQL Server 2012 has made it extremely easy to migrate an on-premises database to SQL Azure. Prior to SQL Server 2012, the options for migration required many steps, were somewhat painful, and didn't really fit the DAC picture, simply because DACPACs didn't migrate data. This all changed with SQL Server 2012 and DAC Fx 2.0. Deploying directly to SQL Azure is as simple as a three-step wizard.

If it's not already open, open SQL Server Management Studio for SQL Server 2012. In Object Explorer, expand the Databases node for your server and right-click the AWMini database. From the context menu, select Tasks ➤ Deploy Database to SQL Azure, which will start the database deployment wizard (see Figure 4-1).

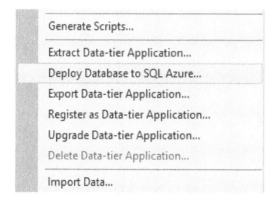

Figure 4-1. *The Deploy Database to SQL Azure menu option*

In the Deploy Database wizard, click Next on the Introduction page. On the Deployment Settings page of the wizard, you need to specify the connection information for the target SQL Azure server to which the database will be migrated. Click the Connect button, which will bring up the familiar Connect to Server dialog. Enter the SQL Azure server name (in the format *server*.windows.database.net), along with the username and password for the SQL Azure server, and then click Connect.

Next, enter a name for the database (see Figure 4-2). As the wizard states, this is a NEW database, not the name of an existing one. Based on the size of your on-premises database, select the Edition needed (Web or Business) and then the size of the database needed. The wizard will automatically fill in the Temporary file name for you, so there is no reason to change that. However, notice that the wizard is creating a BACPAC, not a DACPAC. This means that your data will be migrated as well.

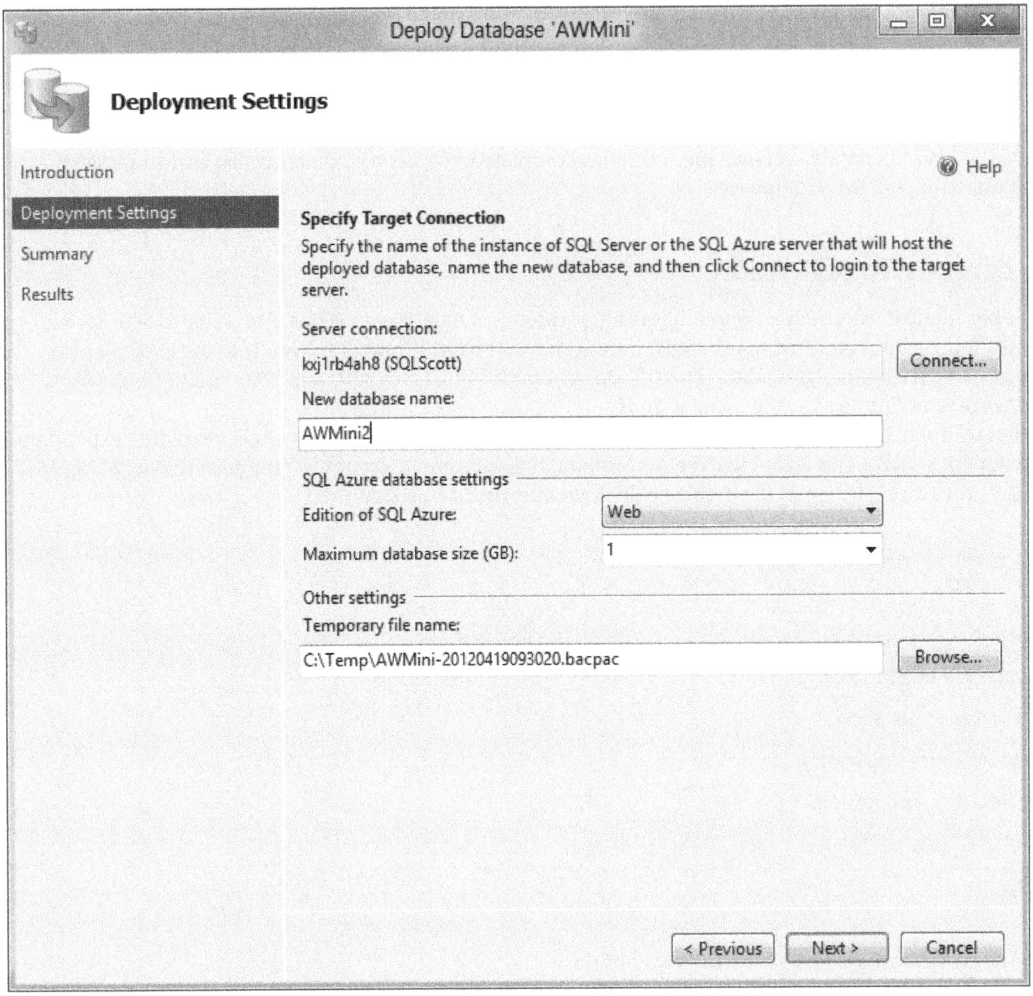

Figure 4-2. *DAC deployment settings*

Click Next, which will then display the Summary page of the wizard. This contains some important information, not just "here are the options you selected in the wizard." Notice that under the Source section of the summary, it lists the Source Database Size, and then informs you that your source database might be larger than the size of the database selected on the previous wizard page. This isn't anything to panic about, but it is a critical piece of information to inform you to be sure that the edition and size of the database you selected will be large enough.

Click Finish on the Summary page to begin the deployment and migration. In Figure 4-3 you can see the steps it takes during the migration process, including creating the target database, creating and verifying a deployment plan, and then executing that plan by applying the BACPAC against the target database. Once the deployment is completed, click Close.

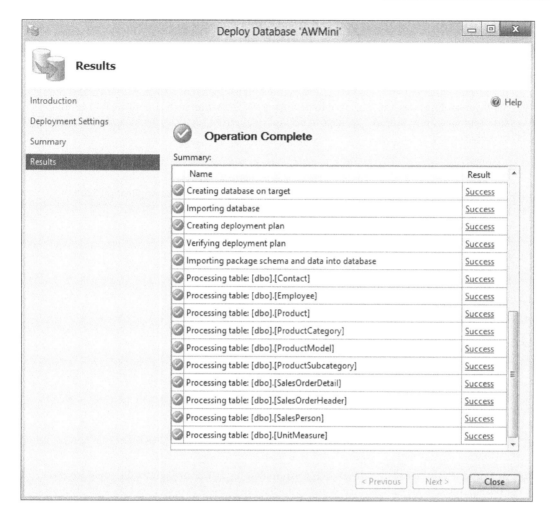

Figure 4-3. *DAC execution results*

This process is quite fast. The AWMini database contains 10 tables with a total of about 200,000 records, and on my system migrating it took less than a minute. Your results may vary (my apologies for sounding like a commercial) depending on your Internet connection, but even larger databases, such as the full AdventureWorks database, didn't take much longer.

This option is a no-stop migration for deploying your SQL Server database to SQL Azure. This means that once you click Finish, the deployment begins. Yet, the BACPAC file specified in the Temporary File Name in Figure 4-2 will still exist once the migration completes. Depending on the size of the database, the DAC file (. bacpac) could be quite large. Even for the AWMini database the file size was 5.5 MB. The great thing is that if you have a program that can open a large XML file (and enough memory), you can look to see the structure of the BACPAC.

The BACPAC file at this point can be archived, deleted, or used for other import services. In this simple example, the BACPAC was stored locally. However, best practices state that if you will be importing the database to multiple servers or multiple times, you'll want to store the BACPAC in Windows Azure storage.

Exporting and Importing to SQL Azure via a BACPAC using SQL Server 2012

As stated earlier, Deploy Your Database to SQL Azure is a no-stop option. Once you click Finish, there is no going back. Also, you have to wait until the deployment is complete to get access to the BACPAC. The great news is that SQL Server 2012 didn't stop with just deploying directly to SQL Azure, but through an additional menu option you can export your on-premises database directly to a BACPAC without deploying directly to SQL Azure. Via this menu option, you have flexibility regarding your BACPAC prior to deploying to SQL Azure, such as copying it to another PC or using the Import option to import the DAC package to multiple SQL Azure servers. This section will begin by discussing the Export option.

DAC Export

To create a DACPAC, right-click the AWMini database and select Tasks ➤ Export Data-Tier Application from the context menu (see Figure 4-4), which will start the DAC export wizard.

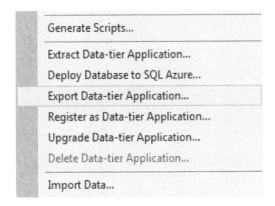

Figure 4-4. *The Export DAC menu option*

Click Next on the Introduction page of the wizard. In the Export Settings page (see Figure 4-5), you have two options; Save to Local Disk and Save to Windows Azure. Select the Save to Local Disk option and click the Browse button to select a file name and location to save the BACPAC file. Click Next.

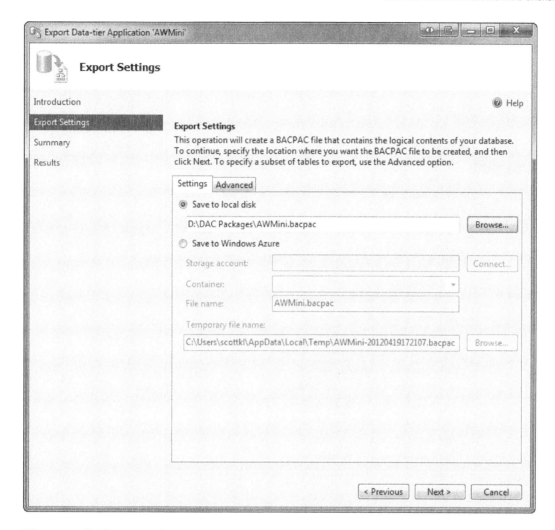

Figure 4-5. *DAC export settings*

On the Summary page, review the specified settings and click Next. The AWMini database will then be exported in a BACPAC format to the file you specified in the Export Settings page of the wizard. Figure 4-6 shows the steps the DAC framework took to construct the BACPAC. In fact, this is the first half of the process that the previous example took to deploy directly to SQL Azure.

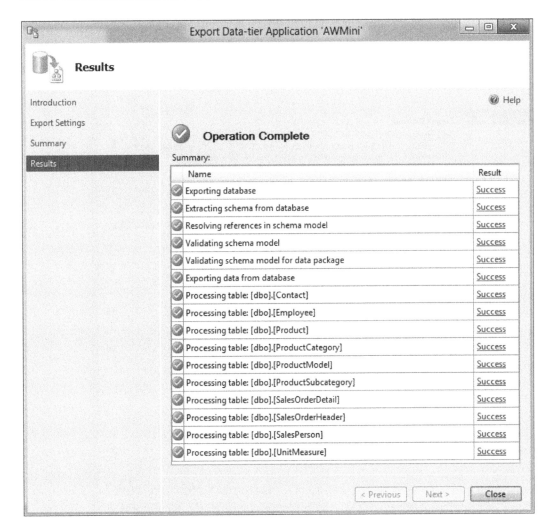

Figure 4-6. *DAC export results*

It should be noted that the first few steps are performed for every export, even if the database isn't SQL Database-ready. Exporting to a BACPAC on a database that isn't SQL Database-ready will fail on the step "Validating schema model for data package." Typical errors you will see will be "[MS-Description] is not supported when used as part of a data package (DACPAC)," and "Full-text Catalog: [*CatalogName*] is not supported when used as part of a data package (DACPAC)." The key is to review the errors, correct them, and rerun the export.

You can see that the schema was first extracted from the database including references, and then the all-important steps of validating that the database is SQL Database-ready were performed. Once the schema is exported and all the validation completed, the data is then exported.

Once the export has completed successfully, click Close. At this point, you have a BACPAC that you can then import to one or multiple SQL Azure servers. Granted, you can't import to multiple SQL Azure servers simultaneously, but unlike the Deploy Database to SQL Azure option, with the Export and Import functionality, you can import the BACPAC multiple times without rerunning the export step again. It's now time to import that DAC package (BACPAC) to SQL Azure.

DAC Import

Connect to your SQL Azure server in SQL Server Management Studio, and in the Object Explorer window right-click the Databases node and select Import Data-Tier Application from the context menu (see Figure 4-7), which will start the Import Data-Tier Application Wizard.

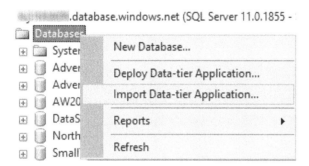

Figure 4-7. *DAC Import menu option*

Click Next on the Introduction page of the wizard. In the Import Settings page of the wizard, shown in Figure 4-8, notice that you have two options; Import from Local Disk and Import from Windows Azure. We saved our DAC file to a local directory, so select the Import from Local Disk option, browse to the location of the DAC package (BACPAC) that you exported in the previous step, and then click Next.

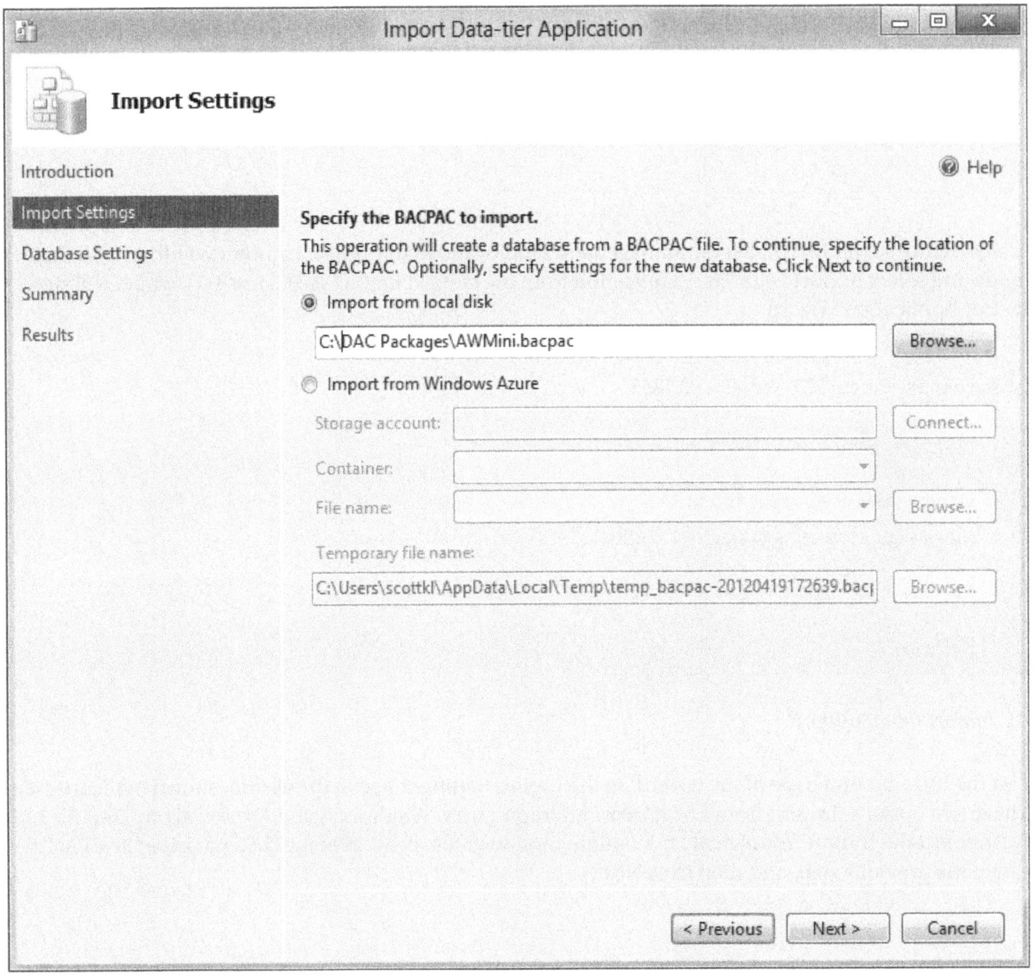

Figure 4-8. *DAC import settings*

The next step of the wizard, Database Settings, shown in Figure 4-9, should look familiar because you saw it earlier as the Deployment Settings page of the Deploy Database wizard in Figure 4-2. Here again you need to connect to your SQL Azure server, and then select the new SQL Azure database edition and size. Once you have done that, click Next.

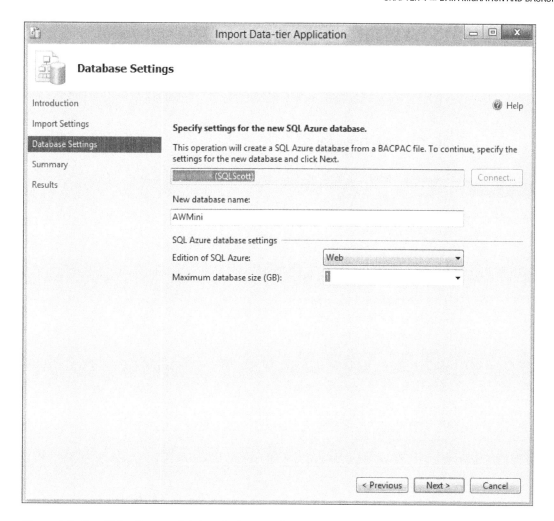

Figure 4-9. *Specifying the new database instance options*

Again you are presented with the Summary page, and if everything looks good, click Next to execute the Import.

In Figure 4-10 you can see the steps that were taken by the DAC Fx to deploy the DAC package (BACPAC) to SQL Azure, which is the last half of the process that the previous example took to deploy directly to SQL Azure. The DAC Fx first created the database and then created a deployment plan, which looks at the current DAC package and determines how it is going to deploy the package to the new database. It then creates the schema and imports the data for each table.

Figure 4-10. *Successful BACPAC import operation*

Granted, while both the Deploy Database to SQL Azure and the Import/Export DAC options accomplish the same tasks, the Import/Export DAC option gives you more control and flexibility, such as the ability to deploy the DACPAC to multiple destinations without the need of re-exporting. However, Deploy Database to SQL Azure is a wonderful option if you need to quickly get your on-premises database to SQL Azure.

The Import/Export Service

Up until now, the focus has been on the client side; importing and exporting from SQL Server to a BACPAC. The Import/Export service is designed to import and export directly between Windows Azure SQL Database and Windows Azure BLOB storage. This service has been available in production since late January 2012 and is free of charge. No sign-ups, no codes to enter. Just go use it. How? The Import/Export service is built directly into the Windows Azure Management Portal via two buttons on the lower Ribbon bar: Import and Export.

Import

In this section, you will upload the BACPAC file to BLOB storage and then import it into an entirely new SQL Database instance using the Import/Export service. The first step is to upload the `AWMini.bacpac` to Windows Azure BLOB storage. If you haven't created a Windows Azure storage account, select the Storage tab in the left navigation pane, and then select New ➤ Storage ➤ Quick Create from the lower New menu. Type in the name of the Storage account into the URL field, select the Region and Subscription, and click Create Storage Account.

With the storage account created, select the account name in the portal; then select the Containers tab. On the lower menu bar, select Add Container to create a container in which to upload the BACPAC. In the New Blob Container dialog, enter a name for the container (I called mine bacpac), and then click the check (OK) button.

The next step is to upload the AWMini BACPAC into the storage account and container. Currently this option is not available in the Windows Azure Management Portal, but there are several tools that can help you do this. On CodePlex is a project called Azure Storage Explorer (`http://azurestorageexplorer.codeplex.com/`), a utility for viewing and managing Windows Azure storage (BLOBs, tables, and queues). RedGate also has a utility called Cloud Storage Studio (`www.cerebrata.com/Products/CloudStorageStudio/`), which provides a rich set of functionality for managing your Windows Azure storage. There are a few more out on the Internet, but these two are the most popular. Either of these two tools will allow you to quickly and easily upload the `AWMini.bacpac` to your BLOB container.

Once the BACPAC is uploaded into BLOB storage, log into the Windows Azure Management Portal at `https://manage.windowsazure.com` with the Windows Live ID that is associated with your Windows Azure subscription. Once logged in to the portal, select the SQL Databases node in the left navigation pane. If you have any SQL Database instances, the lower section of the portal will display Import and Export buttons, as shown in Figure 4-11. Otherwise, only an Import button will be visible.

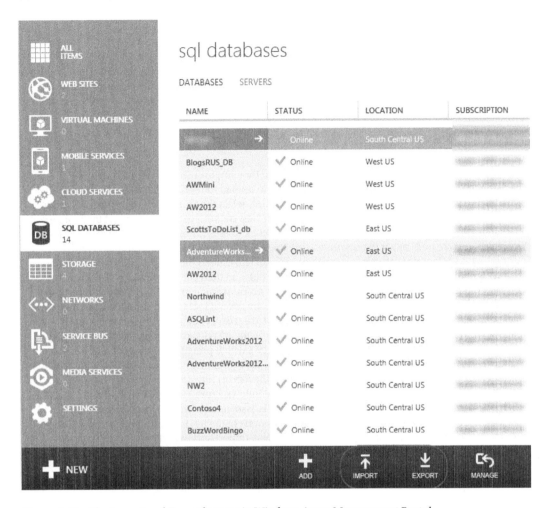

Figure 4-11. *The Import and Export buttons in Windows Azure Management Portal*

Click the Import button, which bring up the Import Database dialog. In this dialog you first need to select the black folder icon in the Bacpac URL field, which will bring up the Browse Cloud Storage dialog, shown in Figure 4-12. On the left side of this dialog, expand the storage account name and select the container in which the BACPAC resides. Then select AWMini.bacpac from the list and click Open.

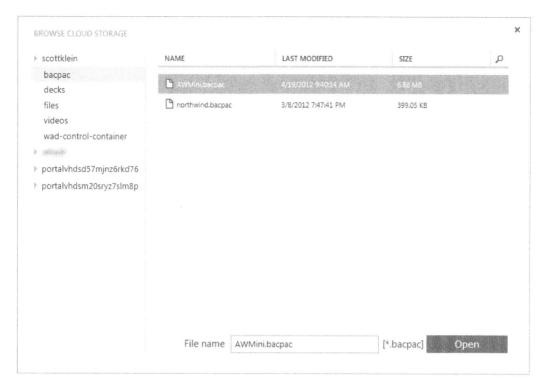

Figure 4-12. The Browse Cloud Storage dialog

Back in the Import Database dialog, enter a name for the new database that will be created during the import process. I called mine AWMini2 so it doesn't conflict with the database created in the previous example.

Next, select the subscription where you will be creating the database and into which you will import the BACPAC into, and then select the server on which the new database will be created.

■ **Note** The storage account and Windows Azure SQL Database instance must be in the same geographical region; otherwise you will receive a warning stating that the Database and Resource are not in the same region and you will not be able to import the BACPAC. This limitation exists to ensure that no outbound transfer costs will be incurred during the import/export process.

Finally, enter the Login name and password to the Windows Azure SQL Database server. The Import Database dialog should now look like Figure 4-13. If you want to specify the new database Edition and Max size, check the Configure Advanced Database Settings box. If you leave the checkbox blank, the import process will create a 1 GB Web Edition database. Therefore, if your database is larger than 1 GB, you should select this option and select the appropriate database size for the Import process.

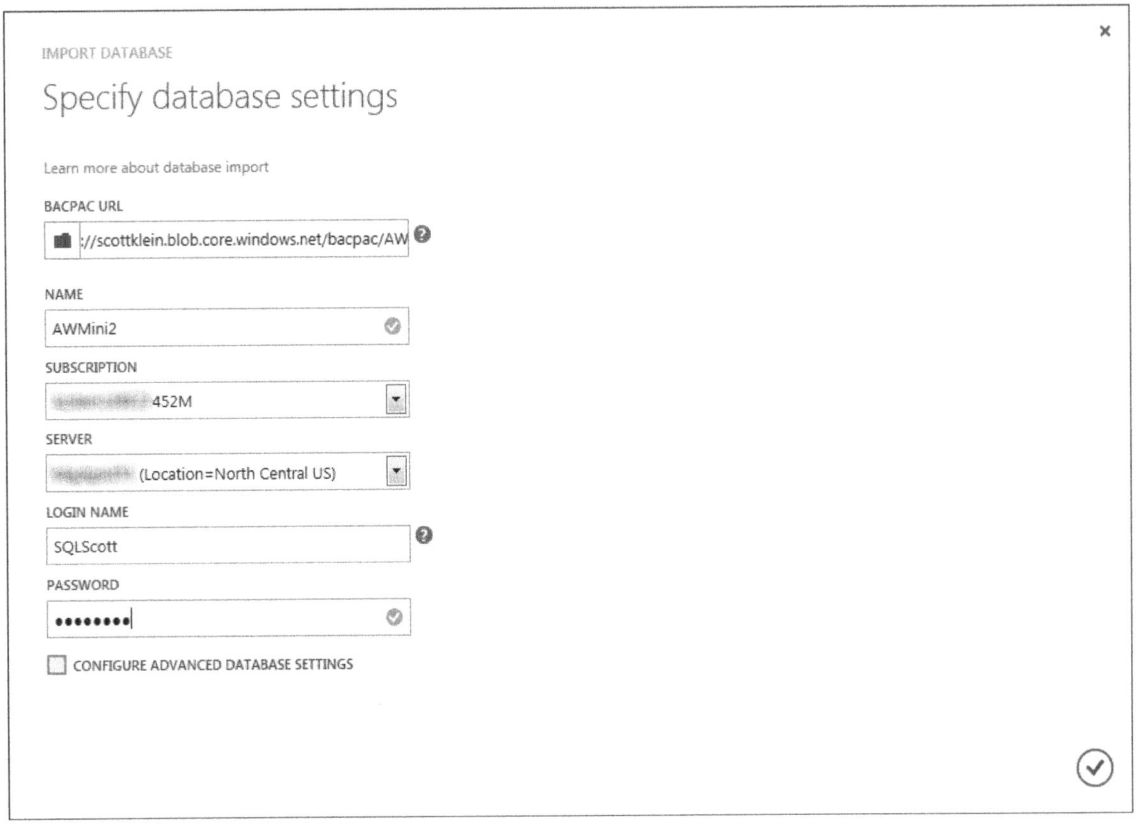

IMPORT DATABASE

Specify database settings

Learn more about database import

BACPAC URL

://scottklein.blob.core.windows.net/bacpac/AW

NAME

AWMini2

SUBSCRIPTION

452M

SERVER

(Location=North Central US)

LOGIN NAME

SQLScott

PASSWORD

••••••••

☐ CONFIGURE ADVANCED DATABASE SETTINGS

Figure 4-13. *The completed Import Database dialog*

When ready, click the check (OK) button on the Import Database dialog to begin the import process. The dialog will go away, but the import process is indeed happening and you can verify this by watching the status of the lower menu bar. Once the import is successful, the new status will display in the lower menu bar, indicating that the import has succeeded.

Export

Exporting a Windows Azure SQL Database instance is similar to the Import process. In the Windows Azure Management Portal, select the SQL Databases node in the left navigation pane, and then select a database from the list of databases. The Export button, shown in Figure 4-11 earlier, will now be visible. Clicking the Export button will bring up the Export Database dialog, shown in Figure 4-14.

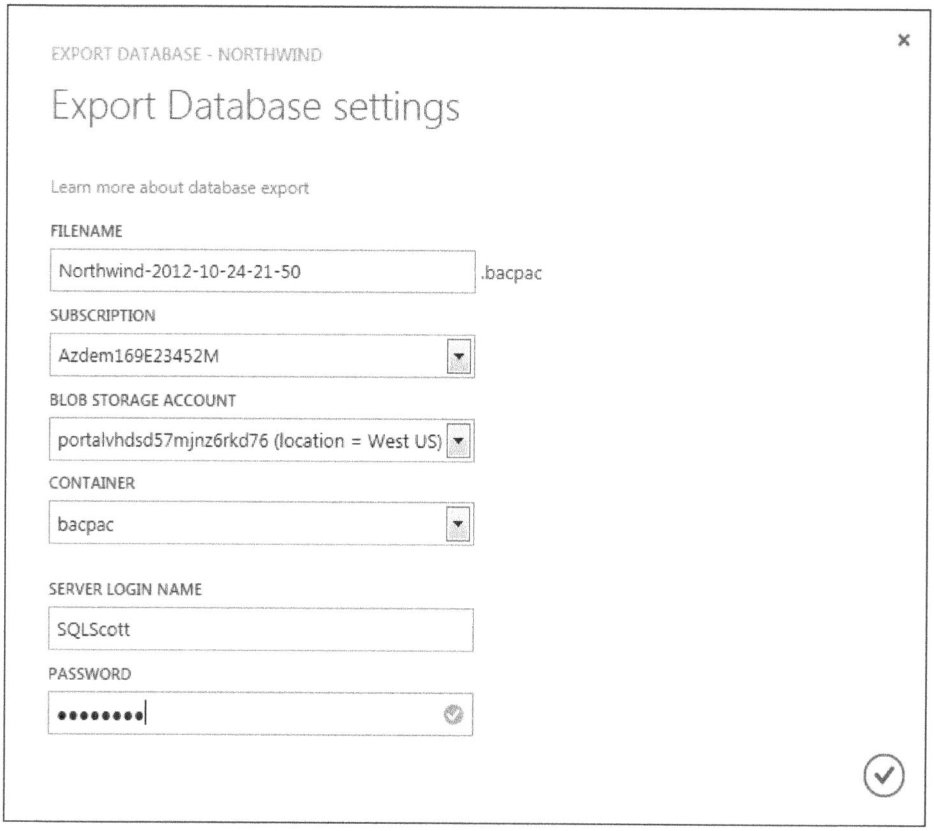

EXPORT DATABASE - NORTHWIND

Export Database settings

Learn more about database export

FILENAME

Northwind-2012-10-24-21-50 | .bacpac

SUBSCRIPTION

Azdem169E23452M

BLOB STORAGE ACCOUNT

portalvhdsd57mjnz6rkd76 (location = West US)

CONTAINER

bacpac

SERVER LOGIN NAME

SQLScott

PASSWORD

••••••••

Figure 4-14. *The Export Database dialog*

In the Export Database dialog, the Filename and Subscription fields will automatically be populated for you. However, you are free to provide a different file name, as well as select a different subscription.

Select the Blob Storage Account and container in which to create the BACPAC. However, as noted earlier, if the storage account and database are in different regions, you will receive a warning message and will not be allowed to execute the Export process.

Once you have entered the appropriate information, click the check (OK) button, which will initiate the Export process. Just as you did in the Import process, you can verify the Export of the database by watching the status of the lower menu bar. Once the export is successful, the new status will display in the lower menu bar, indicating that the export has succeeded. You can then use the same tool you used to upload the BACPAC initially into BLOB storage to verify that the export did indeed succeed.

Generate and Publish Scripts Wizard

The Generate and Publish Scripts Wizard is used to create T-SQL scripts for SQL Server databases and/or related objects within the selected database. You have probably used this wizard, so this section doesn't walk through it step by step; instead, the section briefly highlights a few steps in the wizard and points out the options necessary to work with SQL Azure effectively. SQL Server 2012 and SQL Server 2008 R2 come with the ability to script an on-premises database for the SQL Azure environment.

One of the differences between SQL Server 2012/2008 R2 and SQL Server 2008 (pertaining to object scripting) is a setting in the Advanced Scripting Options dialog of the wizard. There are two properties you can set for the version of SQL Server for which you're scripting database objects: Script for Server Version and Script for the Database Engine Type. The Script for Server Version option lists the version of SQL Server that the Generate and Publish Scripts Wizard supports, which ranges from SQL Server 2000 to SQL Server 2012.

The Script for the Database Engine Type property has two options you can choose from: Stand-Alone Instance and SQL Azure Database. The SQL Azure Database option only works with the SQL Server 2012 and 2008 R2 Server versions. For example, if you set the Script for Server version to SQL Server 2008 (non R2) and then set the Script for the Database Engine Type property to SQL Azure Database, the Script for Server version property value automatically changes to SQL Server 2012/2008 R2.

The Generate and Publish Scripts Wizard does a really nice job of appropriately scripting objects for SQL Azure. The wizard checks for unsupported syntax and data types, and it checks for primary keys on each table. Thus, the following example will set SQL for Server Version to SQL Server 2008 (non R2) for several reasons. First, many people aren't using SQL Server 2012/2008 R2 and therefore don't have the option to script for SQL Azure. Second, this exercise shows you what steps are needed to get a script ready to run in SQL Azure.

The database that will be used in this section is the trusty AdventureWorks database you can get from CodePlex:

```
http://msftdbprodsamples.codeplex.com/releases/view/55330
```

This database download is an .mdf specifically for SQL Server 2012. We will be using SQL Server Management Studio for SQL Server 2012 to do our work, so fire it up and attach the download database.

Starting the Wizard

To start the Generate and Publish Scripts Wizard in SQL Server Management Studio (SSMS), open Object Explorer and expand the Databases node. Select the AdventureWorks2012 database, right-click it, and then select Generate Scripts from the context menu.

On the wizard's Introduction page for SQL Server 2012, you're informed that you must follow four steps to complete this wizard:

1. Select database objects.

2. Specify scripting or publishing objects.

3. Review selections.

4. Generate scripts.

The following sections work through these steps.

Choosing Target Objects

To select your target database objects, follow these steps:

1. On the Introduction page of the Generate and Publish Scripts Wizard, click Next.

2. On the Choose Objects page (see Figure 4-15), select the Select Specific Database Objects option, because for the purposes of this example, you simply want to select a few objects to migrate.

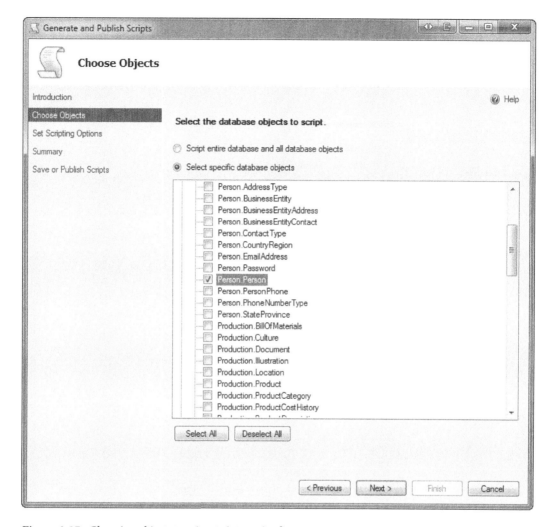

Figure 4-15. *Choosing objects to migrate into script form*

3. In the list of objects in Figure 4-15, expand the Tables and XML Schemas Collection nodes, and select the following objects:

- **Tables:** Person.Person

- **User-Defined Data Types:** Name, NameStyle

- **XML Schema Collections:** IndividualSurveySchemaCollection

- **Schemas:** Person

4. Click Next on the Choose Objects page.

5. On the Set Scripting Objects page, select the Save to New Query Window option shown in Figure 4-16, and then click the Advanced button.

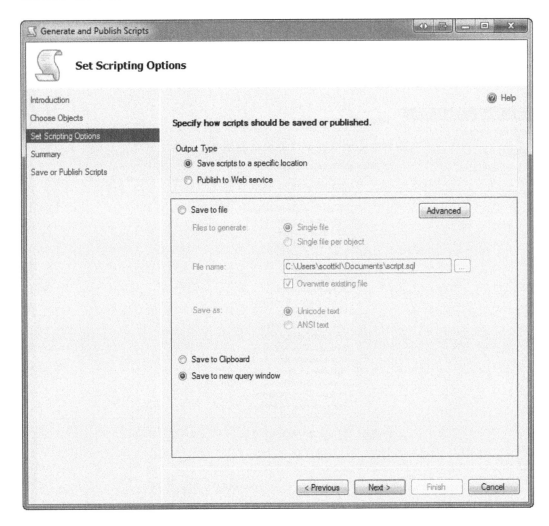

Figure 4-16. *Scripting options*

Setting Advanced Options

Clicking the Advanced button brings up the Advanced Scripting Options dialog shown in Figure 4-17. Follow these steps to set the advanced options for this example's script:

1. In the Advanced Scripting Options dialog, set the following options:

    - **Convert UDDTs to Base Types:** True

    - **Script Extended Properties:** False

    - **Script Logins:** False

    - **Script USE DATABASE:** False

- **Types of data to script:** Schema

- **Script for Server Version:** SQL Server 2012

- **Script for the database engine type:** Stand-Alone Instance

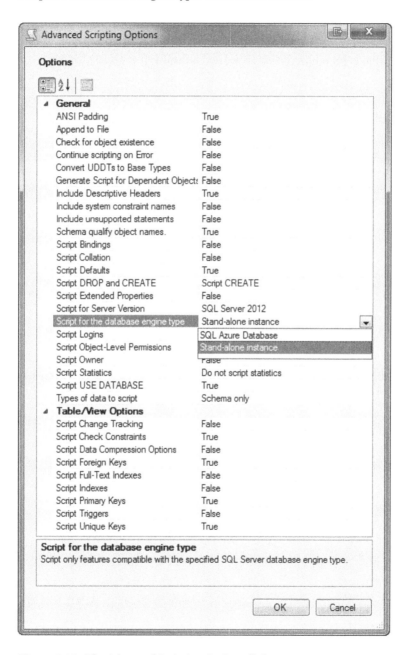

Figure 4-17. *The Advanced Scripting Options dialog*

You can also set the Script DROP and CREATE option to Script DROP and CREATE, as shown in Figure 4-17, but that option isn't required for SQL Azure.

2. Click OK in the Advanced Scripting Options dialog, and then click Next in the Generate Scripts wizard.

3. On the wizard's Summary page, review your selections, and then click Next. The T-SQL script is generated, and you're taken to the Save or Publish Scripts page.

4. Click Finish. At this point your script is finished and is displayed in a query window in SSMS.

Reviewing the Generated Script

Open the file you created, and let's take a quick look at the generated T-SQL. The following snippet from what you see shows the creation of an XML Schema collection and a single table. To save space in the chapter, the majority of the XML Schema Collection has been left out, along with creation of some of the constraints, but your script will show the entire CREATE statement. Also, except for the things you told the script-generation wizard to ignore, the following T-SQL looks like all other object creation T-SQL you typically deal with on a daily basis:

```
/****** Object:  Schema [Person]    Script Date: 4/22/2012 3:38:28 PM ******/
CREATE SCHEMA [Person]
GO
/****** Object:  XmlSchemaCollection [Person].[IndividualSurveySchemaCollection]    Script Date:
4/22/2012 3:38:28 PM ******/
CREATE XML SCHEMA COLLECTION [Person].[IndividualSurveySchemaCollection]
AS N'<xsd:schema xmlns:xsd="http://www.w3.org/2001/XMLSchema"
...
</xsd:schema>'
GO
/****** Object:  UserDefinedDataType [dbo].[Name]    Script Date: 4/22/2012 3:38:28 PM ******/
CREATE TYPE [dbo].[Name] FROM [nvarchar](50) NULL
GO
/****** Object:  UserDefinedDataType [dbo].[NameStyle]    Script Date: 4/22/2012 3:38:28 PM ******/
CREATE TYPE [dbo].[NameStyle] FROM [bit] NOT NULL
GO
/****** Object:  Table [Person].[Person]    Script Date: 4/22/2012 3:38:28 PM ******/
SET ANSI_NULLS ON
GO
SET QUOTED_IDENTIFIER ON
GO
CREATE TABLE [Person].[Person](
    [BusinessEntityID] [int] NOT NULL,
    [PersonType] [nchar](2) NOT NULL,
    [NameStyle] [bit] NOT NULL,
    [Title] [nvarchar](8) NULL,
    [FirstName] [nvarchar](50) NOT NULL,
    [MiddleName] [nvarchar](50) NULL,
    [LastName] [nvarchar](50) NOT NULL,
    [Suffix] [nvarchar](10) NULL,
    [EmailPromotion] [int] NOT NULL,
    [AdditionalContactInfo] [xml](CONTENT [Person].[AdditionalContactInfoSchemaCollection]) NULL,
```

```
    [Demographics] [xml](CONTENT [Person].[IndividualSurveySchemaCollection]) NULL,
    [rowguid] [uniqueidentifier] ROWGUIDCOL  NOT NULL,
    [ModifiedDate] [datetime] NOT NULL,
 CONSTRAINT [PK_Person_BusinessEntityID] PRIMARY KEY CLUSTERED
(
    [BusinessEntityID] ASC
)WITH (PAD_INDEX = OFF, STATISTICS_NORECOMPUTE = OFF, IGNORE_DUP_KEY = OFF, ALLOW_ROW_LOCKS = ON,
ALLOW_PAGE_LOCKS = ON) ON [PRIMARY]
) ON [PRIMARY] TEXTIMAGE_ON [PRIMARY]

GO
ALTER TABLE [Person].[Person] ADD  CONSTRAINT [DF_Person_NameStyle]  DEFAULT ((0)) FOR [NameStyle]
GO
ALTER TABLE [Person].[Person] ADD  CONSTRAINT [DF_Person_EmailPromotion]  DEFAULT ((0)) FOR
[EmailPromotion]
GO
ALTER TABLE [Person].[Person] ADD  CONSTRAINT [DF_Person_rowguid]  DEFAULT (newid()) FOR [rowguid]
GO
ALTER TABLE [Person].[Person] ADD  CONSTRAINT [DF_Person_ModifiedDate]  DEFAULT (getdate()) FOR
[ModifiedDate]
GO
```

Notice that the script enables several options, such as ANSI_NULL and ANSI_PADDING. It then creates the Person table. This table has a rowguid column that uses the uniqueidentifier database. The rowguid column also has a default on it, which uses the newid() function to generate new GUIDs automatically. This table is created on the PRIMARY file group, followed by the setting of several table options via the WITH clause.

Fixing the Script

Because you selected to script for SQL Server 2012, the script includes some syntax and statements that aren't supported in SQL Azure. Figure 4-18 shows some of the errors you will see if you try to run the script as generated.

```
 Messages
  Msg 40510, Level 16, State 1, Line 2
  Statement 'CREATE XML SCHEMA COLLECTION' is not supported in this version of SQL Server.
  Msg 40517, Level 16, State 1, Line 12
  Keyword or statement option 'content' is not supported in this version of SQL Server.
```

Figure 4-18. *SQL Azure execution errors*

In this example, you scripted only a single table, a few UDTs, and an XML index. If you scripted more objects, you would also see errors such as these:

- Keyword or statement option 'pad_index' is not supported in this version of SQL Server.

- Keyword or statement option 'allow_row_locks' is not supported in this version of SQL Server.

- Keyword or statement option 'textimage_on' is not supported in this version of SQL Server.

- 'ROW GUID COLUMN' is not supported in this version of SQL Server.

- 'Filegroup reference and partitioning scheme' is not supported in this version of SQL Server.

Another item you might run into is that SQL Azure doesn't support *heap tables*. A heap table is one without a clustered index. SQL Azure currently supports only clustered tables.

The question then becomes, what changes need to be made in order to make the script runnable for SQL Azure? You need to make some changes for your script to run under SQL Azure. Here's what to do:

1. Delete all instances of SET ANSI_NULLS ON.

2. Delete all instances of ON [PRIMARY].

3. Delete all instances of TEXTIMAGE_ON [PRIMARY].

4. Delete all instances of the following:

   - PAD_INDEX = OFF

   - ALLOW_ROW_LOCKS = ON

   - ALLOW_PAGE_LOCKS = ON

5. In the Person table, modify the rowguid column, removing the ROWGUIDCOL keyword.

6. Add a clustered index to any heap tables.

Appendix B discusses the need for these changes in detail. For now, here's a quick explanation:

- ON [PRIMARY] isn't needed because, as you learned in Chapters 1 and 2, SQL Azure hides all hardware-specific access and information. There is no concept of PRIMARY or file groups, because disk space is handled by Microsoft, so this option isn't required.

- According to SQL Server Books Online (BOL) you can remove the entire WITH clause that contains the table options. However, the only table options you really need to remove are those listed in step 4 (PAD_INDEX, ALLOW_ROW_LOCKS, and ALLOW_PAGE_LOCKS).

- Even though this table didn't use it, the NEWSEQUENTIALID() function isn't supported in SQL Azure, because there is no CLR support in SQL Azure, and thus all CLR-based types aren't supported. The NEWSEQUENTIALID() return value is one of those types. Also, the ENCRYPTION option isn't supported because SQL Azure as a whole doesn't yet support encryption.

- SQL Azure doesn't support heap tables. Thus, you need to change any heap table into a clustered table by adding a clustered index. (Interestingly, if you execute one statement at a time, you can, in fact, *create* a heap table. However, any inserts into that table fail.)

One of the things the SQL Azure documentation suggests, and which is listed earlier, is to set the Convert UDDTs to Base Types property to True. This is because user-defined types aren't supported in SQL Azure.

After you make the changes just described to your SQL script, it should look like the following:

```
/****** Object:  Schema [Person]    Script Date: 4/22/2012 3:38:28 PM ******/
CREATE SCHEMA [Person]
GO
/****** Object:  UserDefinedDataType [dbo].[Name]    Script Date: 4/22/2012 3:38:28 PM ******/
CREATE TYPE [dbo].[Name] FROM [nvarchar](50) NULL
GO
/****** Object:  UserDefinedDataType [dbo].[NameStyle]    Script Date: 4/22/2012 3:38:28 PM ******/
CREATE TYPE [dbo].[NameStyle] FROM [bit] NOT NULL
GO
/****** Object:  Table [Person].[Person]    Script Date: 4/22/2012 3:38:28 PM ******/
SET ANSI_NULLS ON
GO
```

```
SET QUOTED_IDENTIFIER ON
GO
CREATE TABLE [Person].[Person](
    [BusinessEntityID] [int] NOT NULL,
    [PersonType] [nchar](2) NOT NULL,
    [NameStyle] [bit] NOT NULL,
    [Title] [nvarchar](8) NULL,
    [FirstName] [nvarchar](50) NOT NULL,
    [MiddleName] [nvarchar](50) NULL,
    [LastName] [nvarchar](50) NOT NULL,
    [Suffix] [nvarchar](10) NULL,
    [EmailPromotion] [int] NOT NULL,
    [AdditionalContactInfo] [xml] NULL,
    [Demographics] [xml] NULL,
    [rowguid] [uniqueidentifier] NOT NULL,
    [ModifiedDate] [datetime] NOT NULL,
 CONSTRAINT [PK_Person_BusinessEntityID] PRIMARY KEY CLUSTERED
(
    [BusinessEntityID] ASC
)WITH (STATISTICS_NORECOMPUTE = OFF, IGNORE_DUP_KEY = OFF)
)

GO
ALTER TABLE [Person].[Person] ADD  CONSTRAINT [DF_Person_NameStyle]  DEFAULT ((0)) FOR [NameStyle]
GO
ALTER TABLE [Person].[Person] ADD  CONSTRAINT [DF_Person_EmailPromotion]  DEFAULT ((0)) FOR
[EmailPromotion]
GO
ALTER TABLE [Person].[Person] ADD  CONSTRAINT [DF_Person_rowguid]  DEFAULT (newid()) FOR [rowguid]
GO
ALTER TABLE [Person].[Person] ADD  CONSTRAINT [DF_Person_ModifiedDate]  DEFAULT (getdate()) FOR
[ModifiedDate]
GO
```

Now that you've made the necessary corrections, you're ready to create your objects in a SQL Azure database.

Executing the Script Against an Azure Database

You don't have a SQL Azure database to run the script against, so let's create one now:

1. Connect to your SQL Azure instance (refer to Chapter 1 for reference if needed), making sure you're connecting to the master database.

2. Open a new query window, and use the syntax discussed in Chapter 1 to create your SQL Azure database. Name it AWMini, because this is the name the examples use throughout this chapter.

3. Click over to the generated script. This query window is currently connected to your local SQL instance, so you need to change it to your SQL Azure instance and the database you just created. Right-click anywhere in the script, and select Connection ➤ Change Connection from the context menu.

4. In the Connect to Database Engine dialog, enter the information for your SQL Azure instance, and enter the name of the database you just created on the Connection Properties tab.

5. Click Connect.

You now have your script, a database, and a connection to that database. Click the Execute button. Your script should run and create the tables, procedures, and data in your SQL Azure Database.

The SQL Server Generate and Publish Script wizard is a great way to start understanding the required changes that need to be made when migrating to SQL Azure. With this foundation, let's discuss one of the other options, the bcp utility.

The bcp Utility

The bcp utility provides bulk copying of data between instances of Microsoft SQL Server. This utility is installed with SQL Server and requires no knowledge or understanding of T-SQL syntax. If you aren't familiar with the bcp utility, don't confuse or associate its functionality with that of the Import/Export Wizard in SQL Server. Although the bcp documentation refers to what bcp does as a "bulk copy," be aware that you can't bcp data from a source into a destination with a single statement. You must first bcp the data out of the source; then, you can bcp the data in to the destination.

The bcp utility is a great way to move data. Since it doesn't do schema (that is, the schema must already exist), the bcp utility is a very quick way of migrating data. For example, you need to refresh your SQL Database with data from an on-premises database, the bcp option is a great solution to do that.

■ **Note**   The bcp utility is very flexible and powerful, and you can apply a lot of options to it. This section doesn't go into the entire range of bcp options or dive deep into the many uses of the utility. You can find that information in the SQL Server Books Online or on the Microsoft MSDN web site at http://msdn.microsoft.com/en-us/library/ms162802.aspx.

This section describes how to use the bcp utility to export data from a local database and import the data into your SQL Azure database. It also discusses some things you should watch out for when using the bcp utility for SQL Azure.

Invoking bcp

The bcp utility has no GUI; it's a command prompt-driven utility. But don't let that intimidate you, especially given what you're using it for. It's very flexible and can seem a bit overwhelming, but it's quite simple. The basic syntax for the bcp utility is as follows:

```
bcp table direction filename -servername -username -password
```

where:

- *table* is the source or destination table based on the direction parameter.
- *direction* is in or out, depending on whether you're copying data into the database or out of the database.
- *filename* is the filename you're copying data to or from.
- *servername* is the name of the server you're copying data to or from.
- *username* is the username used to connect to either the local or SQL Azure database.
- *password* is the password associated with the username.

Let's get started by exporting the data from your source database.

Exporting the Data

Begin by copying data out of your local SQL instance. Open a command prompt, and type the command shown in Figure 4-19. Enter your own values for the server name, and the target directory for the resulting bcp file. In this example I used the -T parameter to tell the bcp utility to connect to my local instance with a trusted connection using integrated security.

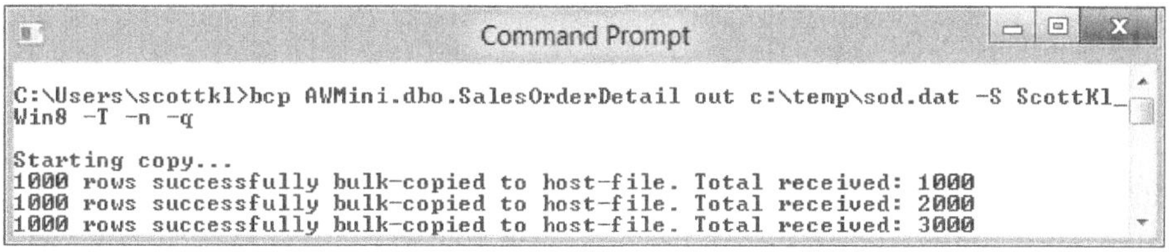

Figure 4-19. *Using bcp to export data*

Notice that in this example you're using the out keyword for the direction parameter. That's because you're copying data *out* of SQL Server.

The -n parameter performs the bulk-copy operation, using the native database data types of the data. The -q parameter executes the SET QUOTED_IDENTIFIERS ON statement in the connection between the bcp utility and your SQL Server instance.

After you type in the command, press Enter to execute the bcp utility. In mere milliseconds, over 71,000 rows are exported and copied to the user.dat file (see Figure 4-20).

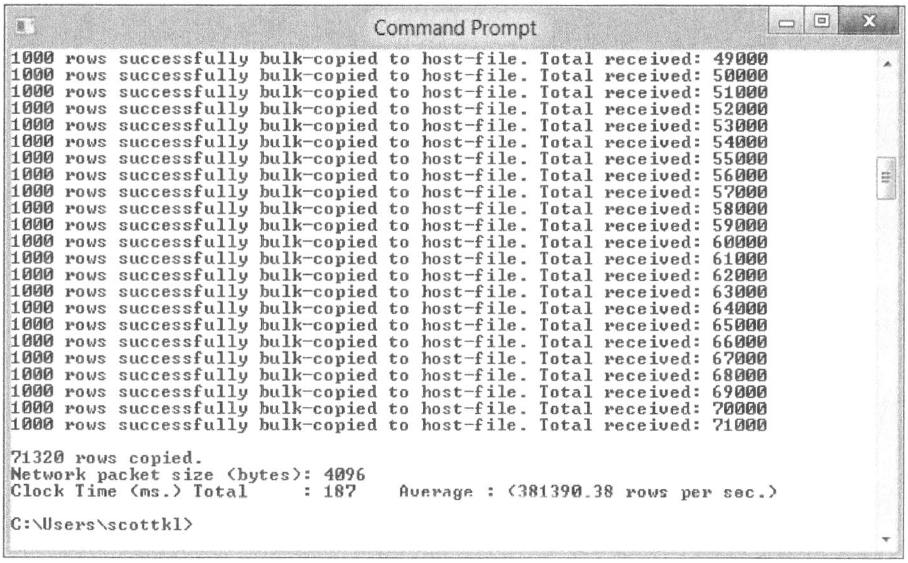

Figure 4-20. *Output from the bcp export command*

Importing the Data

The next step is to copy the data into the cloud—specifically, to your SQL Azure AWMini database. The syntax for copying *into* a database is very similar to the syntax for copying data *out*. You use the in keyword and specify the server name and credentials for your SQL Azure database, as shown in Figure 4-21.

Figure 4-21. *Uniqueidentifier data type error during bcp import*

After you type in the command, press Enter to execute the bcp utility. Notice in Figure 4-22 that importing all 71,320 rows took no time at all.

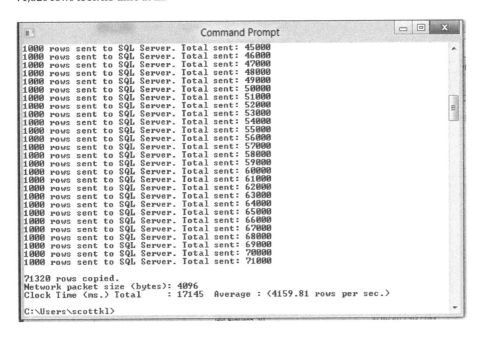

Figure 4-22. *Successful bcp import*

If you ever receive an error stating that an unexpected end-of-file (EOF) was encountered, this error isn't specific to SQL Azure; the bcp utility has issues with columns of the uniqueidentifier data type. You can find posts and blogs all over the Internet about this problem.

The solution is to drop the rowguid column from the table in the SQL Azure table. The cool thing is that you don't need to re-export the data. You can simply re-execute the bcp import command and then put the rowguid column back on the table.

As stated earlier, SQL Server BOL is full of information about how to use the bcp utility. This section is a brief introductory look at how to use this utility to move data from your local SQL Server instance to SQL Azure. The bcp utility is a bulk-copy method of moving data. It lacks SSIS's ability to convert data from one data type to another, and SSIS's workflow components. But if all you're interested in is moving data from one table to a similar destination table, bcp is your best friend.

> ## SQL AZURE MIGRATION WIZARD
>
> The tools discussed so far in the chapter are provided by Microsoft. However, a standout third-party utility is available, which was built specifically for migrating data to SQL Azure. That utility is the SQL Azure Migration Wizard, and it deserves some well-earned attention.
>
> The goal of the SQL Azure Migration Wizard is to help you migrate your local SQL Server 2005/2008 databases into SQL Azure. This utility is wizard-driven, making it very easy to use. It walks you step by step through all that is required, so migration is simple and nearly seamless.
>
> You can find the SQL Azure Migration Wizard on CodePlex at `http://sqlazuremw.codeplex.com/`.
>
> Note that although this nifty utility migrates 2005, 2008, and 2012 databases, it requires a minimum of SQL Server 2008 R2 to run.

SQL Azure Backup Strategies

Your data is in the cloud, but it really doesn't stop there. Much of the functionality that DBAs have at their fingertips when dealing with local data stores doesn't exist in the cloud yet. The operative word in that sentence is *yet*.

Database Copy enables you to copy your database to make a new database on the same SQL Azure server. Alternatively, you can copy to a different SQL Azure server in the same subregion or data center. This functionality is much needed, but at the same time it has some shortcomings; some can be worked around, but others will require future service updates.

Copying a Database

The Database Copy feature allows you to create a single copy of a source database. You do so by adding a new argument to the `CREATE DATABASE` statement: `AS COPY OF`. As a refresher, the syntax for `CREATE DATABASE` is as follows:

```
CREATE DATABASE MyDatabase (MAXSIZE= 10 GB, EDITION= 'Business')
```

To create a copy of a source database, the syntax now becomes

```
CREATE DATABASE MyDatabase AS COPY OF [source_server_name].source_database_name]
```

Thus, if you want to create a copy of your AWMini database, the syntax is

```
CREATE DATABASE AWMini2 AS COPY OF servername.AWMini
```

Figure 4-23 shows the execution of the previous statement. The interesting thing to note is the message in the Messages window. When you execute the `CREATE DATABASE` statement with the `AS COPY OF` argument, you immediately get the "Command(s) completed successfully" message. Does this mean the copy finished that quickly? No. This message means the copy has *started*. You can also see in Figure 4-23 that the AWMini2 database is already listed in the list of databases; however, that doesn't mean the database copy has completed.

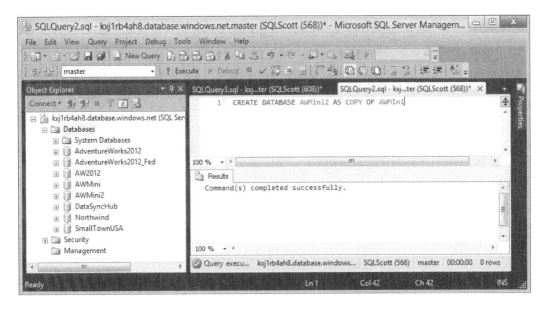

Figure 4-23. *Copying a database*

Knowing When a Copy Is Complete

The question then becomes, how do you know when the copy is finished? The answer is that Microsoft created a new data management view (DMV) to return the details of the database copy operation. This DMV is called sys.dm_database_copies, and it returns a great deal of information about the status of the database copy, such as when the database copy process started and completed, the percentage of bytes that have been copied, error codes, and more. In addition, Microsoft modified the state and state_desc columns in the sys.databases table to provide detailed information about the status of the new database.

Figure 4-24 shows the progress of the database copy. The statement looks at the sys.dm_database_copies DMV and checks the status of the copy, reporting the start date and time, and percent complete of the copy process, and the date and time the status was updated (in the modify_date column). Any copy errors are shown in the error_code and error_description columns. Once the copy is complete, the specific row in the table for the copy is removed from the table.

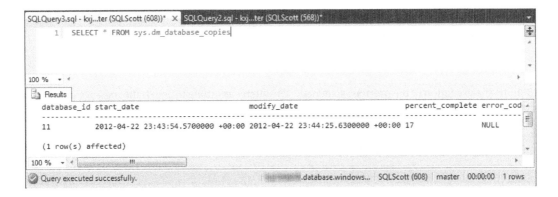

Figure 4-24. *Checking the database copy status*

Automating a Database Copy

You can schedule a database copy via an on-premises SQL Agent job and an SSIS package (as discussed earlier in this chapter). The job can be scheduled like a normal on-premises SQL job, as long as the connection information for the Execute SQL task points to the SQL Azure database.

Although this may not be the most favorable solution, it's certainly an option, and it does provide the scheduling capabilities you're looking for. The key for this solution is to first delete the copy database before you re-create it.

Maintaining a Backup History

The Database Copy functionality lets you create an instant backup of your database, but it doesn't provide a way to create a backup history. In other words, you can't append to the backup and create multiple days' worth of backups. You do have several options, however.

If all you care about is backing up the current day's data, you can delete the current backup copy and recopy the database. This is a viable option and doesn't require a lot of maintenance.

If, on the other hand, you want a backup history, doing so is a bit trickier. Many, if not most, companies like to keep a week's worth of backups. These companies back up their databases each night and keep seven days' worth of backups so they have the option to restore past the previous night's backup. To do this with the Database Copy functionality, you must create seven copies of the source database—you have seven backup copy databases.

This strategy works, but keep in mind that you're billed for those additional seven databases. The key here is that if you're using SQL Azure, a look at your backup plan is critical.

Backing Up Using the Import/Export Features

While the AS COPY OF feature is nice, you are now paying the cost for an additional database. What many companies are now looking at for a backup and restore solution is the Import/Export Services discussed at the beginning of this chapter. Storing database backups in Windows Azure BLOB storage is certainly much cheaper than the cost of a second database, and in addition you can have multiple backups of your database. Now, granted, neither of these give you the Transactional and Differential backup solutions that you are used to on-premises, but the Import/Export service and DAC framework give you a lot more flexibility.

Third-Party Backup Products

Currently on the market there are two very good products that provide excellent backup and restore capabilities for SQL Azure:

- Enzo Backup for SQL Azure
- Cloud Services

Enzo Backup

Enzo Backup for SQL Azure, by a company called Blue Syntax, is a local Windows application that lets you execute backup and restore requests for your SQL Azure database. The flexibility for this tool comes in several ways. First, you can back up and restore to and from BLOB storage or your local file system. Backups are automatically compressed and include both schema and data. Second, you can back up an entire database or a specific schema. You can also restore a specific schema or a specific table within that schema or database.

The backups are transactionally consistent, just like the AS COPY OF feature of the CREATE DATABASE command. The Enzo backup tool also allows you to schedule backup jobs to run in the Azure platform as well. Backups are performed and run entirely in the cloud using a cloud agent. The agent has multiple sizes (matching the Windows Azure Hosted Services sizes), allowing you determine how quickly you want your backup to execute. More information on the Enzo Backup for SQL Azure tool can be found here:

http://www.BlueSyntax.net/backup.aspx

Cloud Services

Red Gate is known for their SQL Server tools. They continue to create great products, and Cloud Services doesn't disappoint. Cloud Services is a suite of tools that help manage your cloud applications. As part of this suite of tools is the ability to back up your SQL Database. You can schedule backups to Windows Azure BLOB storage as well as restore the backup to a new database or an existing SQL Database. More information on Red Gate's Cloud Services can be found here:

http://cloudservices.red-gate.com/

Summary

In this chapter we discussed the various options for migrating your database schema and associated data to SQL Azure. You learned that there are pros and cons to each method; for example, the SQL Server script-generation wizard will script the schema as well as the data, but SSIS and the bcp utility do not. You also learned that if you use SQL Server 2008 R2 or SQL Server 2012, you have the option to script for SQL Azure, which scripts the objects ready for execution in the SQL Azure environment.

We also discussed the SQL Azure Copy feature, which allows you to make a copy of your SQL Azure database for backup purposes.

With your database in SQL Azure, we can now focus on how to program applications for SQL Azure, the topic of Chapter 5.

CHAPTER 5

Programming with SQL Database

The chapters previous to this one have laid the foundation for the rest of the book. You've seen an overview of Windows Azure SQL Database, learned about cloud computing design options, and walked through setting up your Azure account. You've read about SQL Database security, including security compliance and encryption topics; and you spent the last chapter learning about data migration (how to get your data into the cloud) and backup strategies—the types of things a DBA likes to hear.

Starting with this chapter, the rest of the book focuses on developing with SQL Database. This chapter looks at using various Microsoft technologies to program for SQL Database, including ODBC, ADO.NET, LINQ, and others. This chapter also discusses development considerations as you start to design and build new applications to work with SQL Database or consider moving existing applications to SQL Database.

You should begin getting the picture that SQL Database really isn't *that* different from your local SQL Server instances. The last chapter talked at length about some of the T-SQL differences in SQL Database but also said that Microsoft is continually adding features and functionality; so, the differences gap is closing at a very rapid pace (which has made writing this book a fun challenge, but that's another story). The key to developing applications isn't pointing your application to your cloud version of the database, but rather your approach to developing the application and design considerations for accessing your cloud database. Simply moving a database to the cloud and pointing your application to that instance can have disastrous results, such as degraded application performance and unwanted monetary costs.

This chapter first focuses on application design approaches to get the most from SQL Database application development. The rest of the chapter discusses various technologies for accessing your SQL Database instance, showing you how to use those technologies to connect to and retrieve data. You learn the right place to use each of the technologies, because there are many technologies to choose from. The end of this chapter provides a simple, best-practice discussion of testing locally before deploying remotely to ensure a successful SQL Database application deployment.

This chapter will also spend a few pages on application development best practices to help solve many of the issues noted in earlier chapters, such as throttling and latency, all of which affect any type of application whether hosted on-premises or in the cloud.

Application Deployment Factors

As stated earlier, you could use the information from Chapter 4 to push your *entire* database to SQL Database. But is that the right thing to do?

Chapter 2 discussed at length the design aspects of architecting and publishing applications for the cloud, including topics such as storage, high availability, security, and performance. Each of those aspects is important (especially performance) and should be discussed when you're considering moving applications to the cloud. In addition to security, performance is one of the primary items of concern that companies have about cloud computing. One of the last things a company wants to do is decide to take a critical application and move it to the cloud, only to find that it doesn't perform as well as the on-premises version of the app.

Don't get the idea that moving an on-premises application to the cloud automatically results in security issues and a loss of performance—that isn't the case. With planning and the right approach, you can achieve a very successful application deployment into the cloud. The purpose of this discussion, and of Chapter 2, is to get you to think and plan before you deploy, so you take the right approach. The question is, what is that right approach?

This discussion is really about two things. First, when deciding to move an application to the cloud, do you move the entire application (that is, the database and the app) or just a portion? Second, regardless of whether you move all or a portion of the database, do you also move the application, or do you keep the application on-premises? Let's not forget that using SQL Database doesn't mean you automatically have to move your application to the Azure platform. You can move your database to the cloud and still host your application on-premises. As with everything, you have options. Let's discuss the different ways of hosting your SQL Database application.

On-Premises Application

On-premises means your application is hosted locally and not in Windows Azure, but your database is in a SQL Database instance. Your application code uses client libraries to access one or more SQL Database instances. Some companies are reluctant to put business logic or application-specific logic outside of their corporate data center, and the on-premises option provides the ability to house the data in the cloud while keeping the application logic local.

Although this is a viable option, limitations are associated with it. For example, only the following client libraries are supported:

- .NET Framework 3.5 SP1 Data Provider for SQL Server (System.Data.SqlClient) or later

- Entity Framework 3.5 SP1 or later

- SQL Server 2008 R2 Native Client ODBC driver

- SQL Server 2008 Native Client Driver (supported, but with less functionality)

- SQL Server 2008 Driver for PHP version 1.1 or later

If your application uses OLE DB, you have to change it to use one of the client libraries listed here instead.

The biggest consideration related to keeping your application on-premises is the cost. Any time you move data between SQL Database and your on-premises application, there is an associated cost for inbound data transfers (at the time this book went to press, $0.05 - $0.12 per GB for US and Europe, $0.12 - $0.19 for all other areas). If you're using Azure Storage, there is also the cost of using that storage (currently, $0.037 – $0.093 per GB). Again, this is per GB, so the cost is low. An example of an expensive pattern is synchronizing large amounts of data multiple times per day. But keep in mind that synching even a 50GB database costs less than a few dollars.

These costs and limitations shouldn't deter you from using an on-premises solution for your application. However, let's look at what an Azure-hosted solution provides.

Azure-Hosted Application

Azure-hosted means that your application code is hosted in Windows Azure and your database is in SQL Database. Your application can still use the same client libraries to access the database or databases in SQL Database. Most companies right now are taking existing ASP.NET applications and publishing them to Windows Azure and accessing SQL Database. However, you aren't limited to just web apps: you can use a Windows desktop app or Silverlight app that uses the Entity Framework and the WCF (Windows Communication Foundation) Data Services client to access SQL Database as well. Again, you have plenty of options.

The benefit of using an Azure-hosted solution is the ability to minimize network latency of requests to the SQL Database instance. Just as important is the fact that you're cutting the costs of data movement between SQL Database and the application. As long as your Windows Azure and SQL Database are in the same subregion, bandwidth usage between SQL Database and Windows Azure is free.

By putting both your application and database in Azure, you also get the benefit of more efficient transactions between your app and the database, because doing so minimizes the network latency between your application and the database.

But you incur the compute cost, which is currently $0.12 per hour. *Compute hours* is the time your application is deployed to Windows Azure. Even if your application isn't in a running state, you're being billed. Billing is per hour, and partial hours are billed as full hours. When developing and testing your application, you should remove the compute instances that aren't being used. Thus, the key here is *to test locally before deploying remotely*.

Which to Choose?

The decision whether to move your application to the cloud or keep it local is entirely up to you, and it shouldn't be determined solely by what you've just read in the last two sections. The decision isn't that cut-and-dried. You need to look at several other factors, such as costs, data traffic, and bandwidth, and then base your decision on the analysis of this information. For example, it may not be a sound decision for a small company with little web traffic to host an application in Azure, because of the compute costs. However, that same company can keep its database in Azure while keeping the application on-premises because the data-transfer costs are minimal, and still gain the benefits of SQL Database (failover, high availability, and so on).

In many companies, the initial goal isn't an all-or-nothing approach. The companies spend some time looking at their databases and applications, decide what functionality makes sense to put in the cloud, and test functionality on that. They test for performance foremost, to ensure that when the app is deployed to Winodws Azure in production, performance is in the same ballpark as their on-premises solution. The thought is to keep the important things up front to ensure a successful Azure deployment. Roll your application out in pieces, if necessary, and test locally prior to deployment.

Whether you deploy all or part of your database and application is for you to decide. Chapter 2 discussed the issue at length, and this chapter doesn't rehash it except to say that before you make a decision, you should look at all the facts.

Connecting to SQL Database

Developing applications that work with SQL Database isn't rocket science, but it requires knowing what to expect and what functionality you have to work with. You read earlier that not all client libraries work with SQL Database and saw the libraries that are supported. Appendix B will spend some time discussing what T-SQL functionality exists in SQL Database. Even as this book is being written, the list of supported features changes as Microsoft continues to add functionality. This chapter focuses on a client application's perspective.

This section looks at using several technologies to connect to and query a SQL Database instance, including ADO.NET, ODBC, and WCF Data Services. You read at length earlier about taking the right approach to move to the Azure platform. You must consider many things, including the following:

- SQL Database is only available via TCP port 1433.

- SQL Database doesn't currently support OLE DB.

- SQL Database only supports SQL Server authentication. Windows Authentication isn't supported.

- When connecting to SQL Database, you must specify the target database in the connection string. Otherwise, you're connecting to the *master* database.

- Distributed transactions (transactions that affect multiple resources, such as tables, or different databases via sharding) aren't supported in SQL Database.

- You must ensure that your SQL Database firewall is configured to accept connections.

- You must determine whether any embedded (in-line) T-SQL in your application is supported by SQL Database.

- You must use the login name format *<login>*@*<server>* when connecting to SQL Database, because some tools implement Tabular Data Stream (TDS) differently.

Most of the items in this list are self-explanatory, but let's talk about a couple of them. First, it's highly recommended that you read Appendix B, which discusses the T-SQL syntax that is and isn't supported. Also, if you have any inline or embedded T-SQL code, you need to go through your app and make sure the T-SQL meets the requirements listed in Appendix B. It also may behoove you look at the online help for supported T-SQL syntax to get the latest up-to-date syntax.

Second, although distributed transactions aren't supported, Chapter 10 discusses a technique called *sharding* and SQL Federation that you can use to improve performance dramatically. Sharding is the concept of horizontally partitioning your data among several databases based on criteria (such as geolocation) and then using a technology such as the ADO.NET Task Parallel Library (TPL) to add parallelism and concurrency to your application. SQL Federation applies this same concept to SQL Database by applying partitioning at the database level, built in to the SQL Database. These topics were also introduced to you in Chapter 2.

Third, think carefully about OLE DB. SQL Database currently doesn't support connecting via OLE DB, but supporting OLE DB is on Microsoft's radar. However, as you learned in Chapter 3, you can connect using OLE DB using SSIS. It isn't recommended, though, that you try to work in OLE DB—wait until it's fully supported.

Let's get to some coding. The next few sections show you how to connect to SQL Database using different libraries such as ADO.NET, ODBC, the sqlcmd utility, and WCF Data Services to query SQL Database.

The examples in the chapter will use the AdventureWorks2012 database for both SQL Server 2012 and Windows Azure SQL Database. The on-premises version of the AdventureWorks database for SQL Server 2012 can be found here:

`http://msftdbprodsamples.codeplex.com/releases/view/93587`

Download the file called `AdventureWorks2012_Database.zip`. The Windows Azure SQL Database version can be found here:

`http://msftdbprodsamples.codeplex.com/releases/view/37304`

Instructions for installing the database for SQL Database are included in the download file as well as on the download page. You will need to install both of these to work through the examples in this chapter.

ADO.NET

Microsoft makes it very easy to connect an application to a SQL Database instance, by providing the necessary connection strings for a number of client libraries such as ADO.NET, Java and PHP, as shown in Figure 5-1. You can find the connection information in the Windows Azure Management Portal by selecting the SQL Databases option in the Navigation pane, selecting the appropriate database, and then clicking the Show Connection Strings button on the Dashboard page.

Copy the ADO.NET connection to the clipboard. You'll be using this shortly.

Figure 5-1. *Connection strings*

Making the Connection

Let's first look at how to connect to a SQL Database instance using ADO.NET. Fire up an instance of Visual Studio 2010, and create a new C# Windows Forms application. Then, follow these steps:

1. Place a button on Form1, and double-click the new button to view its Click event.

2. Before you place any code in the click event you'll need to declaration to use the appropriate SQLConnection class:

   ```
   using System.Data.SqlClient;
   ```

3. Next, let's add a method to get a connection string. To demonstrate connecting to SQL Database versus a local database, let's first connect to a local copy of the database. Then, you will change the connection string to connect to a SQL Database instance. Below the click event, add a new method called GetConString that returns the connection string for your local instance of SQL Server. If you have a named instance, be sure to enter the server name correctly (using the escape character). Here's the code to write:

```
string GetConString()
{
    return "Server=server;Database=AdventureWorks2012;User ID=sa;Password=password;";
}
```

4. Go back to the button's click event, and add the following code. This code calls the GetConString method you previously added, returns the connection string, establishes and opens a connection to the local database, and then closes the connection:

```
private void button1_Click(object sender, EventArgs e)
{
    string connStr = GetConString();
    using (SqlConnection conn = new SqlConnection(connStr))
    {
        try
        {
            conn.Open();
            MessageBox.Show("Connection made.");
        }
        catch (SqlException ex)
        {
            MessageBox.Show(ex.Message.ToString());
        }
        finally
        {
            conn.Close();
        }
    }
}
```

5. Run the application, and click the button on the form. You should get a message box that says "Connection Made."

Now, let's change this simple application to connect to SQL Database. Instead of returning the connection string to your local database, you want to return the ADO.NET connection string. Continue as follows:

6. Back in your Visual Studio project, paste in the connection string you copied form the Windows Azure Management Portal earlier in the GetConString method with the SQL Database ADO.NET connection string, as shown in the following code. Be sure to enter your correct password into the connection string:

```
string GetConString()
{
    return "Server=tcp:servername.database.windows.net;Database=AdventureWorks2012;
      UserID=username@servername;Password=password;
    Trusted_Connection=False;Encrypt=True;Connection Timeout=30";
}
```

7. Before you run the application, make sure your Azure firewall settings are up to date (via the SQL Database Server Administration page). Then run the application and click the button on the form. If everything is configured correctly, you should get a message box that says "Connection Made."

Granted, this is a very simple example, but it illustrates how easy it is to take an existing application and point it to SQL Database. The caveat is what your application contains. As mentioned earlier, if you have any inline T-SQL, at a minimum you need to ensure that its syntax is supported by SQL Database. The likelihood is that it is, but it's always safest to check and *test*.

Even though you've connected to SQL Database, does that affect your data-access code? The next two sections discuss using a data reader and a dataset when connecting to SQL Azure.

Using a Data Reader

As you become more and more familiar with SQL Database, you'll find that you don't need to make a lot of changes to your application code except possibly any inline T-SQL. The beauty of all this is that you're using a proven and trusted data-access technology, ADO.NET. Thus, nothing really changes. Let's modify the application and click-event code to illustrate this. Follow these steps:

1. Add a new list box to the form.

2. In the click event, add the code in bold in the following snippet. This new code uses the SqlDataReader class to execute a simple SELECT command against the SQL Database instance and then iterate over the SqlDataReader to populate the list box:

```
private void button1_Click(object sender, EventArgs e)
{
    string connStr = GetConString();
    using (SqlConnection conn = new SqlConnection(connStr))
    {
        SqlCommand cmd = new SqlCommand("SELECT FirstName, LastName  FROM Person.Person",
conn);
        conn.Open();
        SqlDataReader rdr = cmd.ExecuteReader();
        try
        {
            while (rdr.Read())
            {
                listBox1.Items.Add(rdr[0].ToString());
            }
            rdr.Close();
        }
        catch (SqlException ex)
        {
            MessageBox.Show(ex.Message.ToString());
        }
    }
}
```

3. Run the application, and click the button on the form. Within a few seconds, the list box populates with names from the Users table.

The key is that you can replace the connection string with your local connection string, and it still works. This is because you're using ADO.NET to handle the connection, and it doesn't care where the database is. Next, let's take this example one step further and look at how you use datasets.

Using a Dataset

In the last example, you found that there is no difference in syntax when using a SqlDataReader to query a SQL Database instance. This example uses the SqlCommand class and the SqlDataAdapter to query SQL Database and populate a dataset. Here are the steps:

1. In the button's click event, replace the existing code with the following:

```
using (SqlConnection conn = new SqlConnection(connStr))
{
    try
    {
        using (SqlCommand cmd = new SqlCommand())
        {
            conn.Open();
            SqlDataAdapter da = new SqlDataAdapter();
            cmd.CommandText = "SELECT FirstName, LastName  FROM Person.Person";
            cmd.Connection = conn;
            cmd.CommandType = CommandType.Text;
            da.SelectCommand = cmd;
            DataSet ds = new DataSet("Person");
            da.Fill(ds);
            listBox1.DataSource = ds.Tables[0];
            listBox1.DisplayMember = "FirstName";
        }
    }
    catch (SqlException ex)
    {
        MessageBox.Show(ex.Message.ToString());
    }
}
```

This code creates a new connection, using the same connection information as the previous example, and then creates a new SqlCommand instance. The connection, text, and type of the SqlCommand are set and then executed using the instantiated SqlDataAdapter. A new dataset is created and filled from the SqlDataAdapter, which is then applied to the datasource property of the list box.

2. Run the application, and click the button on the form. Again, the list box is populated with the names from the Users table in the SQL Database instance. Again, you could change the connection string to point to your local database and the code would work fine.

So, when would code like this *not* work? Suppose your application had code such as the following, which creates a table without a clustered index:

```
using (SqlConnection conn = new SqlConnection(connStr))
{
    try
    {
        using (SqlCommand cmd = new SqlCommand())
```

```
    {
        conn.Open();
        SqlDataAdapter da = new SqlDataAdapter();
        cmd.CommandText = "CREATE TABLE TestTable(ID int, Name varchar(20))";
        cmd.Connection = conn;
        cmd.ExecuteNonQuery();
        cmd.CommandText = "INSERT INTO TestTable (ID, Name)
VALUES (1, 'Scott'), (2, Chris)";
        int val = cmd.ExecuteNonQuery();
    }
}
catch (SqlException ex)
{
    MessageBox.Show(ex.Message.ToString());
}
}
```

Although this code is certainly valid and runs successfully against your local SQL Server instance, it doesn't work when executing against your SQL Database instance. Why? Go ahead and replace the code in the button's click event with this code, and run the application. The error you'll get in the message box states that SQL Database tables without a clustered index aren't supported. If you step through the code, you find out that the table is indeed created, but the error comes from trying to insert data into the table. You need to go through your application and look for these sorts of things, to ensure that the application will run successfully against SQL Database.

We have discussed connecting with ADO.NET and the different options we have with ADO.NET, so let's move on to the other connection option, ODBC.

ODBC

There is nothing earth-shattering or truly groundbreaking here, but let's walk though an example to see how ODBC connections work and illustrate that your ODBC classes still work as you're used to. Follow these steps:

1. Do this the proper way and create an enumeration to handle the type of connection you're using.

2. Modify the GetConString method as shown in the following snippet to take a parameter. The parameter lets you specify the connection type so you can return the correct type of connection string (either ADO.NET or ODBC). Be sure to use your correct password, username, and server name with the correct server. If the value of ADO_NET is passed into this method, the ADO.NET connection string is returned; otherwise the ODBC connection string is returned:

    ```
    enum ConnType
    {
        ADO_NET = 1,
        ODBC = 2
    }
    string GetConString(ConnType connType)
    {
        if (connType == ConnType.ADO_NET)
            return "Server=tcp:servername.database.windows.net;Database=AdventureWorks2012;
                User ID=username@servername;Password=password;
    ```

```
            Trusted_Connection=False;Encrypt=True;";
    else
        return "Driver={SQL Server Native Client
10.0};Server=tcp:servername.database.windows.net;

Database=AdventureWorks2012;Uid=username@servername;Pwd=password;Encrypt=yes;";
}
```

3. Add the following declaration to the project:

```
using System.Data.Odbc;
```

4. Place a second button on the form, along with a DataGridView. In its click event, add the following code. This code is just like the code from the ADO.NET example, but it uses the Odbc data classes versus the Sql data classes. For clarity, change the Text property of this new button to "ODBC" so you know the difference between this button and the first. Notice in the code that the value "ODBC" is passed in the GetConString method, returning the ODBC connection string:

```
string connStr = GetConString(ConnType.ODBC);

using (OdbcConnection conn = new OdbcConnection(connStr))
{
    try
    {
        conn.Open();
        OdbcDataAdapter da = new OdbcDataAdapter();
        OdbcCommand cmd = new OdbcCommand("SELECT FirstName, LastName  FROM Person.
Person", conn);
        cmd.CommandType = CommandType.Text;
        da.SelectCommand = cmd;
        DataSet ds = new DataSet("Person");
        da.Fill(ds);
        listBox1.DataSource = ds.Tables[0];
        dataGridView1.DataSource = ds.Tables[0];
        listBox1.DisplayMember = "FirstName";

    }
    catch (OdbcException ex)
    {
        MessageBox.Show(ex.Message.ToString());
    }
}
```

5. Before the project is run, you need to modify the code behind the first button to pass the appropriate Enum and return the appropriate connection string. Add the following line to the beginning of the code behind Button1:

```
string connStr = GetConString(ConnType.ADO_NET );
```

6. Run the project, and click the ODBC button. As in the previous example, the list box populates with the names from the Person.Person table. The grid also populates with the same set of names (see Figure 5-2).

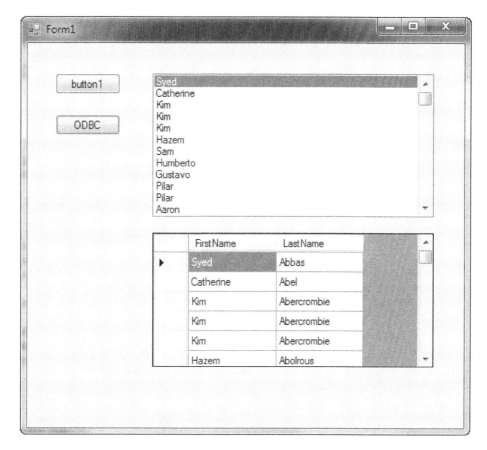

Figure 5-2. *Finished form with data*

From these examples, you can see that connecting to and querying SQL Database is no different from connecting to a local instance of SQL Server. The end of this chapter discusses some guidelines and best practices to help you prepare for your move to SQL Database.

So far we have discussed connecting with ADO.NET and ODBC along with the different options we have with each, so let's continue the discussion and talk about using the sqlcmd utility.

sqlcmd

If you've worked with SQL Server for any length of time, chances are you've worked with the sqlcmd utility. This utility lets you enter and execute T-SQL statements and other objects via a command prompt. You can also use the sqlcmd utility via the Query Editor in sqlcmd mode, in a Windows script file, or via a SQL Server Agent job.

This section discusses how to use the sqlcmd utility to connect to a SQL Database instance and execute queries against that database. This section assumes that you have some familiarity with sqlcmd. This utility has many options, or parameters, but this section only discusses those necessary to connect to SQL Database.

■ **Note** SQL Database doesn't support the -z or -Z option for changing user passwords. You need to use ALTER LOGIN after connecting to the master database in order to change a password.

To use the sqlcmd utility, you first open a command prompt. At the command prompt, you need to provide the options and values necessary to connect to the SQL Database instance. As a minimum, the command syntax is the following:

```
sqlcmd -U login -P password -S server -d database
```

The parameters are nearly self-explanatory, but here they are, just in case:

- -U is the user login ID.

- -P is the user-specified password. Passwords are case sensitive.

- -S specifies the instance of SQL Server to which to connect.

Optionally, you can provide a database name via the -d parameter. Thus, the sqlcmd syntax looks something like the following:

```
Sqlcmd -U providerlogin@Server -P ProviderPassword -S ProviderServer -d database
```

Let's put this syntax to use. Follow these steps:
At the command prompt, use the sqlcmd syntax and type in your connection information, as shown in Figure 5-3. (In the figure, the server name and password are hidden.) Press Enter.

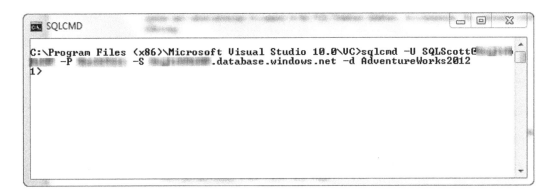

Figure 5-3. *Connecting via sqlcmd*

When the sqlcmd utility connects, you're presented with the sqlcmd prompt 1>, at which point you can begin typing in and executing T-SQL commands. The command to execute any T-SQL statement is GO. For example, in Figure 5-4, the following SELECT statement is entered and executed:

```
SELECT FirstName, LastName FROM Person.Person
```

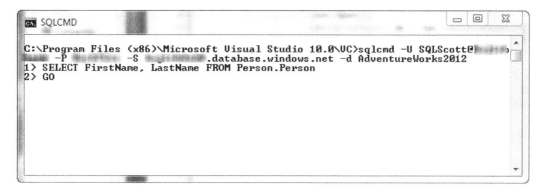

Figure 5-4. *Executing a SELECT*

Press the Enter key on line 1> to create a new line and execute the SELECT query. Type GO on line 2> and press Enter to execute all statements since the last GO statement (see Figure 5-4). Figure 5-5 shows the results of the sqlcmd query entered. As you can see, executing a query isn't difficult.

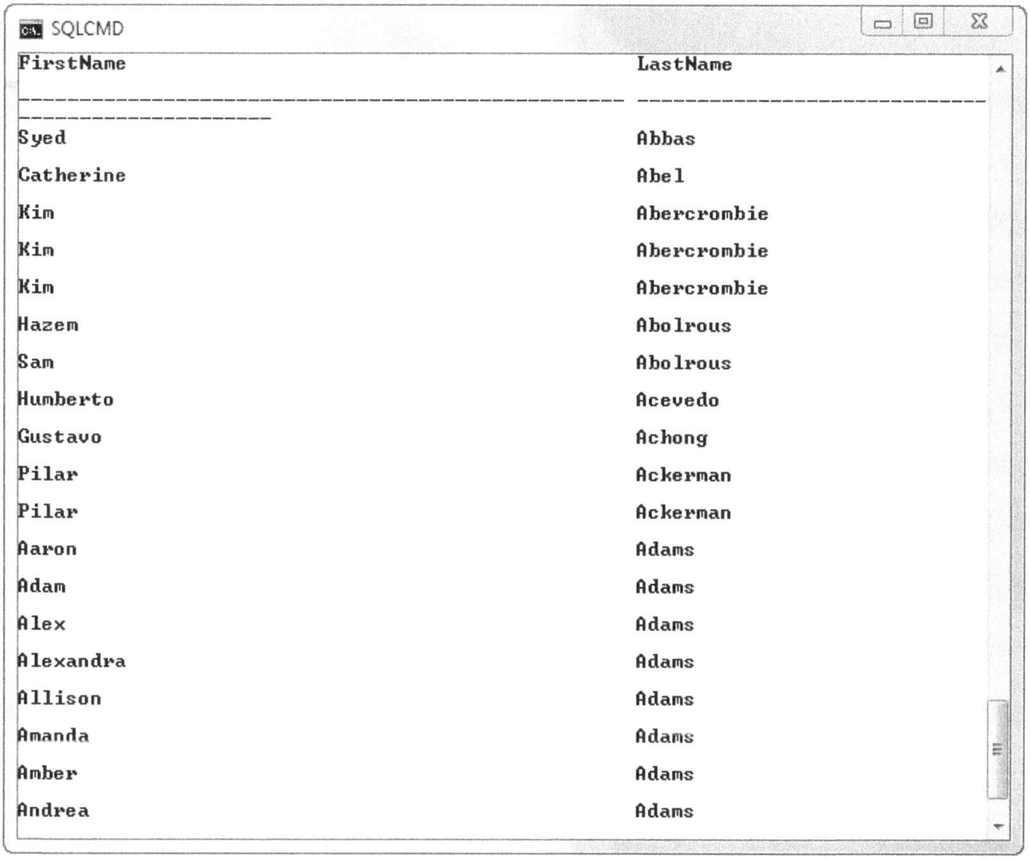

FirstName	LastName
Syed	Abbas
Catherine	Abel
Kim	Abercrombie
Kim	Abercrombie
Kim	Abercrombie
Hazem	Abolrous
Sam	Abolrous
Humberto	Acevedo
Gustavo	Achong
Pilar	Ackerman
Pilar	Ackerman
Aaron	Adams
Adam	Adams
Alex	Adams
Alexandra	Adams
Allison	Adams
Amanda	Adams
Amber	Adams
Andrea	Adams

Figure 5-5. *Sqlcmd query results*

Let's work through another example in which you create a table and add data. Here are the steps:

1. After the previous query is finished, you're back at the 1> prompt. Type in the statement shown in Figure 5-6.

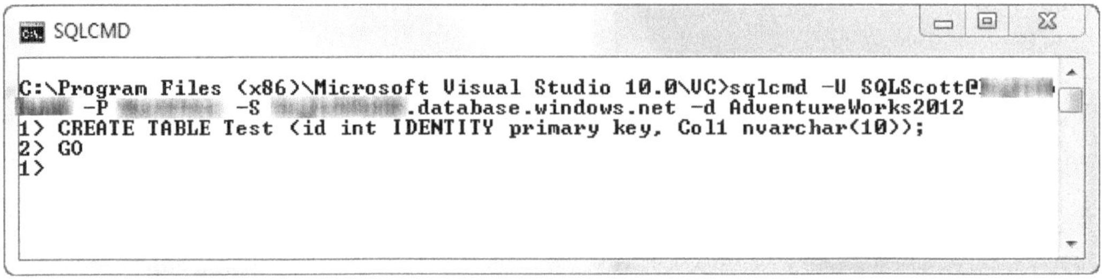

```
SQLCMD                                                              ☐ ☐ ✕

C:\Program Files (x86)\Microsoft Visual Studio 10.0\VC>sqlcmd -U SQLScott@
        -P             -S             .database.windows.net -d AdventureWorks2012
1> CREATE TABLE Test (id int IDENTITY primary key, Col1 nvarchar(10));
2> GO
1>
```

Figure 5-6. *Creating a table*

2. Press Enter, type GO on line 2>, and press Enter again, to execute the CREATE statement.

3. When the T-SQL command that you execute is the type that doesn't return data, the sqlcmd utility doesn't give you back a message but takes you to the 1> prompt. However, you can verify that a statement executed successfully by going into SQL Server Management Studio (SSMS), connecting to your SQL Database instance, and expanding the Tables node of your chosen database. Figure 5-7 shows the results from doing that— you can see that the table was indeed created.

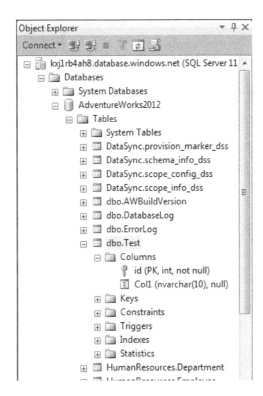

Figure 5-7. *The new table viewed in SSMS*

The table you created is called Test, and it has two columns: an ID column that is the primary key (clustered index), and Col1, an nvarchar column. The table is simple, but it's good enough to demonstrate functionality.

■ **Note**   You know from earlier in the chapter that the ID column must be a primary key clustered index, or you won't be able to add data to the table.

---

4.   Add some data to the table by going back to the command window and typing in the INSERT statements shown in Figure 5-8. The great thing about the sqlcmd utility is that you can enter in as many commands as you want and not execute them until you type GO. Here you use two INSERT statements that add two records the table you created in the previous step.

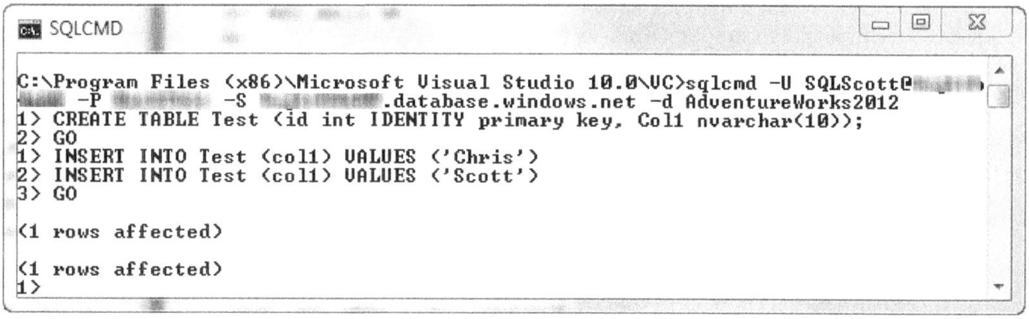

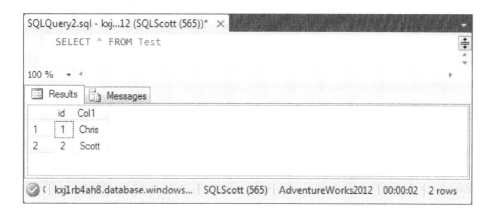

Figure 5-8.   Inserting rows via sqlcmd

5.   Type GO on line 3>, and press Enter. Although the sqlcmd utility tells you 1 rows affected, you can query this new table in SSMS and see the two new rows that were added, as shown in Figure 5-9.

Figure 5-9.   Viewing results via SSMS

As you can see, using the sqlcmd utility is straightforward. Just remember that it doesn't work with SQL Database if you're trying to use heap tables. All tables must have a primary key. Also, as mentioned earlier, the -z and -Z parameters don't work.

This section has discussed the different mechanisms for connecting to and querying SQL Database, including examples for ADO.NET, ODBC, and sqlcmd. You can see that the connection process is quite similar to the way you currently connect to and query an on-premises database. However, given the overall industry push to an SOA architecture, let's take the discussion to the next level and look at using services, specifically WCF Data Services, to connect to our Azure database.

WCF Data Services

WCF Data Services, formerly known as ADO.NET Data Services, is the tool that enables the creation and consumption of OData services. OData, the Open Data Protocol, is a new data-sharing standard that allows for greater sharing of data between different systems. Before it was called WCF Data Services, ADO.NET Data Services was one of the very first Microsoft technologies to support OData with Visual Studio 2008 SP1. Microsoft has broadened its support of OData in products such as SQL Server 2008 R2, Windows Azure Storage, and others. This section discusses how to use WCF Data Services to connect to and query your SQL Database instance.

Creating a Data Service

First you need to create a data service. Follow these steps:

1. Fire up Visual Studio (to be safe, run Visual Studio as Administrator) and create a new C# ASP.NET web application (in the New Project dialog, select the Web option from the list of installed templates), and call it WCFDataServiceWebApp. (You can host data services in a number of different environments, but this example uses a web app.)

2. The next step in creating a data service on top of a relational database is to define a model used to drive your data service tier. The best way to do that is to use the ADO.NET Entity Framework, which allows you to expose your entity model as a data service. And to do that, you need to add a new item to your web project. Right-click the web project and select New Item. In the Add New Item dialog, select Data from the Categories list, and then select ADO.NET Entity Data Model from the Templates list. Give the model the name AW.edmx, and click OK.

3. In the first step of the Data Model Wizard, select the Generate from Database option, and click Next.

4. The next step is Choose Your Data Connection. Click the New Connection button, and create a connection to the AdventureWorks2012 SQL Database instance. Click OK in the connection dialog.

5. Back in the Entity Data Model Wizard, select the "Yes, include the sensitive data in the connection string" option. Save the entity connection settings as AdventureWorks2012Entities, and then click Next.

6. The next step of the wizard is the Choose Your Database Objects page. Select the Person.Person table. Note the option to pluralize or singularize generated objects names. If you leave this option checked, it comes into play later. Leave it checked, and click Finish.

7. The Entity Framework looks at all the tables you selected and creates a conceptual model on top of the storage schema that you can soon expose as a data service. In Visual Studio, you should see the Entity Framework Model Designer with a graphical representation of the table you selected, called *entities*. Close the Model Designer—you don't need it for this example.

8. What you need to do now is create the data service on top of your data model. In Solution Explorer right-click the web application and select Add; then select New Item. In the Add New Item dialog, select the Web category, and then scroll down the list of templates and select the WCF Data Service template. Enter a name of AWDataService and then click Add, as shown in Figure 5-10.

***Figure 5-10.** Adding a WCF Data Service to the Solution*

When the ADO.NET Data Service is added to your project, the associated .cs file will automatically be displayed in the IDE. As you can see, the ADO.NET Data Service template has generated for you the beginnings of your data service.

Connecting the Service to the Model

Now you need to wire up your data service to your data model so that the service knows where to get its data. You know where to do this, because as you can see in the code it tells you where to enter that information. Thus, change the line:

```
public class AWDataService : DataService< /* TODO: put your data source class name here */ >
```

To:

```
public class AWDataService : DataService< AdventureWorks2012Entities >
```

Wiring up your data service to the model is as simple as that. Believe it or not, you're ready to test your service. However, let's finish what you need to do on this page. By default, the WCF Data Service is secured. The WCF Data Service needs to be told explicitly which data you want to see. The instructions in the code tell you this, as you can see in code in the InitializeService method. Some examples are even provided in the comments to help you out.

For your example, you don't want to restrict anything, so you really want to unlock all the entities and explicitly define access rights to the entity sets. You do this by adding the following code to the `InitializeService` method. This code sets the access rule for the specified entities to All, providing authorization to read, write, delete, and update data for the specified entity set:

```
// This method is called only once to initialize service-wide policies.
public static void InitializeService(DataServiceConfiguration config)
{
    // TODO: set rules to indicate which entity sets and service operations are visible, updatable, etc.
    // Examples:
    config.SetEntitySetAccessRule("People", EntitySetRights.All);
    config.DataServiceBehavior.MaxProtocolVersion = DataServiceProtocolVersion.V2;
}
```

If you don't feel like specifying each entity one by one, you can optionally specify all the entities with a single line, as follows:

```
config.SetEntitySetAccessRule("*", EntitySetRights.All);
```

This line assumes that you want to specify the same rights to all the entities. That's not recommended, but it will do for this example. In a production environment you will want to be more specific about the rights you specify for each entity.

There are other `EntitySetRights` options, such as `AllRead`, `AllWrite`, `None`, `ReadSingle`, and `WriteAppend`. This chapter won't cover them all, but you can read about them here:

```
http://msdn.microsoft.com/en-us/library/system.data.services.entitysetrights.aspx
```

So far, you've created your Web application, added your data model, and added your WCF Data Service. Right now your Solution Explorer should look like Figure 5-11.

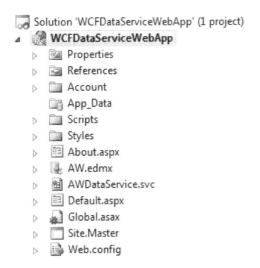

Figure 5-11. *The web application with a data service as seen in Solution Explorer*

Creating the Client Application

The next step is to add the client application. In Solution Explorer right click the solution and select Add New Project. In the Add New Project dialog, select the Cloud project type and then select Windows Azure Project, providing a name of AWSite, as shown in Figure 5-12.

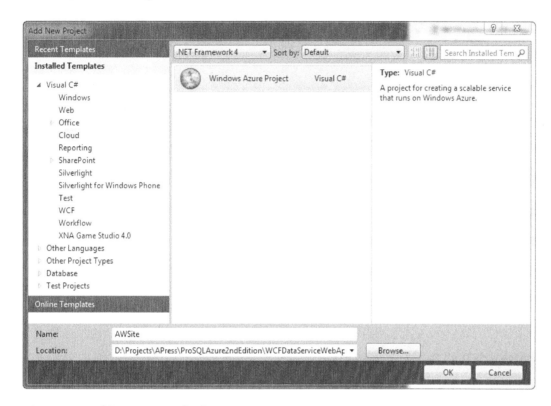

Figure 5-12. *Adding an Azure Cloud Service*

Click OK in the Add New Project dialog.

Next, in the New Cloud Service Project dialog, select ASP.NET Web Role to add it to the Cloud Service Solution pane, leaving the default name of WebRole1, and click OK.

Next, right-click the Web Role project in Solution Explorer and select Add Service Reference from the context menu. This will bring up the Add Service Reference dialog shown in Figure 5-13.

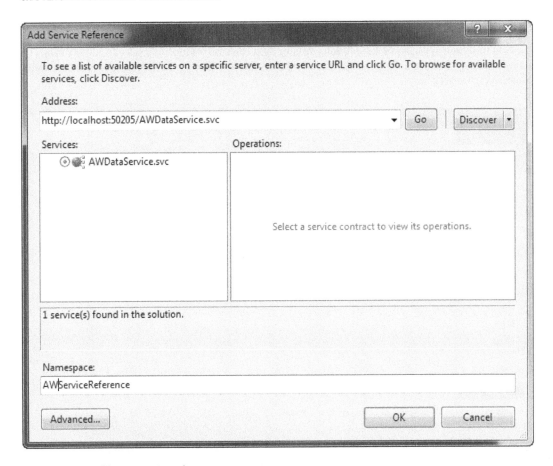

Figure 5-13. *Adding a service reference*

In the Add Service Reference dialog, click the Discover button, which will interrogate your solution for existing services and display them in the Services list. As you can see from Figure 5-13, the discovery function did in fact find your AWDataServices service in your Web application project. The discovery also provides your local URI for the service as well as the entities that are exposed by the service. Give the service a namespace name of AWServiceReference and click OK.

At this point your Solution Explorer will have your AWSite Cloud Service project, your WCFDataServiceWebApp project, and your web role. You should see those items as they're shown in Figure 5-14.

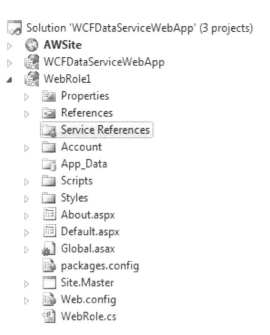

Figure 5-14. *Projects in Solution Explorer*

That was quite the example, but let's discuss some best practices that pertain to the application when connecting to Windows Azure SQL Database.

Best Practices

Let's spend a few minutes talking about some things you should consider when developing applications for the cloud. We've spent a large portion of this chapter discussing how to connect to SQL Database, but even before you start coding, the very first thing you should consider is your connection. First and foremost, secure your connection string from injection attacks and man-in-the-middle attacks. The .NET Framework provides a simple class in which to create and manage the contents of connection strings used by the SqlConnection class. This is the SqlConnectionStringBuilder class.

The following example illustrates how to use this class. I first define four static variables to hold the username, password, database name and server:

```
private static string userName = "SQLScott@server";
private static string userPassword = password;
private static string dataSource = "tcp:server.database.windows.net";
private static string dbName = "AdventureWorks2012";
```

I then modify my GetConString method to use the SqlConnectionStringBuilder class to dynamically build my connection string:

```
string GetConString(int connType)
{
    if (connType == 1)
        SqlConnectionStringBuilder connstr = new SqlConnectionStringBuilder();
        connstr.DataSource = dataSource;
        connstr.InitialCatalog = dbName;
        connstr.Encrypt = true;
        connstr.TrustServerCertificate = false;
        connstr.UserID = userName;
        connstr.Password = userPassword;
        return connstr.ToString();
...
}
```

Thus, consider the following when connecting to a SQL Database instance.

- Use the SqlConnectionStringBuilder class to avoid injection attacks. This class helps protect the user ID and password from being seen and then used in an attack.

- While all SQL Database traffic is encrypted and sent over port 443, be sure to set the Encrypt parameter to True and the TrustServerCertificate to False to ensure a properly encrypted connection to avoid any man-in-the-middle attacks.

- Use MARS (Multiple Active Results Sets) whenever possible to reduce the number of trips to the database.

- Use connection pooling to provide improved code efficiency and application performance by reducing the number of times a new database connection must be opened. Windows Azure SQL Database automatically terminates connections that have been idle for 30 minutes or longer. The best practice is to design your application such that connections are opened late and closed early.

Lastly, let's discuss some connection constraints.

Transient Fault Handling Application Block

The Transient Fault Handling Application Block provides a set of reusable components for adding retry logic into your applications. These components can be used with the many of the Windows Azure services such as SQL Database, Storage, Service Bus, and Caching. These components provide the resiliency applications needed in applications by adding robust transient fault handling logic into applications.

Transient faults are errors that occur due to some type of temporary condition such as network connectivity issues or unreliable service. In most cases, simply waiting for a brief period of time and then retrying the operation results in a successful operation.

This is where the Transient Fault Handling Application Block comes in. The Transient Fault Handling Application Block (we'll call it TFHAB from here to save space. . . and typing) is part of Microsoft's Enterprise Library. It is the result of some great collaboration between the Microsoft Patterns & Practices group and the Windows Azure Customer Advisory team.

The TFHAB works by using detection strategies to identify all known transient error conditions, making it easy for developers to define retry policies based on the built-in retry strategies.

The TFHAB includes three built-in retry strategies which developers can utilize to implement a consistent retry behavior within their applications. The three built-in retry strategies are based on intervals:

- **Fixed**: Wait a fixed number of time between retries.

- **Incremental**: Increment the wait time by 1 between each retry.

- **Exponential back-off**: Exponentially increment the wait time between each retry.

You'll see an example of each of these shortly.

Adding the Transient Fault Handling Application Block to Your Project

The TFHAB is a NuGet package that is added through the Package Manager Console in Visual Studio. However, before you can use the Package Manager Console, you need to install NuGet. Open a browser and navigate to the NuGet web site at http://nuget.org/. On the main home page, click the Install NuGet button. NuGet supports Visual Studio 2010 and 2012.

Once NuGet is installed, open Visual Studio and create a new WinForms application. Once the project is created, from the Tools menu in Visual Studio, select Library Package Manager ➤ Package Manager Console.

In the console window type the following command, as shown in Figure 5-15, to install the Transient Fault Handling Application Block:

```
Install-Package EnterpriseLibrary.WindowsAzure.TransientFaultHandling
```

Figure 5-15. *Adding the TFHAB in Package Manager Console*

Press Enter once you have typed in in the `Install` command. The appropriate assemblies and references will be added to your project. Once the install is done, expand the References node in Solution Explorer and you will see over six new Microsft.Practices references added to your project.

Using the Transient Fault Handling Application Block

With the TFHAB installed, the first thing that needs to be done is to add a couple of directives to the code:

```
using Microsoft.Practices.EnterpriseLibrary.WindowsAzure.TransientFaultHandling.SqlAzure
using Microsoft.TransientFaultHandling
```

These directives are like any other directive in that they allow the use of types in a namespace. The next thing to do is to define the retry policy. This policy simply defines the number of times to retry the command and the length of time to wait between the number of retries, as well as several backoff times. Setting this is actually quite easy; a single line of code:

```
RetryPolicy myretrypolicy = new RetryPolicy<SqlAzureTransientErrorDetectionStrategy>
(3, TimeSpan.FromSeconds(3));
```

The RetryPolicy constructor has five overloads, as shown in Figure 5-16, but the most commonly used overload takes two parameters; the count of retries and the wait time between retries.

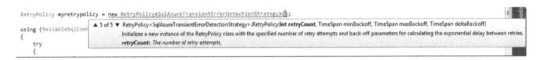

Figure 5-16. *Retry policy constructors*

This example simply defines the number of tries as three and sets the retry interval at three seconds. With the retry policy defined it can be applied to the connection through the ReliableSqlConnection class. This class provides a way to reliably open a connection and execute commands through the policy just defined.

The ReliableSqlConnection class also has three overloads: the connection string, the defined retry policy to the connection, and optionally the command.

Add to Button2 the following code, which uses the ReliableSqlConnection class and applies the retry policy to both the connection and the command:

```
using (ReliableSqlConnection cnn = new ReliableSqlConnection(connString, myretrypolicy,
myretrypolicy))
{
    try
    {
        cnn.Open();

        using (var cmd = cnn.CreateCommand())
        {
            cmd.CommandText = "SELECT * FROM HumanResources.Employee";

            using (var rdr = cnn.ExecuteCommand<IDataReader>(cmd))
            {
                //
            }
        }
    }
    catch (Exception ex)
    {
        MessageBox.Show(ex.Message.ToString());
    }
}
```

Alternatively, the TFHAB also provides the `ExecuteReaderWithRetry` method, which sends the specified connection to the connection using the specified retry policy:

```
using (var rdr = cmd.ExecuteReaderWithRetry(myretrypolicy))
```

Retry policies can also be applied and used with the Entity Framework. The following code illustrates how to apply a defined policy to a LINQ to Entities query:

```
using (NorthwindEntities dc = new NorthwindEntities())
{
    RetryPolicy myPolicy = new RetryPolicy<SqlAzureTransientErrorDetectionStrategy>(3);
    Employee e1 = myPolicy.ExecuteAction<Employee>(() =>
        (from x in dc.Employees
            where x.LastName == "King"
            select x).First());
}
```

The Transient Fault Handling Application Block provides a simple but very necessary mechanism for building "best practice" fault-tolerant applications. Retry policies are a way to handle transient conditions and things that happen externally to your application, such as network and internet connectivity or service interruption.

To see this in action, run the app first as-is to ensure it runs properly. Next, set the number of retries in your policy to 3 and the retry interval to 3 as well. Unplug your network cable and rerun the app. You will notice that the application does not error immediately; instead, after 9 seconds it will error. Pretty slick.

Summary

We began the chapter with a discussion of the different factors for deploying your application, such as keeping your application on-premises or hosting your application in Azure. We also covered application deployment from the database side, providing some ideas and concepts to consider when moving your database to the cloud, such as how much of your data to move.

We then discussed the different programming approaches for connecting to and querying a SQL Database instance, providing examples for each method including ADO.NET and ODBC.

Next, we discussed accessing your SQL Database instance through WCF Data Services. With today's strong emphasis on SOA architecture coming not only from Microsoft, the discussion of WCF Data Services offered a solid foundation for providing a services layer for your SQL Database instance.

Lastly, we discussed some crucial best practices, such as implementing Reply Policies in your application that can drastically improve the end-user experience and add the resiliency needed in cloud-based applications. Along with retry, we also discussed other best practices including connection pooling and using the `SqlConnectionStringBuilder` class. An important component to all application development, regardless of whether the application is cloud-based or not, is the implementation of fault handling and retry logic. This chapter spent a few pages on retry login because of how critical it is in cloud-based applications. All of these best practices, if implemented, will help ensure a well-operating application.

CHAPTER 6

SQL Reporting

A lot has changed in the two years since the first release of this book. What at one time was in CTP (Community Technology Preview) and still being fleshed out has seen the light of day. Not long after we released the first version of this book, SQL Reporting, formally known as SQL Azure Reporting Services, hit the market in Beta form.

By the time this book hits the shelves, Windows Azure SQL Reporting will have been officially released. This chapter will first provide an overview of SQL Reporting by looking at its architecture and how fits into the Windows Azure SQL Database picture to support a wide variety of reporting needs. We will then spend the rest of the chapter looking at how to work with SQL Reporting, including how to deploy reports and access those reports from your application. This chapter will also look at managing SQL Reporting security via different roles, as well as discuss some best practices for securing SQL Reporting.

We'll also spend some time in this chapter looking at the differences between on-premises SQL Server Reporting Services and SQL Reporting, including the security model as well as the different data sources for reports. This chapter assumes that you're familiar with SQL Server Reporting Services and how to create and work with reports and subreports. Plenty of great books on SSRS are available if you need an introduction.

Let's get started.

SQL Reporting Overview

When Microsoft set out to create a reporting service for the SQL Database, their goal was to provide many of the great reporting capabilities that currently exist in SQL Server Reporting Services and to ensure that the same cloud benefits that all of the Azure services benefit from (such as elasticity and high availability) were extended to SQL Reporting, without making developers learn a whole reporting structure. With SQL Reporting, they succeeded. SQL Reporting is a cloud-based reporting platform based on the tried-and-true SQL Server Reporting Services. Simply stated, SQL Reporting is SQL Server Reporting Server running as a highly available cloud service.

This is good news because it means several things. First, you don't need to install your own Reporting Services instance, and you don't need to maintain those instances (such as applying updates). Second, as part of the SQL Database platform, SQL Reporting can take advantage of the benefits of the Azure platform, providing high availability and scalability of your reporting services. Third, you can build reports using the same familiar tools that you currently use for building on-premises reports. Lastly, developers can deliver reports as an integrated part of a Windows Azure-based solution.

Think about this for a minute. In an on-premises environment, how long does it typically take to provision a new SQL Server Reporting Services server? Even if you have an extra server lying around, to get that server added to your SQL Server environment would typically take several hours. What if you could provision a new report server in a matter of minutes? Now you can do that with SQL Reporting, while enjoying the benefits of the Azure platform (letting Microsoft manage the physical administration).

With SQL Reporting you can quickly and easily provision and deploy reporting solutions while taking advantage of the enterprise-class availability, scalability, and security of the Windows Azure platform.

So, with that introduction it will be helpful to look at the architecture of SQL Reporting to help you get a feel for how reporting works in SQL Database.

Architecture

The architecture of SQL Reporting Services has load balancing and high availability automatically built in. Figure 6-1 illustrates the different components of the SQL reporting architecture which we'll discuss.

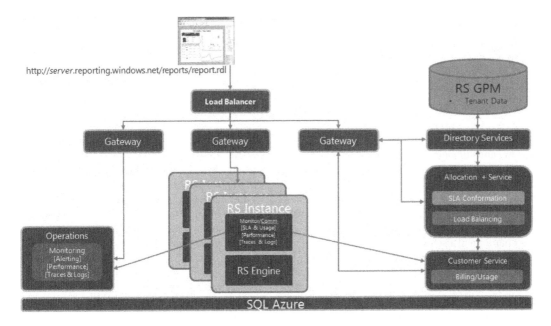

Figure 6-1. *SQL Reporting Services Architecture*

Each SQL Reporting report is accessed via the service endpoint and referencing a specific report. Notice that this isn't any different than accessing your on-premises report server, except that in this case you are accessing a service endpoint instead of a physical machine.

The request is routed through the load balancer, which routes the request through two more application tiers in the architecture:

- Reporting Service Gateway
- Reporting Service Nodes

Gateway

The Reporting Services Gateway handles all of the intelligent metadata routing. For example, the Gateway implements Smart Routing, which means that as requests for a report come in, each request is processed and sent to the best available report server to handle that request. This allows for increased security and control over the availability of the system. For example, if a report (request) takes down a specific node, the Gateway can intelligently stop routing requests to that specific Reporting Services node.

Nodes

The nodes are the actual reporting servers. They are described as multi-tenant, meaning that each node has its own catalog and tempDBs (from SQL Database). The nodes are built on top of SQL Database; thus the data tier that is used for SQL Reporting is SQL Database.

It is important to note that the services that the Gateway provides are very similar to the way the SQL Database intelligent metadata routing tier operates; in fact, some of the design patterns have been replicated in the SQL Reporting architecture.

Feature Comparison

Before we get to the "hands-on" portion of the chapter it will be very beneficial to highlight some of the similarities and differences between SQL Server Reporting Services and SQL Reporting (see Table 6-1).

Table 6-1. *SQL Server Reporting Services and SQL Reporting Feature Comparison*

Category	SQL Server Reporting Services	SQL Reporting
Tooling	Business Intelligence Development Studio (BIDS)	Business Intelligence Development Studio (BIDS)
Data Sources	Built-in or customizable data sources	SQL Database Instance
Report Management	Report Manager for native mode, SharePoint application pages. Can display and render reports to different formats. Can create subscriptions and schedule deliveries. Reports can be viewed in browsers, Report Viewer via Windows Forms, and ASP.NET and SharePoint.	Windows Azure Management Portal Reports can be viewed in browsers, Report Viewer via Windows Forms and ASP.NET.
Extensibility	Custom extensions for data, processing, rendering, delivery, and security	No extensions are supported in this release
Security Model	Windows authentication and other supported authentications	SQL Database username and password authentication

Both SQL Server Reporting Services and SQL Reporting share the ability to apply permissions to reports and report-related items via role assignments.

The list in Table 6-1 is a brief feature comparison; in addition, the following SQL Server Reporting Services features are not currently supported in SQL Reporting:

- Creating subscriptions or schedule report snapshots.

- Creating SMDL report models.

- Creating reports from Report Builder version 1.0, 2.0, or 3.0. However, you can create reports using version 3.0 and then deploy the reports by addingz them to BIDS.

- SharePoint integrated mode is not supported. Native mode is supported.

It should be noted that Report Manager is not available, but the SQL Database Reporting portal provides similar features.

It is time to get "hands-on," so the rest of the chapter discusses how to create a SQL Reporting Server and deploy a report to that server. This chapter uses the full AdventureWorks database for Windows Azure SQL Database. This database, and instructions for installing it, can be found here:

`http://msftdbprodsamples.codeplex.com/releases/view/3704`

Download the file called AdventureWorks2012Full_SQLAzure. Instructions for installing the database can also be found on this same page. The download file is a zip file containing two different installations. Follow the instructions for the non-Federated version (you will learn all about SQL Federation in Chapter 10).

Provisioning Your SQL Reporting Server

Creating your SQL Reporting Server is a simple and quick process. It should be noted that up until now you have spent the majority of the time in the new Windows Azure Management Portal. As of this writing, both SQL Reporting and SQL Data Sync have not been ported over to use the new portal. In the short term, the current Silverlight-based portal will continue to function as it always has so that SQL Reporting and SQL Data Sync remain accessible until they are ported to the new portal.

1. Open your web browser, navigate to https://windows.azure.com/, and log in with your LiveID.

2. Once you are in the portal, click the Reporting option in the Navigation pane. If you have previously created any SQL Reporting servers, they will be listed per subscription at the top of the Navigation pane. Figure 6-2 shows the Navigation pane with the Reporting option selected but no servers yet created.

Figure 6-2. *Windows Azure portal navigation pane*

3. You have two options for creating a server. Either select the Create button on the ribbon to begin, or click the Create a New SQL Reporting Server section in the Items List section of the portal. Either one will open the Create Server dialog, shown in Figure 6-3.

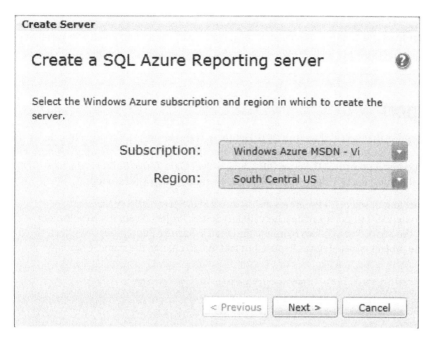

Figure 6-3. *The Create Server dialog*

4. Select the Subscription and Region in which to provision the server. Click Next.

5. Enter an Administrator username and Password, and then click Finish. Your SQL Reporting Server will provision quickly, at which point the Management Portal will display your new server and the associated information, as seen in Figure 6-4.

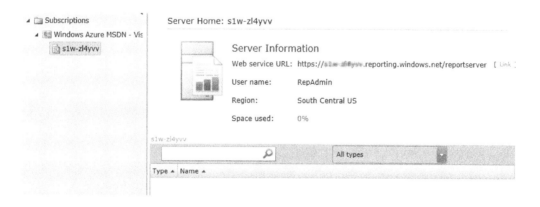

Figure 6-4. *A new SQL Reporting server viewed in the Management Portal*

Notice that the server "name" is actually a service endpoint. This is how you will access your report server when deploying and accessing reports.

At this point, your server is provisioned and ready to be used. In the rest of the chapter you will create a report and deploy it to your new SQL Reporting Server.

■ **Note** SQL Server Data Tools is a central and unified development environment integrated into Visual Studio which allows database developers and DBAs to perform all of their database design work all within a single tool.

Creating a Report

The process of creating reports that access data from SQL Database is the same as for reports that access local data, with one slight difference: the connection to the data. The example in this chapter for creating a report will use SQL Server Data Tools, which is installed with SQL Server 2012. SQL Server Data Tools (SSDT) is the new BIDS (Business Intelligence Development Studio) for SQL Server 2012. To create a report, follow these steps:

1. From the Start menu, select All Programs ➤ Microsoft SQL Server 2012 ➤ SQL Server Data Tools. When SSDT opens, create a new Report Server Project. From the New Project dialog select the Reporting Services template and then select the Report Server Project. In Figure 6-5 the project is called AzureReport, but feel free to change the name. Click OK.

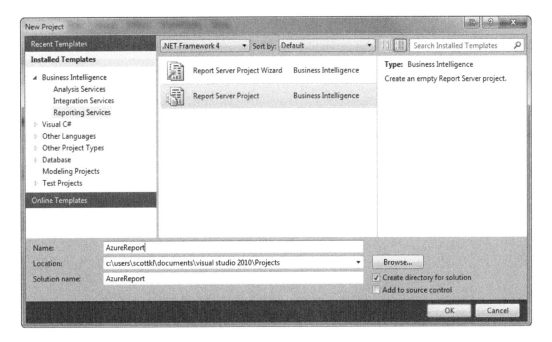

Figure 6-5. *New Report Server Project*

2. In Solution Explorer, right-click the solution and select Add ➤ New Item from the context menu.

3. In the Add New Item dialog, select the Report template, and click Add, as shown in Figure 6-6.

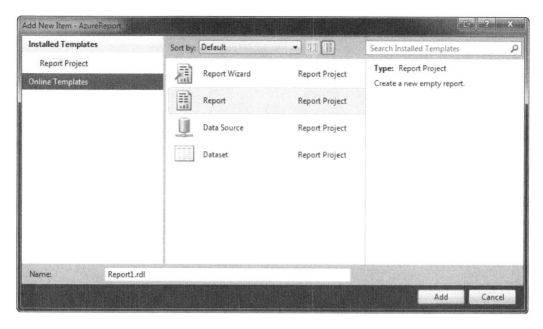

Figure 6-6. *Adding a report*

At this point, you're staring at a blank report, but you also see a new Report Data tab displayed in the Visual Studio IDE. Your task is to tell the report where to get its data from, and starting with SQL Server 2008 R2 (and continuing in SQL Server 2012) it became very easy via the ADO.NET (SqlClient) and OLE DB data providers. However, SQL Server 2008 R2 and above also add a new SQL Database–specific provider. You'll see this shortly.

Creating the SQL Database Data Source

Continue with these steps:

1. In the Report Data window, right-click the Data Sources node, and select Add Data Source from the context menu, as shown in Figure 6-7.

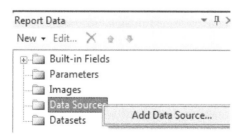

Figure 6-7. *Adding a data source*

2. In the Data Source Properties dialog, you define the type of connection and the connection properties. Select the "Embedded connection" option, and then click the Type down arrow. You read earlier that beginning with SQL Server 2008 R2 a SQL Database-specific provider was included, and this is where you find it, along with other data source types. As shown in Figure 6-8, select the new data provider for SQL Database, called Microsoft SQL Azure (what else are they going to call it?).

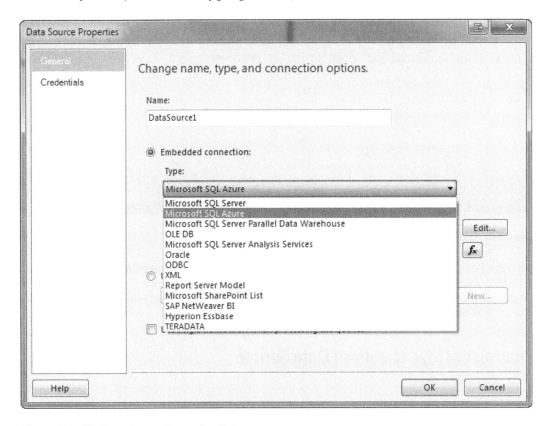

Figure 6-8. *The Data Source Properties dialog*

When you select this provider, the Connection String text box defaults to

Encrypt=True;TrustServerCertificate=False

These two parameters and associated values are defaulted for you. It's recommended that you not change them. The Encrypt parameter indicates that SQL Server will use SSL encryption for all data sent between the server and client if the server has a cert installed. The TrustServerCertificate property tells the transport layer to use SSL to encrypt the channel and bypass walking the cert chain to validate trust. When both Encrypt and TrustServerCertificate are set to True, the encryption level specified *on the server* is used even if the value of the Encrypt parameter in this connection string is set to False.

However, even with this default string set, you still need to add the SQL Database connection information.

3. Click the Edit button to open the Connection Properties dialog, shown in Figure 6-9. Enter your SQL Database instance name, username, and password. You should know by now that you can't use Windows Authentication with SQL Database, so make sure you enter the SQL Database account username and password.

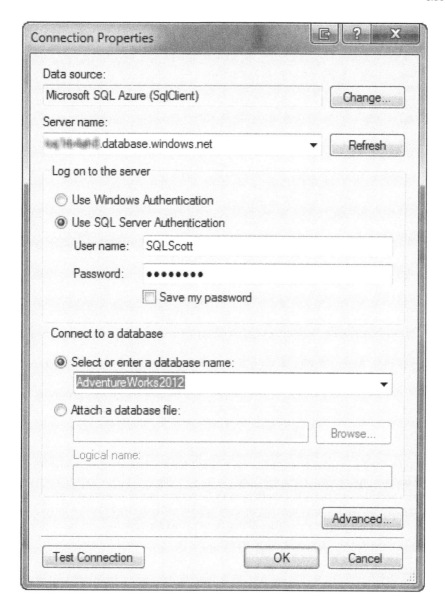

Figure 6-9. *The Connection Properties dialog*

4. Select (or type in) the database you want to pull the data from, and then click Test Connection to ensure that all your settings are correct.

5. Click OK to close this dialog and return to the Data Source Properties dialog. It should now look like Figure 6-10, which shows the appropriate connection type and connection string.

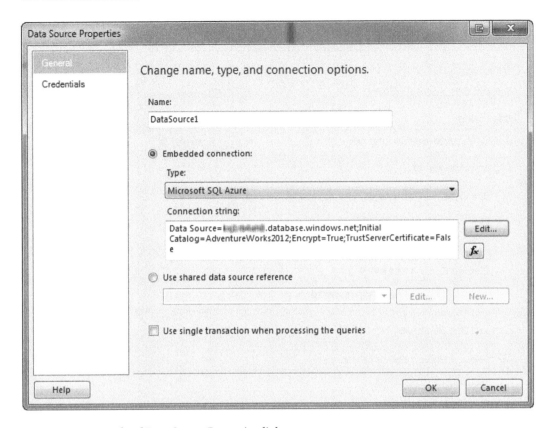

Figure 6-10. *Completed Data Source Properties dialog*

Granted, these steps are no different than those for connecting to a local database. But although the steps are the same, some of the key selection components are different, such as those in Figures 6-8 and 6-9, where you select the specific Microsoft SQL Azure provider and the SQL Database–specific connection information.

Your data source definition also allows you to specify the credentials with which to connect to your data source. Selecting Credentials at left in the Data Source Properties dialog shows you four options:

- Windows Authentication (integrated security)

- Prompt for credentials

- Use this user name and password

- Do not use credentials

Obviously, you need to use credentials, so not specifying credentials isn't the option you want. And integrated security isn't available with Azure, so that won't work either. You can either prompt for credentials or specify a username and password. The default value is to prompt for credentials; if you leave that setting, the report prompts you to enter a username and password every time you run the report.

6. Best practice says that in a production environment, you should use integrated security. But because that isn't an option with SQL Database, select the "Specify a user name and password" option, and enter the username and password of an account that has access to the appropriate database.

With your data source created, you now need to add a dataset for the report. For each data source, you can create one or more datasets. Each dataset specifies the fields from the data source that you would like to use in the report. The dataset also contains, among other things, the query used to get the data and any query parameters to filter the data.

7. In the Report Data window, right-click the Datasets node, and select Add Dataset from the context menu. Doing so opens the Dataset Properties window, shown in Figure 6-11.

8. The Query page of the Dataset Properties window allows you to do two primary things: specify the data source on which this dataset is based, and specify the query type and associated query. For this example, base your dataset on the data source you created earlier. The query type is Text, meaning that you type a T-SQL statement in the Query field. For this example, four tables will be joined to return contact information, such as name and address, so enter the SELECT statement shown in Figure 6-11. The Name of the dataset defaults to DataSet1, which is fine for this example. Click OK.

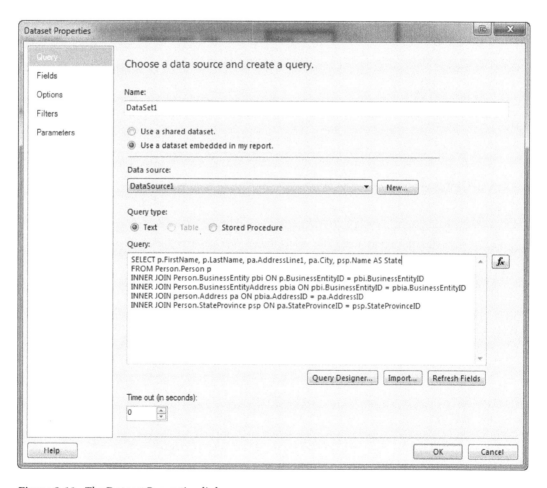

Figure 6-11. *The Dataset Properties dialog*

There is nothing else you need to do for your dataset; you're ready to define and lay out your report.

Creating the Report Design

With your report in Design view, you can now start laying it out. In this example you don't do anything flashy or extensive, just something simple to demonstrate your connectivity to SQL Database. Follow these steps:

1. From the Toolbox, drag a text box and table onto the Report Designer window. Move the text box to the top of the report: it's the report title. Change the text in the text box to My First SQL Azure Report.

2. The table you placed on the report has three columns, but you need five. Right-click any of the existing columns, and select Insert Column ➤ Right from the context menu to add an additional column. Add one more column for a total of five.

3. From the Report Data window, drag the First Name, Last Name, Address Line 1, City, and State columns from the dataset to the columns in the table, as shown in Figure 6-12.

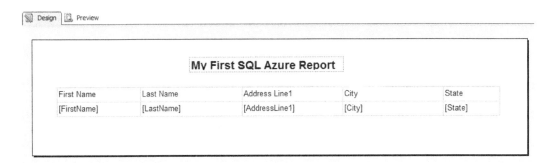

Figure 6-12. *Report Design view*

4. Your simple report is finished—it isn't complex or pretty, but it's functional. You're now ready to test the report: to do that, select the Preview tab. You'll see the result shown in Figure 6-13.

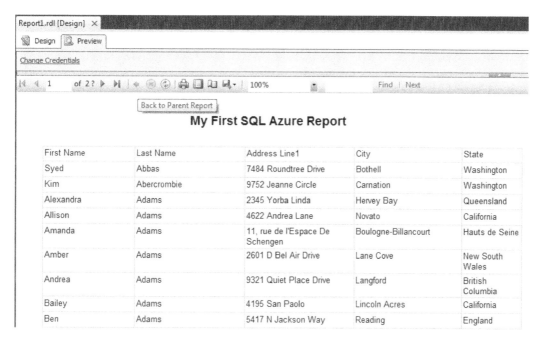

Figure 6-13. *Report Preview view*

Figure 6-13 shows the results of your labors, displaying the First Name, Last Name, Address Line 1, City, and State data from several tables in your SQL Database instance. If your report looks like this, congratulations are in order—you just created a report that queries a SQL Database. However, the power of this chapter now comes from deploying the report.

Deploying the Report

To deploy a report, follow these steps:

1. Back in the Windows Azure Management Portal, select the Reporting option in the Navigation pane, and then select the report server created earlier.

2. Highlight and copy the Web service URL from the Server Information section of the portal.

3. Back in SSDT, right-click the report solution, and select Properties from the context menu.

4. In the Property Pages dialog, the only thing you need to enter is the TargetServerURL, shown in Figure 6-14. Notice also the name of the TargetReportFolder, which in this case is AzureReport—the name of your Visual Studio solution.

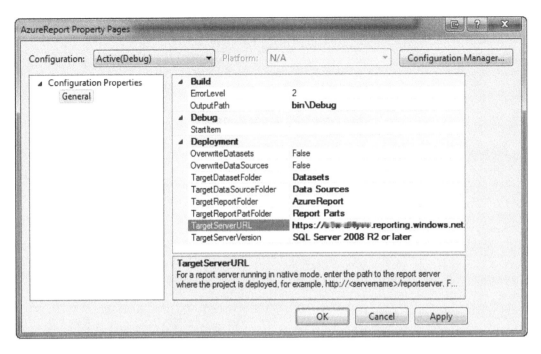

Figure 6-14. *The Solution Property page*

5. Click OK on the Properties page.

6. Right-click the solution in Solution Explorer, and select Deploy from the context menu.

    After several seconds you will be prompted for the Reporting Services Login. This is the administrator username and password you entered when provisioning your server.

7. Once the report has been deployed, go back to the Windows Azure Management Portal and click the Refresh button on the ribbon. Your report will then show in the Items List section of the portal, as seen in Figure 6-15.

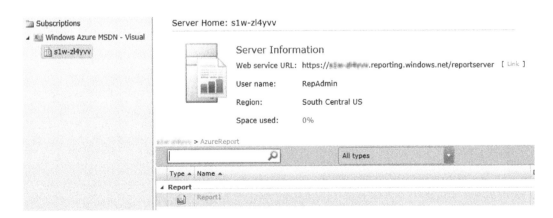

Figure 6-15. *The report shown in Management Portal*

8. Open your browser, and navigate to

   `https://[servername].reporting.windows.net/reportserver/AzureReport/Report1`

9. You should be presented with your SQL Reporting Service Home folder and the `AzureReport` folder listed. In the `AzureReport` folder is your newly created report. To view the report, click the report link.

You've just walked through a simple example of creating a report that pulls data from SQL Database. However, before we close this discussion of SQL Reporting, we also need to talk about security.

Security

This section contains some guidelines and best practices for managing the security of your SQL Reporting server and reports.

- When embedding reports into your application, secure your connection string to the report server.

- Because reports can only use SQL Database instance as a data source, the recommended way to provide access to shared data sources is to create and deploy shared data sources for reports to a folder on the report server. Store the credentials for each shared data source on the report server.

- By default, report items inherit security based on report folder permissions. Thus, the folder to which you deploy your report items matters greatly. By assigning specific permissions to a folder, you break the inheritance for permissions in the folder hierarchy.

SQL Reporting requires not only a username and password to access reports, but a URL as well. These three pieces of information are the URL, username, and password to the report server account. However, you can create users in the Management Portal and assign them to roles that grant permissions. You can then provide the report readers with those usernames and passwords.

When creating new users, you assign them to Item roles, and optionally, System roles.

Roles

As part of creating new users, you also assign them to an Item role and, optionally, a System role. The Item roles and System roles are similar to those available on a native mode report server:

- Item roles: Browser, Content Manager, My Reports, Publisher, and Report Builder.

- System roles: System Admin and System User.

Roles are a concept that helps organize in terms of functions or goals. Roles represent one or more people who perform one or more functions or tasks that require specific permissions. For SQL Reporting, the preceding roles help determine which users can perform specific functions such as viewing or editing reports, publishing reports, creating and managing additional users, and managing database objects.

For example, the Browser role can run reports, subscribe to reports, and navigate through the folder structure. The My Reports role can manage a personal workspace for storing and using reports and other items.

It should be noted that these roles are not specific to Windows Azure SQL Database, but to the underlying SQL Server Reporting service. More information about these roles can be found here:

`http://msdn.microsoft.com/library/ms157363.aspx(v=SQL.105)`

Take the following steps to create a user and assign it a role:

1. In the Management Portal for SQL Reporting, click the Manage button on the ribbon. This will display the Manage Users dialog shown in Figure 6-16.

Figure 6-16. *The Manage Users dialog*

2. To add a user, click the Create User button to open the Create User dialog, as seen in Figure 6-17.

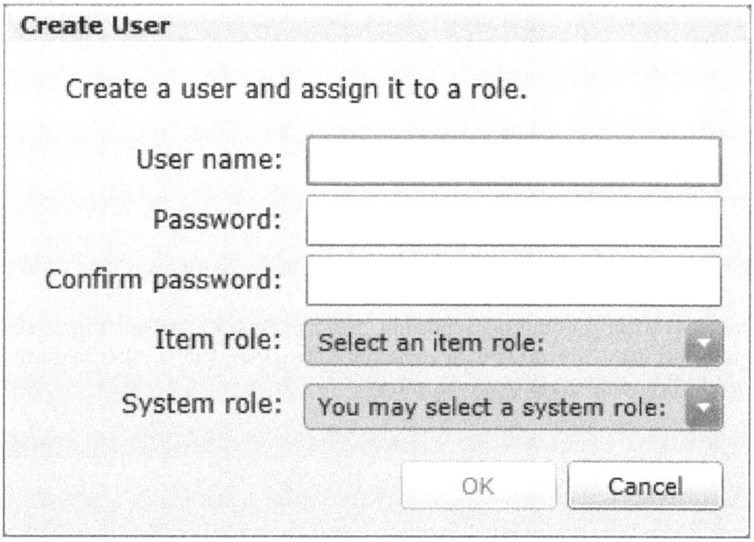

Create User

Create a user and assign it to a role.

User name: _____

Password: _____

Confirm password: _____

Item role: [Select an item role: ▼]

System role: [You may select a system role: ▼]

[OK]   [Cancel]

Figure 6-17. The Create User dialog

3. In the Create User dialog, enter a username and password. Select an Item role and an optional System role. Click OK.

4. Click OK on the Manager Users dialog.

Even though both My Reports and Report Builder are listed in the Item role drop-down list on the Create User dialog, they are not available nor supported in SQL Reporting. However, depending on role assignments, users can perform different tasks on the server. By granting users the Browser role, you give those users permission to read reports. You can assign users to multiple roles, and via the combination of roles and permission create users who have the appropriate permissions for our reporting environment.

Using the Management Portal

Except for provisioning the Report Server and managing users, the majority of this chapter has used tools such as SQL Server Data Tools to create and deploy reports. However, a lot of what you did in this chapter can also be done through the Management Portal, which provides additional functionality. Figure 6-18 shows the ribbon in the Management Portal when a SQL Reporting server is selected. Notice that you can create a shared data source, create and set permissions on a folder, upload a report, and look at server usage statistics. Server statistics provides the ability to look at the overall usage of SQL Reporting over a given time span. By default it will show you the usage over a single day, but you can also view usage data over a 2-day period, 1-week period, 1-month period, and 3-month period.

Figure 6-18. The Management Portal ribbon

Also from the ribbon, you have the ability to look at the report execution log. You are not limited to a time span with this option. You can simply select start and end dates for which you want to view. The execution report can be saved locally.

Pricing

Starting August 1, 2012, users of SQL Reporting are billed for using it. SQL Reporting use is charged for each clock hour of a reporting instance (reporting server), a minimum of one reporting instance for each clock hour that a SQL Reporting server is provisioned, even if no reports are deployed.

The price per reporting instance is $0.88 per hour per reporting instance. This charge covers up to 200 reports each clock hour. For each clock hour during which more than 200 reports are generated, another Reporting Instance Hour at $0.88 will be billed (for each additional block of 200 reports).

Summary

In this chapter you first learned what Windows Azure SQL Reporting is and the many benefits this cloud-based reporting solution provides. This chapter then discussed the architecture of SQL Reporting and how this architecture provides the high availability and scalability needed in a cloud-based reporting solution.

It's also important to understand the functional differences between on-premises SQL Server Reporting Services and SQL Reporting, so we spent some time discussing these differences and how they might impact report development.

Lastly, this chapter discussed provisioning a new SQL Reporting server, creating and deploying a report, and the security around hosting reports in SQL Reporting. Much of the functionality is shared between on-premises development tools and the Management Portal when developing reports, such as defining folders and data sources and applying permissions. This provides great flexibility in report development.

CHAPTER 7

■ ■ ■

SQL Data Sync

When I first wrote this chapter for the first edition of this book, SQL Data Sync was part of SQL Azure Labs and called SQL Azure Data Sync Services. Not too much later it was moved out of the SQL Azure Labs and has been in CTP (Community Technology Preview) and available in the Windows Azure Management Portal. Since that time, SQL Data Sync Services, or DSS, has been gaining tremendous momentum and acceptance and by the time you read this, will be out of CTP and in full general availability.

A bit of background is due. In November 2009, at the Microsoft Professional Developers Conference (PDC) in Los Angeles, Microsoft announced Project Huron, which allows database synchronization capabilities in the cloud. If you've been following the hype and keeping up with the blog posts regarding Huron, you know that Microsoft has been billing it and associated database sync functionality as "friction free," meaning easy to set up and maintain. Microsoft's goal with Huron was to eliminate many of the emblematic complexities and idiosyncrasies that are associated with data sharing between databases, such as scalability and configuration. Along with these goals, Microsoft also wanted to include user-friendly tools that let administrators easily configure and synchronize their data.

In June 2010, at the start of Tech-Ed in New Orleans, Microsoft announced the public preview availability of the Data Sync Service for SQL Azure, part of the Huron project. This is Microsoft's solution to allow users to easily and efficiently share data between databases without regard to database locations or connectivity. Sharing data is only the beginning: Microsoft also has visions of including data collaboration, providing users and developers the ability to use and work on data regardless of the data's location.

In May 2012, Microsoft formally implemented a new approach to the naming and branding of the services in Windows Azure, including SQL Azure Data Sync Services. As such, SQL Azure Data Sync Services is now called SQL Data Sync.

This chapter focuses entirely on the capabilities and features of SQL Data Sync. It begins with a brief overview and then shows you how to get started by setting up and configuring the Data Sync service. You will then work through several examples of using SQL Data Sync in different scenarios and situations. You also see some patterns and best practices along the way to help ensure a solid understanding of the Data Sync Service.

Understanding SQL Data Sync

SQL Data Sync provides bidirectional synchronization between two or more databases. On the surface, it's as simple as that; but even behind the scenes, it doesn't get much more complicated. With zero lines of code, you can quickly and easily configure your SQL Database to be synchronized with other SQL Database instances in any of the Microsoft Azure data centers or even with on-premises SQL Server.

Why the Need?

Why is the ability to sync data between SQL Database instances important? That's a fair question to ask. Let's explore a couple of answers.

First, you may be a fan of SQL Server replication, but it isn't the easiest feature to set up and configure. Granted, transactional replication gives you real-time updates, but setting up and maintaining transactional replication isn't a cake walk.

Second, although SQL Data Sync doesn't give you real-time updates, it does allow you to extend your data to the location closest to your users *without* a lot of headaches. The Data Sync service lets you move data changes between databases seamlessly. It ensures that the appropriate changes are proliferated to all the other databases in the current data center as well as other databases in other data centers.

SQL Data Sync is part of Windows Azure and runs in Windows Azure, so it can take advantage of the web and worker roles. A key component of SQL Data Sync is its use of the Microsoft Sync Framework, a synchronization platform provided in the .NET Framework. The great thing is that all this synchronization functionality is provided for you; there is no application you need to run or installation you need to perform when synchronizing SQL Database instances. However, if you need to sync to a database on-premises with SQL Database, a Client Sync Agent must be installed to allow each on-premises SQL Server database to be registered and then added to a sync group.

By providing the synchronization flexibility between multiple SQL Database instances and SQL Server, you can create custom and flexible sync groups that are tailored to your needs and business requirements.

The Basic Scenario

Every SQL Database synchronization environment includes a single database *hub* and has one or more database *members*, or *spokes*, as shown in Figure 7-1. The hub is the central database in a synchronization group. A spoke is a member database which synchronizes with the hub. Setting up synchronization includes creating and defining a synchronization group in which you specify the hub database and then assigning the database members to that hub.

Figure 7-1. *Data Sync scenarios*

Let's talk about the initial synchronization for a minute, because it's helpful to understand the process and changes that take place. When the initial sync takes place, it's a two-step process:

1. The hub database schema is copied to the member database(s).

2. The data is copied from the hub database to the member database(s).

This may seem simple, but let's discuss what happens during these two steps. First, you don't have to generate the target (member) database schemas yourself. During the first step, the Data Sync service does that for you (for the tables you specify to sync). As part of this process, foreign key constraints are *not* copied. This is because a full schema synchronization capability hasn't been built into the Data Sync service as of yet.

Because foreign keys aren't copied, you may be wondering what happens in the scenario where data is entered at the member that could potentially break synchronization back to the hub. The answer is that you can control the order in which data is applied, and this helps make certain the changes that are applied don't affect any foreign key constraints. During the initial sync, changes are made to both the hub and member databases to effectively track data changes. You'll see this behavior in the example later in this chapter.

The next step in the process is the data synchronization that takes place after all the member databases are provisioned. Provisioning of the members takes place during the initial sync. Data synchronization is as simple as copying the data from hub to member in the order specified in the configuration. Because there are no foreign keys on the member databases, there is no particular order in which the tables need to be synchronized. However, it's a good practice to add the tables in the order in which the changes will be applied when a data sync occurs. This helps you ensure that the changes are applied in a way that doesn't affect any foreign-key constraints.

Common Data Sync Scenarios

A common requirement in many businesses is the need to distribute data among different locations. These locations could be located geographically close or spread out globally in different parts of the world. Regardless of where offices are located, the need to share, consolidate, or migrate data between locations is a necessary commonplace.

As the move toward cloud computing becomes more mainstream, the ability to move, distribute, and synchronize that data becomes more critical. In cloud computing, data synchronization typically falls into one of four categories:

- Bursting data from on-premises data into the cloud

- Aggregating data from multiple locations into a single, central location

- Backing data up from the cloud to on-premises

- Data geo-distribution

The first two scenarios focus on situations where on-premises applications can leverage and utilize the cloud to easily expand their on-premises infrastructure and take advantage of the cloud environment. For example, a company may have the need of additional computational power but doesn't have the on-premises resources. By bursting the data into the cloud it can easily take advantage of the readily available cloud resources.

Data aggregation is a common scenario among many businesses, in which data from two or more satellite locations or partner businesses need to be pulled into a single, central location. In scenarios like this today you will typically see solutions involving BizTalk or SQL Server Integration Services.

The last two scenarios focus on cloud-based application requirements. Common situations include the need to provide a "backup" of cloud data to an on-premises location. Yet more commonly seen is the need to distribute data geographically, moving data closer to the users who need access to it.

Regardless of the scenario, however, Windows Azure SQL Data Sync provides the data synchronization and data migration solutions needed by businesses. The ease and speed of configuration, scalability and availability of the service, and powerful features make SQL Data Sync a viable solution for all four of these common scenarios.

Architecture

It will be helpful to look at the architecture of SQL Data Sync to get a feel for how reporting works in SQL Database. Figure 7-2 shows the basic architecture of SQL Data Sync.

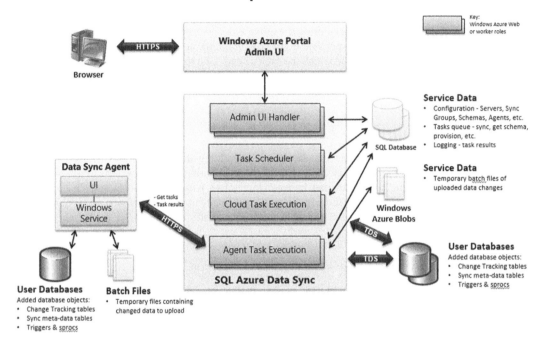

Figure 7-2. *SQL Data Sync service architecture*

SQL Data Sync comprises four main components:

- SQL Data Sync service

- Windows Azure SQL Database

- Windows Azure Storage

- Data Sync Agent

The Windows Azure Administration portal is the user interface to the SQL Data Sync service. This service is responsible for executing the synchronization, communication with the Windows Azure SQL Database and Windows Azure Blob storage, and handling receiving incoming requests from the Data Sync agent and the Windows Azure Administration portal.

Windows Azure Blob storage is used for the temporary storage of batch files containing the uploaded data changes.

The key in the architecture is the SQL Data Sync service itself. It is the heart of the synchronization process. The SQL Data Sync service communicates with all the other components in the architecture and manages the flow of data execution of all tasks.

The basic idea and concept behind this architecture is the following:

- Data Sync is built on the Windows Azure public platform.

- You can configure a sync group and perform a sync quickly and easily on the Windows Azure Platform.

As with SQL Reporting, SQL Data Sync management is not yet available in the new Preview portal, so this chapter will illustrate using SQL Data Sync in the existing Silverlight portal.

Configuring Synchronization

Now that you're familiar with the foundation of how the Data Sync service works, let's dive in and configure a new sync for SQL Data Sync, in order to sync two databases. This example synchronizes the same AdventureWorks database for Windows Azure SQL Database used in Chapter 6. You can find this database and instructions for installing it here:

`http://msftdbprodsamples.codeplex.com/releases/view/3704`

This database will be the hub database. Additionally, this example will utilize two member databases; one located on-premises and another SQL Database. My second SQL Database will be located in a second region to illustrate regional synchronization, but if you are walking through this example feel free to put the second SQL Database in the same region.

Provision a SQL Data Sync Server

Log in to the portal with your LiveID at `https://windows.azure.com`. The first task is to provision a Data Sync server. The Navigation pane is broken into two sections. The lower section contains the components and services available in the Management Portal. The top section shows either a list of available subscriptions linked to your LiveID, or helpful links to get started as shown in Figure 7-3.

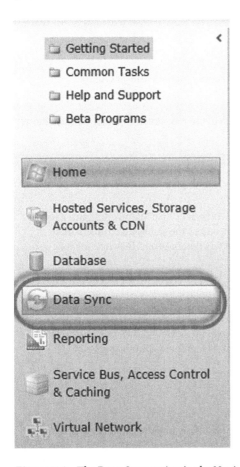

Figure 7-3. The Data Sync option in the Navigation pane

Follow these steps to provision the Data Sync server:

1. Select the Data Sync option in the Navigation pane, and then select the subscription in which you would like to provision and configure SQL Data Sync. The menu bar along the top and the list item section in the center of the portal will change based on the options selected. When you select the subscription, the only option on the menu bar and in the list item section is to provision a new Data Sync server.

2. To provision a new Data Sync server, simply click either the button on the menu bar or the link in the list item section. Either option will display the Provision dialog. First you'll see the Terms of Use. Click the "I agree to the Terms of Use statement above" check box and click Next.

3. The next step of the Provision dialog asks you to select the Subscription in which you want to provision the Data Sync server. Yes, you selected the subscription in the Navigation pane but in case you change your mind and want to select a different subscription, you can do it here instead of starting over. Select the subscription and click Next.

4. Lastly, select the region in which you want to provision the server. Typically you'll want to provision this server wherever your hub database is to limit the amount of data traffic. Select the region and click Finish.

The provisioning process takes only a few seconds. However, you'll notice that you don't get a server name per se, but a logical server in which you can configure your data synchronization. For example, if you provision your server in North Central US, your Data Sync server is listed as "North Central US."

Creating a Sync Group

The next step is to create and configure a *sync group*. A sync group is a collection of SQL Database instances and SQL Server databases that are configured for mutual synchronization. A sync group contains a single *hub* database and one or more *member* databases. The hub database must be a SQL Database instance.

In the top section of the navigation pane, expand the node that lists your new Data Sync server. Underneath that node you will see two subnodes, labeled Sync Groups and Member Databases. Select the Sync Groups node, and as shown in Figure 7-4 there are several options for creating a sync group.

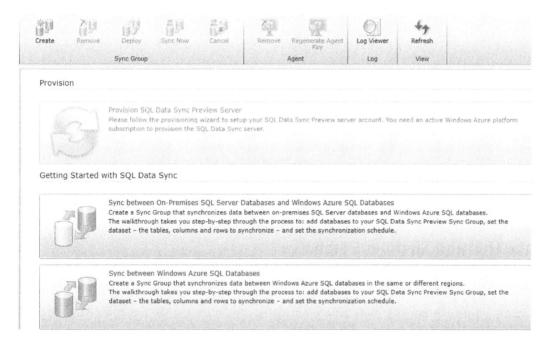

Figure 7-4. *Creating a sync group*

If you are new to SQL Data Sync, the two options under Getting Started with SQL Data Sync provide a step-by-step walkthrough of creating different sync groups types. The first option creates an on-premises–to–SQL Database sync group. The second option creates a sync group between multiple SQL Database instances.

Notice, however, that there is a third option. In the Sync Group section of the ribbon is an enabled button called Create. The example in this chapter will use that button. Go ahead and click that button. Instead of providing a step-by-step walkthrough, you are presented with the entire template to configure, as shown in Figure 7-5.

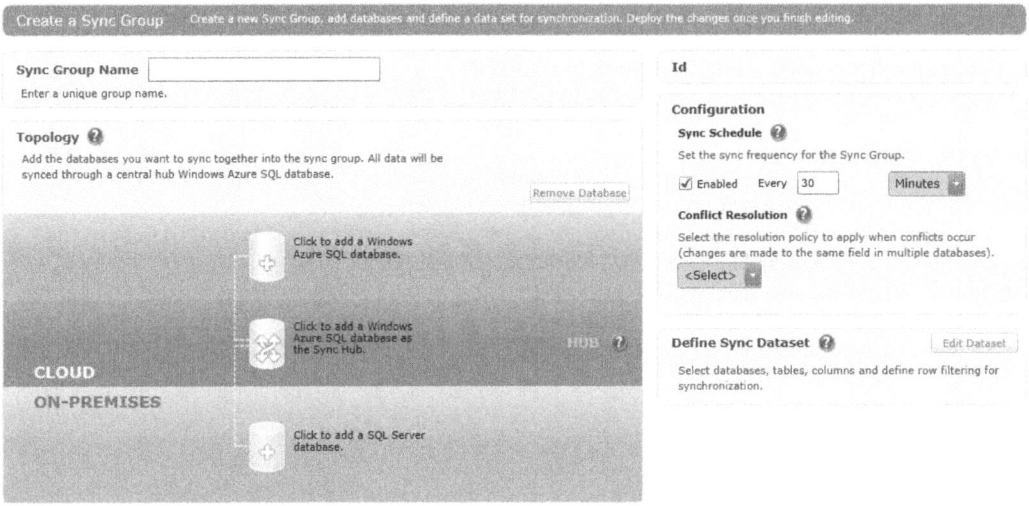

Figure 7-5. *Creating a Sync Group*

This "template" is quite easy to navigate through. The blue section is where you add "cloud" or SQL Database instances and the yellow section is where you add on-premises SQL Server databases. The section on the right is for Sync Group configuration such as defining the sync schedule, the data you want to synchronize, and the conflict resolution policy. Again, keep in mind that all of this is accomplished without writing a single line of code.

Whether you use one of the walkthrough options or simply decide to work from a blank template to create your sync group, either way you need to name the sync group. It doesn't matter what you call it, but make it meaningful. Later on we'll discuss best practices and believe it or not, what you name your sync group is important.

Defining the Hub and Member Databases

The first step is to define the hub database. To do so, simply click the center icon labeled "Click to add a Windows Azure SQL Database as the Sync Hub." Yeah, pretty obvious. Clicking that icon brings up the Add Database to Sync Group dialog shown in Figure 7-6.

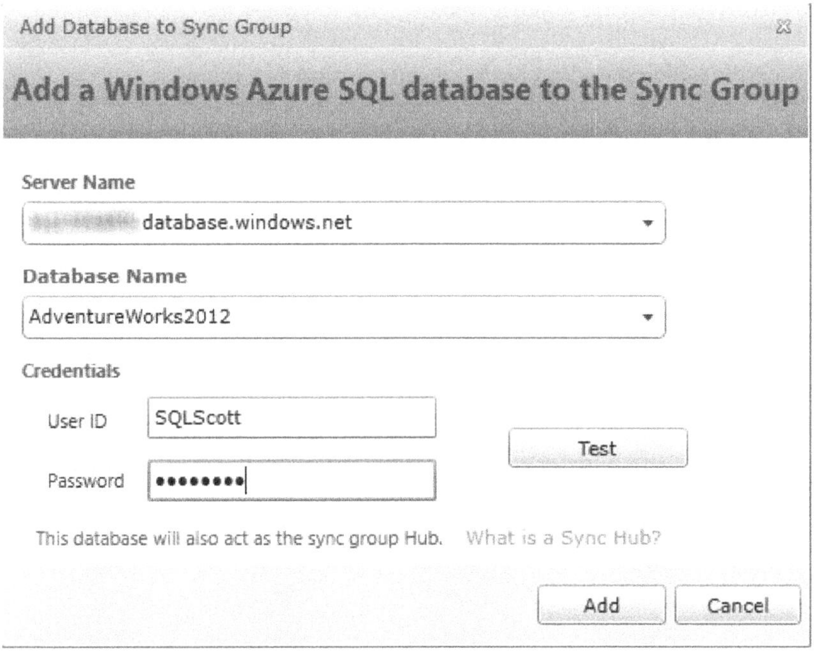

Figure 7-6. *Adding the hub*

In the Add Database to Sync Group dialog, enter the server name, database name, and credentials for the hub database, and then click Add. For this example, you should use the AdventureWorks2012 database.

Notice now that the icon in the sync group now displays the database name and server name. It also contains two vital pieces of information. First, it says "Not Deployed." This means that even though we have marked this database as the hub, we actually haven't provisioned the database for synchronization.

Second, the icon shows a small, green circle, indicating that the Data Sync service can successfully connect to and communicate with the SQL Database instance.

■ **Note**　The icon will display a red X if it cannot communicate with the SQL Database instance. If this is the case, you should either look at the Firewall rules to ensure that a rule has been added for your IP Address, or check the credentials to ensure they were entered correctly.

The next step is to provision the member databases. We'll first provision the SQL Database member by clicking the icon labeled "Click to add a Windows Azure SQL Database." Again, pretty obvious. This brings up a dialog similar to the one for the hub. Enter the server name, database name, and credentials for the member database.

This dialog, however, contains an additional configuration for setting the Sync Direction. Sync Direction simply specifies which direction the data is being synchronized. There are three options:

- **Bi-Directional:** Data is synchronized in both directions between hub and member.

- **Sync to the Hub:** Data is synchronized from the member to the hub only.

- **Sync from the Hub:** Data is synchronized to the member from the hub only.

The default is Bi-Directional, and that is the option this example will use. Click Test to test the connection and make sure all the information entered is correct; then click Add. Notice that the member icon now looks similar to the Hub icon, indicating that it also is awaiting provisioning.

The next step is to provision the on-premises member. This requires a few more steps but is still fairly easy. Click the icon in the yellow section of the Sync Group template labeled "Click to add a SQL Server database." This brings up the same dialog as before but with a few different options.

Previously it was stated that in order to synchronize with an on-premises SQL Server database it is necessary to install a client agent on a computer in the local environment (see the "Data Sync Best Practices" section for more information). This agent is a Windows server that sits between the SQL Server database and the SQL Database hub, enabling bidirectional HTTPS-based communication.

Figure 7-7 shows this dialog. This time, however, the interface is a multi-step wizard that walks you through the installation and registration of the client agent.

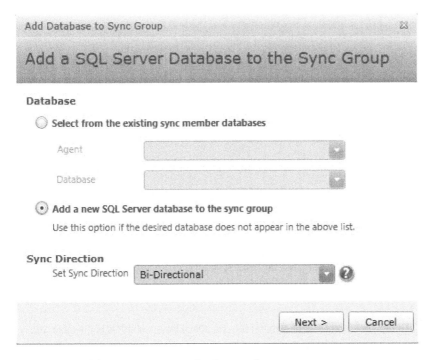

Figure 7-7. *Adding an on-premises database to the sync group*

If you are installing the client agent for the first time and registering a new on-premises database, the option to select on the Add Database dialog is "Add a new SQL Server database to the sync group." Had the client agent been installed and a SQL Server database been registered previously, the first option could have been selected. Select the option for adding a new database, set the Sync direction to Bi-Directional, and click Next.

In the next step of the dialog you decide whether to install a new agent or use an existing agent. This step is straightforward. As stated previously, had the client agent already been installed, the on-premises database could be registered via that agent. However, in this example the agent has not been installed previously, so the option to select here is to install a new agent. Select that option and click Next.

This next step of the Add Database to Sync Group dialog is where you begin installing and configuring the agent and on-premises database, which is itself a multi-step process. The Install a New Agent dialog lists the steps needed in order to install and configure the client agent (see Figure 7-8).

Figure 7-8. *Installing the client agent*

First, click the Download button. This will take you to a web site where you can download the client sync agent. Download the file called SQLDataSyncAgent-Preview-ENU.msi and run the install. The installation of the client agent consists of three easy steps:

1. Agree to the license agreement.

2. Enter the account you want to run the service under.

3. Select the installation folder.

As explained earlier, the account used in configuring the client agent must have network access to reach the Data Sync service through your network's proxy. Enter the appropriate information, accept the default installation folder, and click Install.

Once it is installed you will find a new Windows service listed, called Microsoft SQL Data Sync. If it installed successfully, the service status will be Running.

There are still a few more things to do in the client agent, but first we need to go back to the Management Portal. In the Install a New Agent dialog, enter an Agent Name in Step 2. While the name of this agent is not as critical as the Sync Group name, giving it a meaningful name will still be helpful.

Once the Agent Name has been entered, click the Generate Agent Key button. A key will be generated and displayed in the dialog (along with a Copy button). Click the Copy button to copy the key to the Clipboard.

Don't click Next yet. The next thing to do is launch the SQL Data Sync Agent, which can be found in the Start menu. Once it is launched, the first thing to do is to enter the configuration key that was just copied to the Clipboard. Click the Submit Agent Key button and enter the key in the Agent Key dialog. Click OK.

Once the key is registered, the next step is to click the Ping Sync Service button to make sure that the client agent can communicate with the Data Sync Service. If the client agent can successfully ping the Data Sync service, a dialog will be displayed informing you so.

Next, click the Register button to register an on-premises SQL Server. A SQL Server can be registered using Windows or SQL authentication. This example is using Windows Authentication. Enter the server name and database name; then click the Test Connection button to ensure that the client agent can connect to the selected database. Click OK on the connection test dialog, and then click Save on the SQL Server registration dialog shown in Figure 7-9.

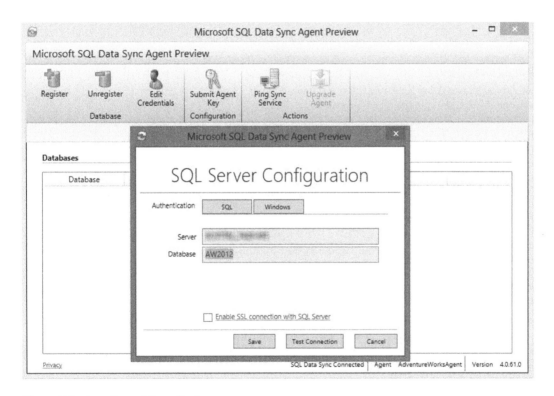

Figure 7-9. *A configured Sync client*

Finally, go back to the Management Portal and click Next on the Install a New Agent dialog. The dialog now displays a Prerequisite check with information for the next steps. Click the Get Database List button in the Step 2 section. This will communicate with the Data Sync agent and return a list of registered databases that populate the Step 3 drop-down list, as shown in Figure 7-10.

Figure 7-10. *Select your on-premises SQL Server database*

In Step 3, select the database from the dropdown list of databases and click Finish. Your Sync Group template should now look like Figure 7-11.

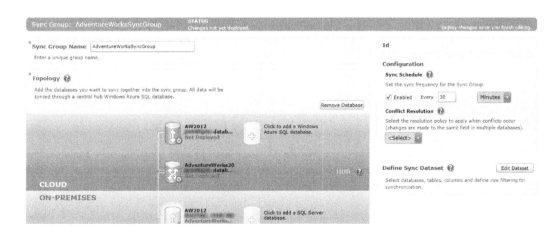

Figure 7-11. *The configured sync group*

With the database registered, but not provisioned, the next step is to configure the sync group to define the data to be synchronized and the Conflict Resolution policy.

Selecting Tables to be Synchronized

Significant enhancements have been made to SQL Data Sync since the last edition of this book, including how the sync dataset is defined. In the Configuration section of the Sync Group window, click the Edit Dataset button, which will display the Define Dataset dialog. This dialog is quite powerful, in that you can select not only the tables to be synchronized, but also the columns of each table. Additionally, row filtering can be applied to the dataset to synchronize specific data. In this example each of these features will be illustrated.

As you scroll through the list of tables you will notice that some are red. You should also notice a nice red warning at the top of the dialog stating the some of the tables do not meet schema requirements.

Tables that appear in red cannot be selected for synchronization. This example will select two tables that are OK for synchronization; HumanResources.Employee and Person.BusinessEntity. As you select the HumanResources.Employee table, you'll notice that even though the table itself is not red (OK for synchronization), some of the columns are red. That means that those columns cannot be selected and are not available for synchronization. You can see this in Figure 7-12.

Figure 7-12. Selected tables and columns to be synchronized, and two columns that cannot be selected

Applying a Filter

The table and columns have been selected. At this point the dataset could be complete, but for this example a filter will be applied. Applying a filter is quite easy. As shown in Figure 7-13, click the Filter checkbox next to the column you want to filter on and apply the row filtering criteria in the Row Filtering section. In this example the BusinessEntityID column of the Person.BusinessEntity table has been selected. Enter a value of 10000 in the filter Value field to filter all Persons with an `BusinessentityID` greater than 10,000.

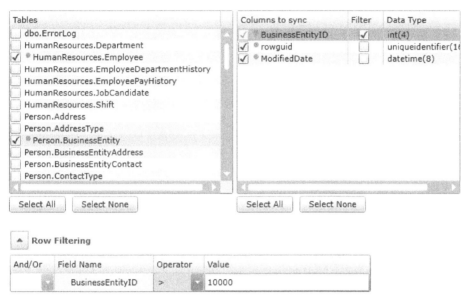

Filter Clause: Person.BusinessEntity.[BusinessEntityID] > 10000

Figure 7-13. *Row filtering*

Querying the Person.BusinessEntity table in the hub database will reveal IDs 1 to 20777, which were added during the creation of the database. Because of the filter applied to this sync group, only rows with BusinessEntityID greater than 10,000 will be synchronized to the member databases.

Applying Conflict Resolution

Configuring the sync group is almost complete. The next step is to set the Conflict Resolution. A data conflict occurs whenever the same data in two or more databases within a sync group is changed between synchronizations. In the current release of SQL Data Sync you can select between two resolution policies: Hub Wins and Client Wins.

- **Hub Wins:** The first row change written to the hub is kept. Subsequent attempts to write to the same row in the hub are ignored. The first write to the hub is propagated out to all member databases.

- **Client Wins:** Each row change in a member database is written to the hub, overwriting prior changes to the same row. The last write to the hub is then propagated out to all member databases.

No matter which policy you adopt, one of the changed rows is kept and the others are lost whenever a conflict arises.

157

Setting the Sync Schedule

Data synchronization can be scheduled from a minimum of 5 minutes to a maximum of 1 month. The default is 30 minutes, but this example won't wait for the scheduler to pick it up. For the purposes of this example, we'll do the synchronization manually. Thus, disable the automatic synchronization by unchecking the Enabled check box.

The complete configuration of the sync group should look like Figure 7-14.

Figure 7-14. *The complete sync group configuration*

The configuration is done; it is now time to deploy and provision.

Deploying the Sync Group

Provisioning the databases and deploying the sync group is as easy as clicking the Deploy button on the ribbon. Figure 7-15 shows that each database will be set to a status of Provisioning during the deployment process. Once each database is ready to go, its status will be set to Ready.

AW2012
.datab...
Provisioning...
AdventureWorks20
.data...
Provisioning...
AW2012
AdventureWorks...
Provisioning...

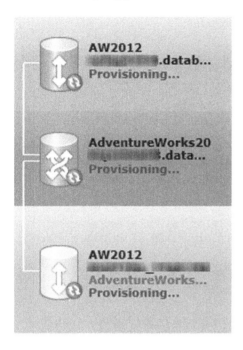

Figure 7-15. *Database provisioning*

The on-premises database will more than likely finish provisioning before the other two, and then would be a good time to look at what changes were applied during the provisioning process. Figure 7-16 shows the changes made to the on-premises database.

AW2012
Database Diagrams
Tables
System Tables
FileTables
DataSync.BusinessEntity_dss_tracking
DataSync.Employee_dss_tracking
DataSync.provision_marker_dss
DataSync.schema_info_dss
DataSync.scope_config_dss
DataSync.scope_info_dss
HumanResources.Employee
Person.BusinessEntity

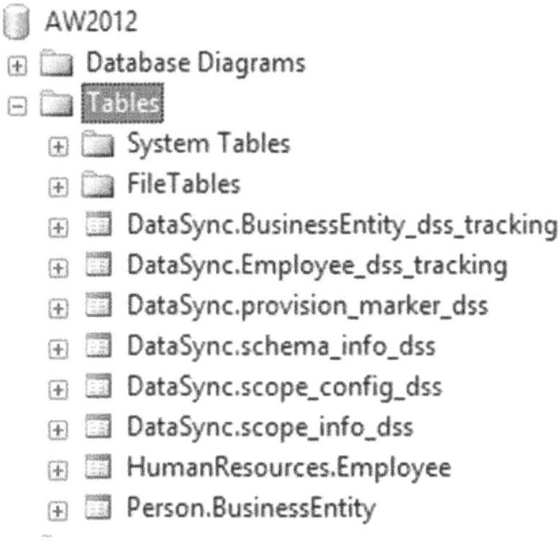

Figure 7-16. *Selected tables in the on-premises database*

Along with the data tables (HumanResources.Employee and Person.BusinessEntity), SQL Data Sync created six new tables, system synchronization tables, in both databases:

- **schema_info:** Tracks member schema information.

- **scope_config / scope_info:** Used by the Sync Framework to determine what tables, filters, and so on are being synchronized. Each database that is participating in a sync includes these tables and includes at least one scope (if they're being synchronized).

- **<table>_dss_tracking:** Tracks changes to the related user table.

- **provision_marker:** A metadata table used internally as part of the change-tracking mechanism.

Each relationship has its own scope—thus the need for the scope tables. For example, the hub-to-Member1 relationship has a scope, and the hub-to-Member2 relationship has its own, different scope. Just like sync groups, these scopes define the data to be shared among members; multiple scopes make up a sync group. Scopes aren't exposed, in order to simplify management of the Data Sync Service.

In this example, four tables were created, but keep in mind that a tracking table is created for each table included in the sync. For example, had you included the Docs and UserDocs tables in the sync, you would also see Docs_tracking and UserDocs_tracking tables. Each tracking table is responsible for storing the changes for its respective table.

Also added, but not shown in Figure 7-16, are *triggers*. A trigger is added to each base table that updates the tracking table when a change occurs. Some stored procedures are also added to each database; the Data Sync Service uses them to get and apply changes efficiently.

Debugging and the Log Viewer

By now you will have realized that both members of the sync group provisioned correctly, but the hub did not. The icon for the hub database turned red, with an error message stating that the provision failed. Why?

There is a wonderful way to find out what happened, and that is through the Log Viewer. On the toolbar, click the Log Viewer button. Figure 7-17 shows a list of different types of information display, including Errors. To view the detail of the error, click the [copy] link at the end of the Message column, which will copy the contents of the error message to the Clipboard.

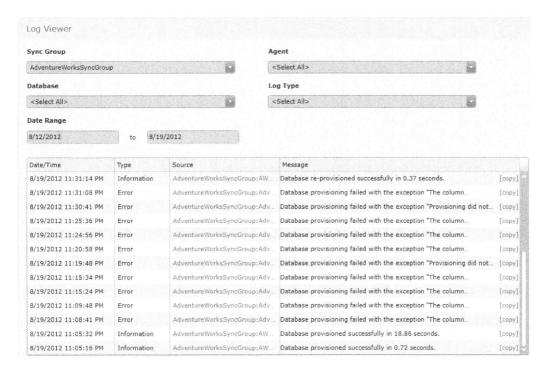

Figure 7-17. *Selected tables*

Open Notepad and copy the contents of the Clipboard, which will reveal that even though the OrganizationLevel column of the HumanResources.Employee table was not red when defining our dataset, SQL Data Sync cannot sync that column because "it is either a computed column or is the result of a UNION operator." Well, indeed that column is a computed column.

Luckily, this is easy enough to fix. Go back into the Sync Group window, and click the Edit Dataset button. Select the HumanResources.Employee table and uncheck the OrganizationLevel column. Click the Deploy button on the toolbar to re-provision all the databases. This time the deployment will succeed and launch the initial synchronization.

Looking at the Synchronized Data

To validate that the synchronization was successful, jump over to SQL Server Management Studio and open a query window to the on-premises member database AW2012. Type in the following query:

```
SELECT * FROM Person.BusinessEntity
```

Figure 7-18 shows that indeed all rows greater than 10,000 were synchronized to the member databases.

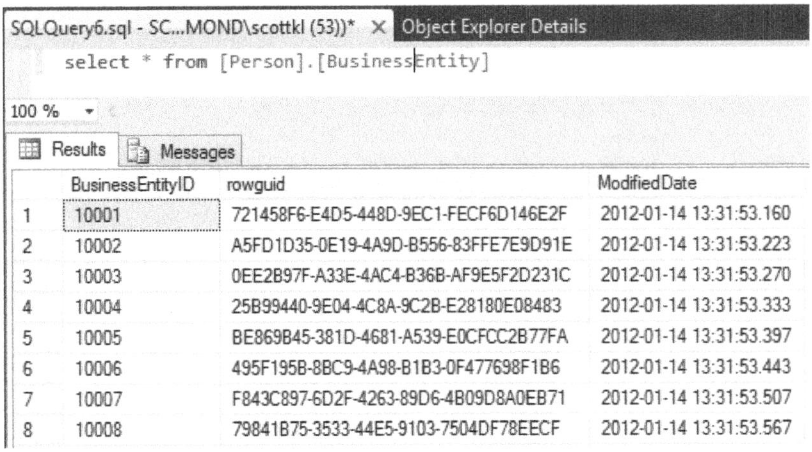

Figure 7-18. *Data validation*

Editing Data and Resynchronizing

Now let's edit some data and resynchronize, and then validate that the changes were made by requerying the data. Go back to SQL Server Management Studio and open a query window to the on-premises member database AW2012. Type in the following query:

```
UPDATE HumanResources.Employee SET Job Title = 'Head Geek' WHERE BusinessEntityID = 1
```

Open up another query window connected to the SQL Database member instance and execute the following query:

```
UPDATE HumanResources.Employee SET Job Title = 'VP of Techy Stuff' WHERE BusinessEntityID = 2
```

Instead of waiting for the scheduled sync to pick up, click the Sync Now button on the toolbar. The synchronization should only take a few seconds, at which point you should be able to query the HumanResources. Employee table in the hub database and validate that the changes made to the member databases where indeed synchronized to the hub database.

Testing Conflict Resolution

In this example the Conflict Resolution was set to Hub Wins. For a quick test, change the Conflict resolution to Client Wins and deploy the changes. Once the deployment is done, go back to SQL Server Management Studio and execute the following query against the on-premises database:

```
UPDATE HumanResources.Employee SET Job Title = 'Chief Executive Officer' WHERE BusinessEntityID = 1
```

Wait 1 minute and then execute the following query against the SQL Database member instance:

```
UPDATE HumanResources.Employee SET Job Title = 'Chief Head Officer' WHERE BusinessEntityID = 1
```

Manually resynchronize; this should only take several seconds. Once the sync is done, query the HumanResources.Employee table in both the hub database and the on-premises member database. The value of the Title column for BusinessEntityID 1 should now be "Chief Head Officer" in all three locations.

Following the Client Wins rule, the last write to the hub overwrote the previous change ("Chief Executive Officer") then propagated out "Chief Head Officer" to all member databases.

Data Sync Limitations

While SQL Data Sync is quite functional and very flexible, there are some limitations in the pre-release version. The following is a list of the current limitations for SQL Data Sync.

- Maximum number of SQL Data Sync Servers per subscription: 1

- Maximum number of sync groups any database can belong to: 5

- Filters per table: Up to 12 (optionally 13 if one is on the primary key column)

- Database, table, schema, and column names: 50 characters per name

- Tables in a sync group: 100

- Columns in a table in a sync group: 1000

If you query the HumanResources.Employee table, you'll notice that it contains BusinessEntityID 1 to 290, well below the filter of 10,000. Even though there is a PK/FK constraint on the hub database, why were records less than 10,000 synchronized in the HumanResources.Employee table?

The answer is that currently filtering is on individual tables. In this example the filter would need to be applied to both tables. In all reality, the filter would be for records less than 10,000 and applied to both tables.

Additionally, in some cases this *might* mean denormalizing the schema of your database so that the value on which you want to filter is available in each table.

Existing triggers on source tables, CHECK constraints, and indexes on XML-type columns are not provisioned. Indexes are created only for the columns selected to be synchronized.

Data Sync Best Practices

A lot has been learned since the last release of this book, so this section will focus on best practices learned over the last couple of years. We will discuss topics that will help in the design and planning phase for SQL Data Sync. The key is to keep in mind that SQL Data Sync is a global solution, allowing you to move data around the world.

Design Considerations

- **Avoid synchronization loops:** A synchronization loop results when there are circular references within a sync group so that each change in one database is replicated through the databases in the sync group circularly and endlessly. Sync loops degrade performance and significantly increase costs. Synchronization loops can be avoided by not including circular references within a database or table, or between two sync groups.

- **On-premises-to-cloud scenario:** Keep your hub database close to the greatest concentration of the sync group's database traffic to minimize latency.

- **Cloud-to-cloud scenario:** When all the databases in a sync group are in the same data center, the hub database should also be located in the same data center. When databases in a sync group are in different data centers, the hub database should be located in the data center where the majority of the traffic takes place.

Initial Synchronization

- SQL Data Sync treats prepopulated rows as data conflicts. Whenever possible, start with an empty destination database.

- To increase performance, use the auto-provisioning capability only for testing. For production, pre-provision the destination databases with the schema.

- Views and Stored Procedures are not created on the destination database. You can use the Generate Scripts wizard in SQL Server Management Studio or SQL Server Data Tools to deploy these objects.

Security

- Install the client agent using the least privileged account with network service access.

- Install the client agent on a computer separate from the on-premises SQL Server.

- Databases should not be registered with more than one client agent to avoid any challenges with deleting sync groups.

Sync Schedule

No bullet points here but a few words of caution. It is good practice to schedule synchronizations such that each synchronization has time to complete. If one synchronization tries to execute before the prior one completes, the second sync attempt won't even start. There is no indication via the logs or management portal that the sync did not take place.

For example, if the sync schedule is set for every five minutes but it takes the group six minutes to complete then your synchronizations will only happen every 10 minutes, not every 5.

Currently, SQL Data Sync is offered without a charge. Yet, there are data transfer charges for data that leaves any data center. Inbound data transfer (ingress) is free, but there are charges for outbound data (egress). Thus, be cognizant of how frequently data needs to be refreshed per table.

Summary

Although SQL Data Sync is yet to be officially released, this chapter has provided a detailed walkthrough of the functionality you can expect to see when it's released.

The chapter began with an overview of SQL Data Sync, including why it is needed and a basic scenario of SQL Data Sync. From there, the majority of the chapter focused on building a SQL Data Sync example, illustrating how to create, configure, and manage a sync group.

Lastly, a few pages were spent on SQL Data Sync security and design best practices, considerations, and limitations.

Windows Azure and ASP.NET

This chapter walks you through the steps of creating a Windows Azure application and deploying it in the cloud. By now, you know you can't create WinForms applications in Windows Azure. However, you can create an ASP.NET application that runs locally in IIS and connects to SQL Database, or build an ASP.NET application that runs as a cloud project which can then run entirely in the cloud. This chapter will show you how to build a small web application in ASP.NET that can be deployed in the cloud, and implements the Direct Connection pattern discussed in Chapter 2.

An application published in the Microsoft cloud is referred to as a *cloud service*, even if it's a web site. So, you first need to create a new Windows Azure cloud service to host the web site.

Creating a Cloud Service

First, you need to set up a Windows Azure cloud service so you can deploy a Windows Azure application later. Each Windows Azure service created in the cloud is mapped to a virtual machine. In most cases you do not need to have control over the Virtual Machine (VM) itself; you can simply deploy your applications and configure certain parameters. However, you can also perform advanced tasks such as running startup scripts and establishing a remote connection to the VM. To create your Windows Azure cloud service, follow these steps:

1. Open Internet Explorer, and go to http://manage.windowsazure.com. You're prompted to sign in with your Windows Live account.

2. When you've logged in, select Cloud Services. You will see the list of cloud services you've created so far (if you have been granted administrative access to someone else's Azure account, you will see their cloud services, too), as shown in Figure 8-1.

Figure 8-1. *Windows Azure cloud services*

■ **Note** This chapter assumes you've signed up for the Windows Azure service. Signing up for the service automatically creates a Windows Azure project in the cloud.

---

3. Click New and then select Quick Create to create your first Windows Azure service. Doing so changes the panel in which you provide information about the cloud service you want to create.

4. As shown in Figure 8-2, the panel allows you to select a unique service name to use for your URL. This URL is available on the public Internet and as such must be globally unique; if it is not unique, you will see an error message like the one shown in Figure 8-3. You also need to select a region or a Service Affinity group. Figure 8-2 shows that you're creating a new service, which will be made available through http://AzureExample.cloudapp.net and hosted in South Central US.

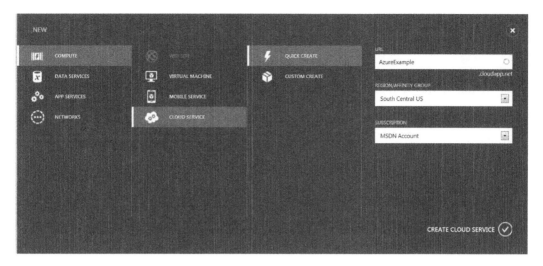

Figure 8-2. *Creating a new Azure Cloud Service*

Figure 8-3. *URL already in use*

When creating a new cloud service, you should consider using an affinity group. To keep things simpler, we are not doing that in this example but creating an affinity group is very important for two reasons:

- **Price**. When a Windows Azure service connects to a SQL Database instance located in the same region, there are no additional charges when transferring data between the service and the database.

- **Failover**. If something happens and either the Windows Azure service or the SQL Database instance must fail over to another region, all the services in the same affinity group are moved together if possible, keeping the performance and cost structure of the service consistent.

5. Click on Create Cloud Service. When the service is created, you'll see a page similar to the one shown in Figure 8-4.

Figure 8-4. *A new Windows Azure service created*

■ **Note**   As long as no code is deployed on this service, you aren't charged. However, as soon as you deploy something, the clock starts ticking from a billing standpoint.

Creating a Windows Azure Project

Let's create a simple Windows Azure application in Visual Studio that displays a list of database users. The Windows Azure project is an ASP.NET application created with a special project template: Cloud. Other project types are available when creating cloud projects and are discussed later in this section. Although you can create the same project as a regular ASP. NET application first and convert it to a cloud project later, it is easier to start with a cloud project right away to avoid additional conversion steps.

Configuring Your Development Environment

You must first install the Windows Azure Tools on your development environment to be able to develop a Windows Azure ASP.NET application. You must be running Windows Server 2008 or later, or Windows Vista or later. The Windows Azure Tools provide a runtime environment on your machine that allows you to develop and test a Windows Azure project. It basically runs a local cloud for development purposes. After it's installed, you see a new project type: Cloud. When creating your project in Visual Studio, you can select the Cloud project type; an option to install the Windows Azure Tools is available the first time you do so.

■ **Note**   If you need to download the Windows Azure Tools, go to the Microsoft Download Center at www.microsoft.com/downloads/. Search for Azure Tools, and pick the version that applies best to your Visual Studio version. Make sure to download and install this extension, and then restart Visual Studio if necessary.

Creating Your First Visual Studio Cloud Project

To create a Visual Studio cloud project, follow these steps:

1. Start Visual Studio in elevated mode (as an Administrator). To do so, right-click Microsoft Visual Studio (2008 or higher), and select "Run as administrator," as shown in Figure 8-5. Running as Administrator is required by the Windows Azure simulation tools that give you the ability to test your Azure solution locally.

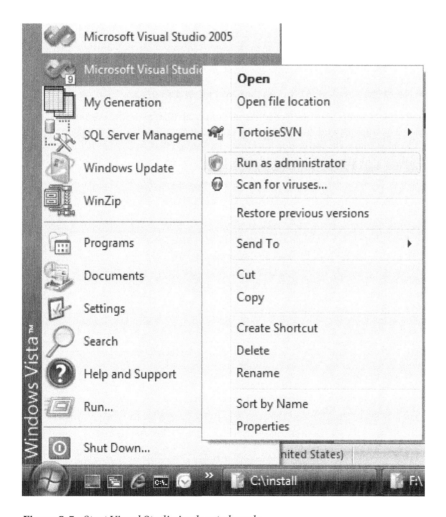

Figure 8-5. *Start Visual Studio in elevated mode*

If you don't start Visual Studio in elevated mode, you're able to create the project but you can't run it. If you try, you get an error message telling you to restart Visual Studio, as shown in Figure 8-6.

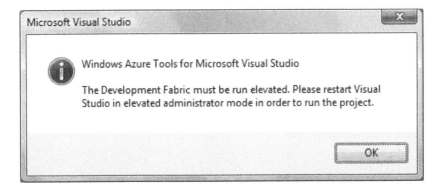

Figure 8-6. *Error trying to run an Azure project when not in elevated mode*

2.   Choose File ➤ New ➤ New Project to bring up the New Project dialog box.

3.   Select the Cloud project type (Cloud Service in Visual Studio 2010), choose the Windows Azure Cloud Service template, and name your project (AzureExample here), as shown in Figure 8-7 for Visual Studio 2008 and Figure 8-8 for Visual Studio 2010.

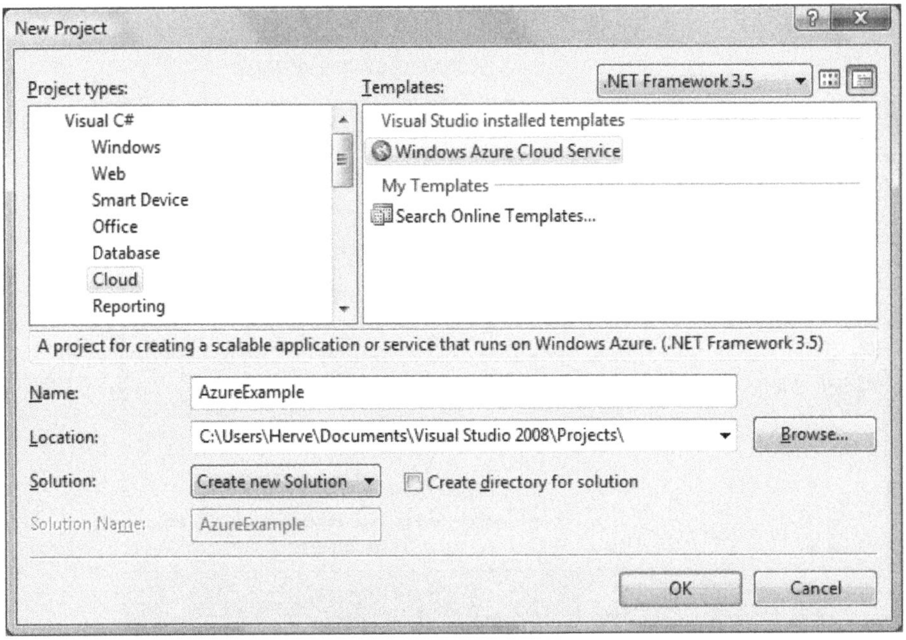

Figure 8-7. *Cloud project type in Visual Studio 2008*

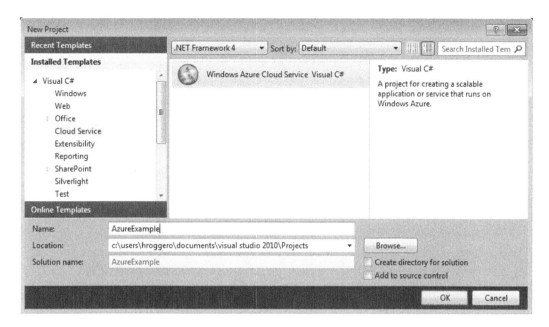

Figure 8-8. *Cloud Service project type in Visual Studio 2010*

4. Now click OK. The New Windows Azure Project dialog box comes up (see Figure 8-9); here you can select a role for your application. The role of your ASP.NET application dictates its primary purpose and what you're able to do with the project. The following roles are available:

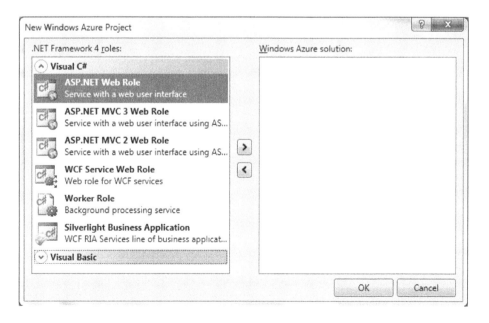

Figure 8-9. *Role Types in Visual Studio 2010*

- **ASP.NET Web Role**. Lets you create a web site with ASP.NET.

- **ASP.NET MVC 3 Web Role**. Lets you create an MVC 3 web application (only available in Visual Studio 2012).

- **ASP.NET MVC 2 Web Role**. Lets you create an MVC 2 web application (only available in Visual Studio 2010).

- **WCF Web Service Role**. Allows you to create a WCF service in Windows Azure.

- **Worker Role**. Equivalent to a background service in Windows Azure that has no user interface.

- **CGI Web Role**. Lets you create a web application using a technology other than ASP.NET, such as Python.

- **Silverlight Business Application**. Lets you build a Silverlight application using WCF RIA Services as the middle tier.

5. For this example, select the first option (ASP.NET Web Role), and click the right arrow (⊳). Doing so adds a new ASP.NET web role in the list of services, initially named WebRole1.

6. To change the name, select WebRole1 and press the F2 key or click the Edit link. To see the Edit link, place your mouse somewhere on the WebRole1 service list item; you'll see two icons come up on the right. The first one (with the pencil) allows you to edit the name, and the second lets you remove this web role (see Figure 8-10).

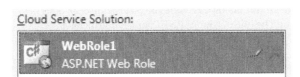

Figure 8-10. *Editing the web role's name*

7. Change the name to **wrAzureExample**, and press the Enter Key. Don't use AzureExample as the web role name, or there will be a conflict with the solution name provided earlier. The web role should now look like Figure 8-11.

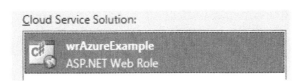

Figure 8-11. *Web role name changed*

8. Click OK.

At this point, you've created a new cloud solution. Solution Explorer looks a little different than it does for a typical ASP.NET project. Your cloud solution contains two projects: the AzureExample project and the wrAzureExample web role, which is itself a project, as shown in Figure 8-12. The AzureExample project contains configuration files that will be deployed later in Windows Azure.

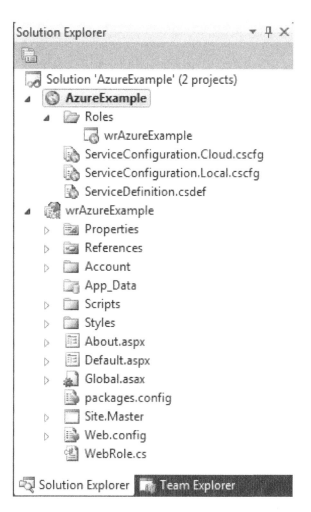

Figure 8-12. *Project layout for the ASP.NET web role*

▨ **Note** At the time of this writing, Windows Azure supports .NET 3.5 SP1 and .NET 4.0.

Connecting a GridView to SQL Database

Now that you have created a sample ASP.NET project, let's connect to a database in the cloud that will return data that we will display on the web page. Continue the example by following these steps:

1. Add a SQL Data Source and a GridView control on the Default.aspx page, and connect it to the data source. These steps next show you how to configure the SqlDataSource manually.

2. Open the Default.aspx page, and select Design view.

3. Drag a SqlDataSource from the Toolbox. Drag a GridView control on the page as well, and set its Data Source property to SqlDataSource1, as shown in Figure 8-13.

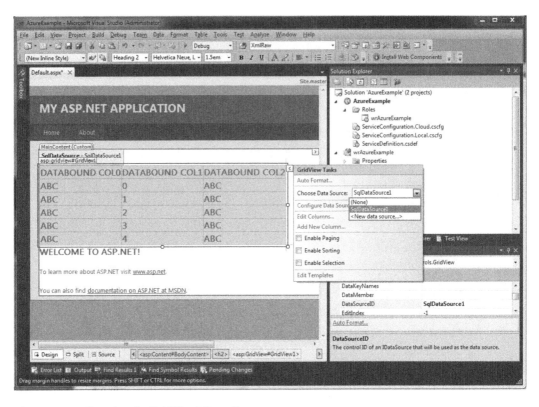

***Figure 8-13.** Changing the GridView's Data Source property*

4. Open the web.config file, and enter your connection string. You need to add a connectionStrings node under the configuration node, as shown in the following example:

```
<connectionStrings>
    <add
        name="Connection1"
        providerName="System.Data.SqlClient"
        connectionString="Server=tcp:yourServer.database.windows.net;
        Database=yourDatabase;User ID=test@yourServer;
        Password=yourPasswordHere;
        Trusted_Connection=False;Encrypt=True;"/>
</connectionStrings>
```

■ **Note** Make sure to specify the user ID as *<user name>@<server name>*.

5. Go back to the Default.aspx page, and change the SqlDataSource settings as follows by adding the ConnectionString and the SelectCommand settings manually.

```
<asp:SqlDataSource ID="SqlDataSource1" runat="server"
    ConnectionString="<%$ ConnectionStrings:Connection1 %>"
    SelectCommand="SELECT uid, name FROM sys.sysusers ORDER BY 1" >
</asp:SqlDataSource>
```

6. Running the project should give you output similar to that shown in Figure 8-14.

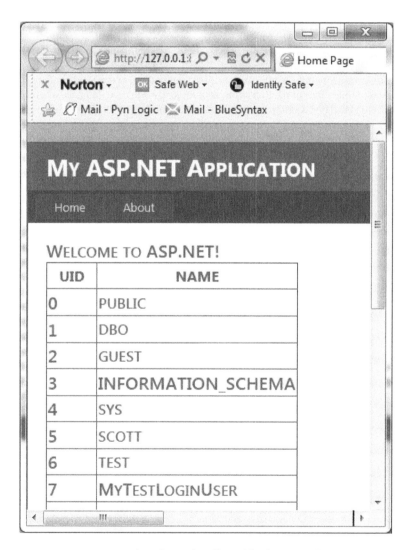

Figure 8-14. *Running the solution locally and fetching data from SQL Database*

So far, you're running this project on the local machine. Although the Windows Azure Tools are required, this project doesn't use any of the Windows Azure storage options; it connects directly to a live SQL Database instance.

■ **Note**   This chapter assumes you've configured the SQL Database firewall correctly as discussed in Chapter 1. Also, connecting from a Windows Azure service requires you to set the "Allow Microsoft Services access to this server" option in the firewall configuration. If you get a connection error stating that you aren't allowed to connect from a specific IP address, see Chapter 1 for detailed information about correctly setting up the SQL Database firewall.

Deployment and Configuration Files

You probably noticed that there are multiple configuration files in your solution. You can find a Web.Config file in your project, along with two additional files underneath: Web.Debug.Config and a Web.Release.Config. These two additional files allow you to perform transformations to your Web.Conf file depending on the build configuration. You can use this feature when you want to modify the connection string to point to a production database when you target a Release build. For more information about Web.Config transformations visit this link: http://go.microsoft.com/fwlink/?LinkId=125889.

You also probably noticed that the web role itself has configuration files. The project created previously has three configuration files:

- **ServiceDefinition.csdef**. Lets you control the definition of the service itself, such as the HTTP endpoint the application will be listening on.

- **ServiceConfiguration.Local.cscfg**. The configuration file being packaged when choosing the Local deployment mode.

- **ServiceConfiguration.Cloud.cscfg**. The configuration file being packaged when choosing the Cloud deployment mode.

Although the web.config build mode changes the web.config file using transformations, the ServiceConfiguration.cscfg does not; it uses the Local or the Cloud version depending on the deployment mode selected. Figure 8-15 shows how to apply the Release build configuration transformation and the Cloud service configuration file when packaging the project.

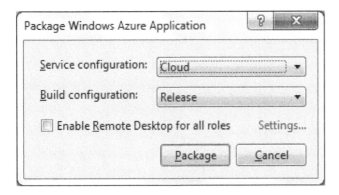

Figure 8-15. *Selecting the deployment and build configuration settings*

The ServiceConfiguration.cscfg file allows you to provide service-level settings that your code can read. Because your code can read this file, you could place the database connection string in this configuration file rather than in the web.config file. Placing a connection string in ServiceConfiguration.cscfg may make sense if your objective is to be able to change the connection string easily through the Windows Azure Management Portal. Indeed, when you place the connection string in the web.config file, you need to redeploy the application to Azure every time you want to change the connection string.

The project created in this chapter contains a simple deployment model shown in Figure 8-16. Whether you build the Release or Debug configuration, the database connection string is the same because you are not using web configuration transformations.

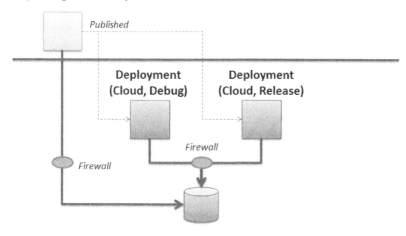

Figure 8-16. *Simple deployment scenario using a single database*

You may want to create a web configuration transformation allowing you to point to the staging database using the Debug build configuration and to the production database using the Release build configuration. When done correctly, the deployment options would look like Figure 8-17.

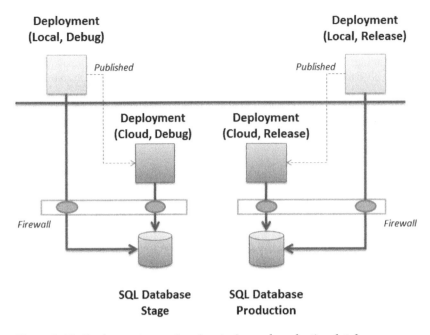

Figure 8-17. *Deployment scenario using staging and production databases*

You can also use code to override the database connection string altogether if you detect that you are running locally or in the cloud, so that you always point to a local database during development (regardless of the build configuration) but use the production database when deploying a release build with a cloud service configuration as shown in Figure 8-18.

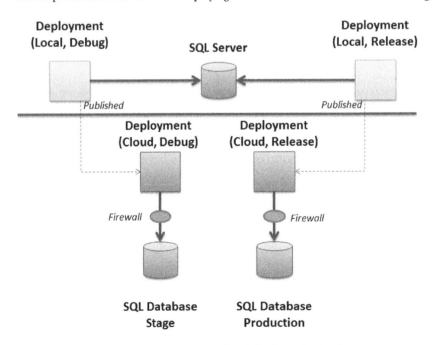

Figure 8-18. *Deployment scenario using a local database for development*

As you can see from the above discussion, you can configure your deployment strategy in many ways. You should establish the deployment model ahead of time so that you do not end up pointing to the wrong database when you are developing.

▓ **Note**   For more information about the Azure configuration files, read the following MSDN link:

http://msdn.microsoft.com/en-us/library/windowsazure/ee405486.aspx

---

Deploying an ASP.NET Application in Windows Azure

You're almost there. In this section, you walk through the steps of deploying the ASP.NET application in the cloud. You can publish an application directly from Visual Studio or package deployment files and deploy them manually. Because publishing directly from Visual Studio requires the creation of certificates and may require changing firewall settings, I'll show you the manual deployment steps to make things simpler to follow.

1. You need to package your project. Right-click AzureExample (the cloud project), and click Package. This action opens the dialog box seen previously in Figure 8-15. Select your Build and Service configuration and click Package. Once the package is created successfully, Windows Explorer opens where the deployment files are located. You will need these files shortly, so do not close that window.

2. Open Internet Explorer, navigate to the Azure Management Portal (http://manage.windowsazure.com), and log in using your Live ID.

3. When you've logged in, the Internet Explorer window shows you the home page for your Azure account. Click on Cloud Services.

4. You should see the page shown in Figure 8-1 at the beginning of this chapter. Click the AzureExample service and then click the Staging link. You now see the staging dashboard of the AzureExample service.

5. Click Upload. Deploying in staging creates a temporary service that you can use to test before promoting to the final public URL. This way, you can test that your application is working as desired before deploying it in production.

6. You now see the Upload a package dialog box (see Figure 8-19) with the following fields:

    •   **Deployment Name**. Under Service Deployment Name, you need to enter a label for your service. Type **TEST001**, for example. To avoid a warning about our test deployment, check the option at the bottom of the screen (Deploy even if one or more roles contain a single instance). You can click the question mark to learn more about this warning.

    •   **Package**. This is the package that Visual Studio built for you. It's the file with extension .cspkg in the Windows Explorer window. Clicking Browse opens an Open form. You may find it easier to copy the entire path from the Windows Explorer window and paste it in the Open form. Select the package file, and click Open.

    •   **Configuration** . This is the configuration file of your cloud service project with a .cscfg extension. Again, click Browse and select the configuration file from the Open form.

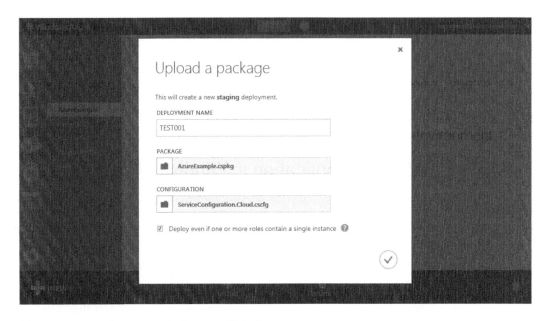

Figure 8-19. *Windows Azure deployment dialog box*

7. When the information provided looks like Figure 8-19, click OK. Doing so first copies the appropriate files to the cloud and creates the virtual machine in which your project will be deployed (see Figure 8-20). After it's deployed, your service starts running immediately and you start incurring charges.

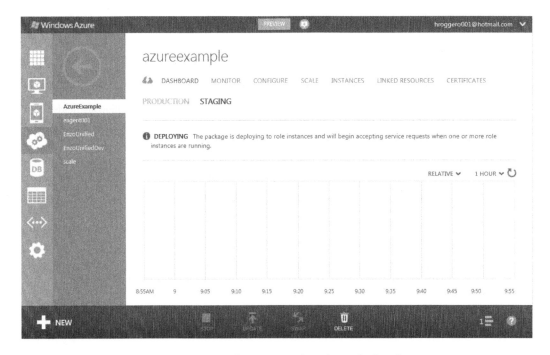

Figure 8-20. *Azure management interface showing a package being deployed*

To check that your website is running, you may first need to refresh your screen. Click the Site URL link located on the right side of the screen, which is the area that lists the properties of the deployment. Clicking the link opens another browser and runs your web application in the cloud (see Figure 8-21).

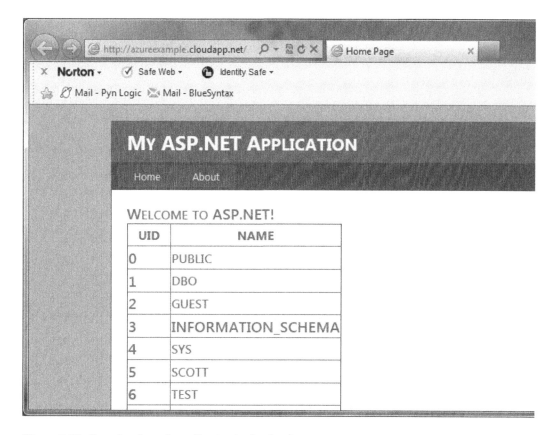

Figure 8-21. *Running the web application in the cloud*

■ **Note**   As mentioned previously, you're now paying for this Windows Azure service. To remove this service and stop accruing charges, select the AzureExample cloud service, click on Staging, and click on the Delete button on the bottom menu.

Summary

This chapter showed you how to create a simple ASP.NET application that connects to a SQL Database instance. This requires a few configuration steps, including the creation of a Windows Azure service in the cloud and the installation of a Visual Studio extension called the Windows Azure Tools.

While this chapter focused primarily on deploying an ASP.NET application in the cloud, you can very easily deploy ASP.NET projects on your enterprise IIS servers and configure the connection string to connect to a SQL Database instance. This gives you multiple deployment options to consider, although you must keep in mind that each deployment option has a different cost structure. Data transfer between Windows Azure and SQL Database is free within the same region, but you pay for compute time in Windows Azure.

■ ■ ■

Designing for High Performance

This chapter focuses on a few key topics that can help you design high-performance applications that consume data in SQL Database and SQL Server databases. The approach used in this chapter builds a simple but effective WinForms application that consumes data stored both on premises and in the cloud. You'll first explore a few general concepts and then quickly go into the design and development of a shard library that reads data from multiple databases. Finally, you'll see how to add multithreading to the shard library using the Task Parallel Library (TPL) and caching using the Enterprise Library (formally known as the caching application block).

General Performance Concepts

Before diving into the details, let's discuss a few concepts related to performance. The first thing you should know is that achieving high performance is difficult. Although making sure applications perform to acceptable levels is important, advanced performance tuning requires careful planning and should be included as a design goal only if requirements drive you to believe that high performance is necessary. For example, if you expect your application to be used by thousands of concurrent users, then you may need to use caching and even multithreading. On the other hand, certain high-performance techniques can make code difficult to read and maintain, and in such cases knowledge transfer may be difficult.

Chatty vs. Chunky

The encrypted network connection to SQL Database yields slower applications and may impact your application design significantly. An application that opens a database connection for every database call and performs a roundtrip for every update (that is, a *chatty* application) performs slower than an application that loads data for multiple objects in a single call and sends changes in bulk (a *chunky* application). LINQ to SQL and the Entity Framework are data access layers that provide good control over the use of bulk operations (the SaveChanges method on the object context).

For example, if you design a data access layer that contains a lot of business rules, your code may perform many roundtrips to the database to load the data needed to execute the business rules. If this is the case, you can implement certain data-intensive business rules in stored procedures (close to the data) and/or use caching to avoid unnecessary roundtrips.

Lazy Loading

On the other hand, although it's good to have fewer roundtrips from a performance standpoint, you should load only the data you need, for two reasons: the more data you load, the more you pay for the SQL Database service if the data is consumed outside of the data center where it resides; and loading more data than necessary can slow down your applications. So, you may want to consider using a *lazy loading* mechanism, by which certain properties of your objects are loaded only when necessary. LINQ to SQL and the Entity Framework 4.0 support lazy loading (through the use of the DeferredLoadingEnabled property).

Although lazy loading minimizes the amount of data loaded, it can create chattier applications. It's important to strike the right balance between using bulk data transfers and minimizing the amount of data needed to run an application function.

Caching

Another important technique used to minimize roundtrips is *caching*. Your application (or service) may use caching to avoid unnecessary roundtrips if some of your data doesn't change often. This may also impact your database design choices. For example, if you have a table that stores a list of states, the table will probably remain unchanged for a long time, which makes it a great candidate for caching.

Caching can be performed in memory or on disk (in a local database, for example). You have a few options:

- **ASP.NET caching.** ASP.NET offers a cache object that provides good caching capabilities. However, ASP.NET caching is tied to IIS. Restarting IIS clears the ASP.NET cache unless you've taken the necessary steps to persist the cache.

- **Windows Server AppFabric.** The AppFabric offers a next-generation distributed cache (previously known as Velocity). This cache can run on multiple computers and is made available through a .NET API. This caching library is only available on premise and cannot be used in Windows Azure.

- **Windows Azure Caching Service.** This caching service is a subset of Windows Server AppFabric caching. Some of the methods are not supported in Azure. The Azure Caching Service is only practical for storing IIS session state, or for other key-value pair storage needs in which the key is always known in advance. However the Azure cache can run on local instances, a method that leverages the memcache protocol.

- **Enterprise Library.** The Enterprise Library offers a collection of application blocks that Microsoft makes available under public license. The Enterprise Library contains a cache mechanism that doesn't depend on ASP.NET. This caching mechanism is provided natively in .NET 4.0 and can be found under the System.Runtime.Caching namespace.

Asynchronous User Interface

Ultimately, performance is a measure that impacts the user experience and can be controlled to a certain degree by offering highly responsive user interfaces. A Windows application that becomes unresponsive while loading data, or a web page that doesn't load until all the data has been retrieved, is perceived as slow. As a result, developing with multithreading techniques may become more important to provide a better experience to your users.

For web development, you should consider using asynchronous controls (such as AJAX) that give you more control over partial page loading. For Windows development, you may need to use a multithreaded user interface development approach.

To implement a highly responsive application in WinForms, use the Invoke method, shown on line 3 of the following example, to refresh your user interface on the UI thread:

```
1. void OnPassCompleted()
2. {
3.     this.Invoke(new EventHandler(UpdateProgressBar), null);
4. }
5.
```

```
6. private void UpdateProgressBar(object o, System.EventArgs e)
7. {
8.    if (progressBarTest.Value < progressBarTest.Maximum)
9.    {
10.       progressBarTest.Value++;
11.    }
12. }
```

In this example, `OnPassCompleted` is a custom event received by the main form, which then calls the `Invoke` method to refresh a progress bar. The call to `Invoke` forces the execution of the progress bar refresh on the UI thread, which is different from the thread on which the `OnPassCompleted` event was raised.

Parallel Processing

In addition to asynchronous user interfaces, your code may need to execute on multiple processors. Two primary scenarios can lead you to choose parallel processing for your application:

- **Many calculations.** Your application is CPU-intensive, especially if computations can be independent from each other. Advanced graphics or complex mathematical computations are examples of CPU-intensive operations.

- **Many waits.** Your application needs to wait between each call, and the cost of creating parallel threads and aggregating results is insignificant. Database shards are an example: calling five databases in parallel is roughly five times faster than calling five databases serially.

Two choices are available to write parallel processes. If you can, you should use the Task Parallel Library (TPL), because it's easier:

- **Task Parallel Library.** The TPL is a newer library that Microsoft is providing as part of .NET 4.0. It allows you to take advantage of multiple CPUs quickly and easily. You can find the TPL under `System.Threading.Tasks`.

- **Threads.** Managing threads the old-fashioned way using the `System.Threading` namespace gives you the most flexibility.

Shards

Shards offer another mechanism by which your code can read and write data against any number of databases almost transparently. Later in this chapter, you'll create a horizontal partition shard (HPS) using the read-write shard (RWS) design pattern as described in Chapter 2, with the round-robin access method. A horizontal partition implies that all the databases have identical schema and that a given record can be written in any database that belongs to the shard. From a performance standpoint, reading from multiple databases in parallel to search for records yields greater performance; however, your code must keep breadcrumbs if you need to perform updates back to the correct database. Finally, using a shard requires parallel processing for optimum performance. In Chapter 10 you will explore *federations*, a SQL Database feature providing built-in capabilities to build database shards.

Coding Strategies Summary

Table 9-1 provides a summary of the concepts discussed so far regarding some of the coding strategies available to you when you develop against a SQL Database instance with performance in mind.

Table 9-1. *Coding Strategies to Design for Performance*

Technique	Comments
Bulk data loading/changing	Minimizes roundtrips by using a data access library that supports loading data in bulk, such as the Entity Framework.
Lazy loading	Allows you to create objects for which certain properties are loaded only when first called, to minimize loading unnecessary data (and improve performance). The Entity Framework 4.0 supports this.
Caching	Lets you to keep in memory certain objects that don't change frequently. The caching application blocks provided by Microsoft offer this capability as well as expiration and scavenging configuration settings.
Asynchronous user interface	Not technically a performance-improvement technique, but allows users to use the application while your code is performing a long-running transaction and thus provides a better user experience.
Parallel processing	Allows you to run code on multiple processors for optimum performance. Although complex, this technique can provide significant performance advantages.
Shards	Lets you to store data in multiple databases to optimize reads and spread the load of queries over multiple database servers.

Because shards are considered a newer technology, the remainder of this chapter focuses on building an HPS using caching and parallel processing in order to improve performance and scalability.

Building a Shard

Let's build a shard library that can be used by applications that need to load and update data against multiple SQL Database instances as quickly and transparently as possible. The shard we are building uses a collection of databases as its underlying storage; however, there is no data affinity. A record could be located in any database; the approach uses a round-robin insert mechanism when adding data. For the purpose of building an efficient shard library, you stipulate the following requirements for the shard:

1. Adding new databases should be simple and transparent to the client code.

2. Adding new databases shouldn't affect performance negatively.

3. The library should function with SQL Server, SQL Database, or both.

4. The library should optionally cache results for fast retrieval.

5. The library should support mass or selective reads and writes.

6. Data returned by the library should be accepted as a data source for controls.

These requirements have very specific implications from a technology standpoint. Table 9-2 outlines which requirements are met by which technology.

Table 9-2. *Technologies Used to Build the Shard*

Technology	Requirement	Comment
Configuration file	1	The configuration file stores the list of databases that make up the shard, keeping the shard definition transparent to the code.
Multithreading	2	Using the TPL lets the library spawn multiple threads to use computers with multiple CPUs, allowing parallel execution of SQL statements and thus improving performance.
SqlClient	3	Using SqlCommand objects allows the shard to connect to both SQL Database and SQL Server databases.
Caching	4	Caching lets the library store results temporarily to avoid unnecessary roundtrips.
Breadcrumbs	5	The library creates a virtual column for each record returned that stores a breadcrumb identifying the database a record it came from, which supports selective writes.
DataTable	6	The library returns a DataTable object that can be bound to objects easily and serve as a data source.

Designing the Shard Library Object

The library accepts requests directly from client applications and can be viewed as an API. Note that you're using extension methods to make this API blend in with the existing SqlCommand class; this in turn minimizes the amount of code on the client and makes the application easier to read.

Figure 9-1 shows where the library fits in a typical application design. It also shows how the library hides the complexity of parallel processing and caching from the client application. Finally, the shard library abstracts the client code from dealing directly with multiple databases.

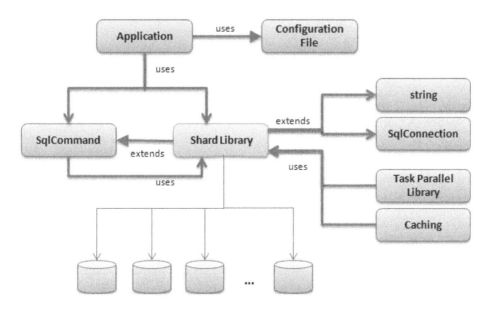

Figure 9-1. *Shard library object diagram*

A sample application is provided to demonstrate how to use the shard library. Although the application you'll build in the following sections is very simple, it uses all the features of the shard for reference.

■ **Note**   Check `http://EnzoSqlShard.Codeplex.com` for the latest shard library. This shard library is made available as an open source project. This project also contains a version of the library that understands SQL Database Federations.

Managing Database Connections

This section walks through a few coding decisions that are necessary when creating this shard. Because the shard library needs to be able to connect to multiple databases, the client has two options to provide this list: it can provide the list of connections to use whenever it makes a call to the library, or it can preload the library with a list of connection objects that are then kept in memory for all future calls.

The shard library declares the following property to hold the list of preloaded connection objects. The `ShardConnections` property is declared as static so it can be used across multiple calls easily; the client application only needs to set this property once:

```
public static List<SqlConnection> ShardConnections {get;set;}
```

In addition, an extension method is added to `SqlConnection` to provide a GUID value that uniquely identifies a connection string. The connection GUID is critical for the shard; it provides a breadcrumb for every record returned by the shard. This breadcrumb is later used by the shard to determine, for example, which database to use when performing an update statement.

The following code shows how a connection GUID is calculated. It uses the `SqlConnectionStringBuilder` helper class and another extension method on strings called `GetHash()` (on line 8). This extension method returns an SHA-256 hash value. Note that if the connection string doesn't specify a default database (Initial Catalog), you assume the user is connected to the master database. This assumption is correct for SQL Database, but it may not hold true for SQL Server:

```
1. public static string ConnectionGuid(this SqlConnection connection)
2. {
3.    SqlConnectionStringBuilder cb = new SqlConnectionStringBuilder(connection.ConnectionString);
4.    string connUID =
5.    ((cb.UserID != null. ? cb.UserID : "SSPI". + "#" +
6.    cb.DataSource + "#" +
7.    ((cb.InitialCatalog != null. ? cb.InitialCatalog : "master");
8.    string connHash = connUID.GetHash().ToString();
9.    return connHash;
10. }
```

For reference, here is the extension method that returns a hash value for a string. Technically, you could use the string's native `GetHashCode()` method. However, the built-in `GetHashCode` method varies based on the operating system used (32-bit or 64-bit) and the version of .NET. In this case, you create a simple `GetHash()` method that consistently returns the same value for a given input. The string value is first turned into an array of bytes using UTF-8 (on line 3). The hash value is then computed on line 4. Line 5 returns the hash as a string value:

```
1. public static string GetHash(this string val)
2. {
3.    byte[] buf = System.Text.UTF8Encoding.UTF8.GetBytes(val);
```

```
4.    byte[] res = System.Security.Cryptography.SHA256.Create().ComputeHash(buf);
5.    return BitConverter.ToString(res).Replace("-", "");
6. }
```

By default, the application code loads the initial set of connections using the application configuration file. In the current design, it's the application's responsibility to load the connections. This sample application reads the configuration file on startup and adds every entry in the ConfigurationStrings of the configuration file that contains the word *SHARD*:

```
1. foreach (System.Configuration.ConnectionStringSettings connStr in System.Configuration.
            ConfigurationManager.ConnectionStrings)
2. if (connStr.Name.ToUpper().StartsWith("SHARD"))
3.    Shard.ShardConnections.Add(new SqlConnection(connStr.ConnectionString));
```

The application can also add connections based on user input. The following code shows how the application adds a new connection to the shard:

```
Shard.ShardConnections.Add(new SqlConnection("connection string here"));
```

When running the test application, you can add a connection to the shard by clicking Add Connection on the Shard Connections tab. The GUID value for this connection is calculated automatically and displayed. Figure 9-2 shows the screen that allows you to add a connection manually, and Figure 9-3 displays all the connections defined in the shard.

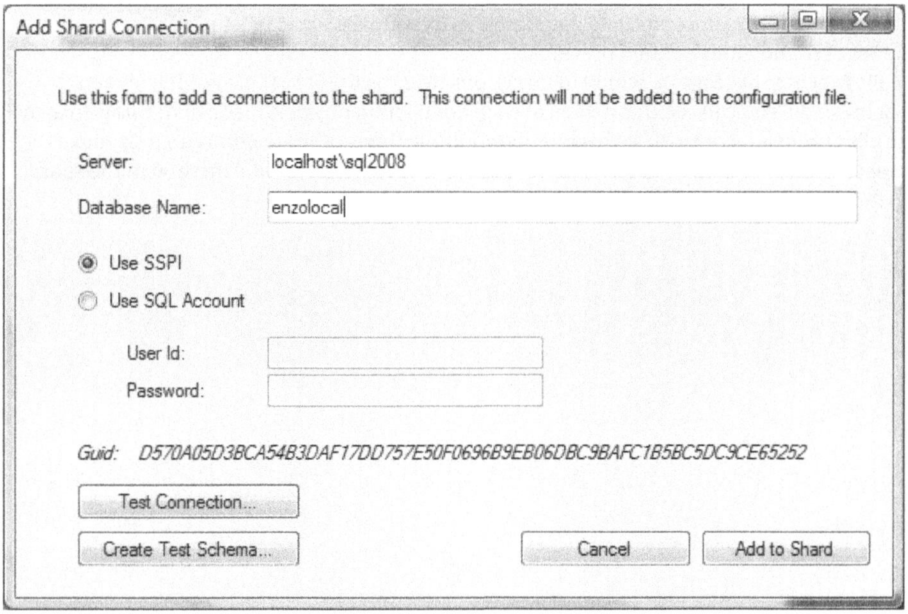

Figure 9-2. *Adding a custom connection to the shard*

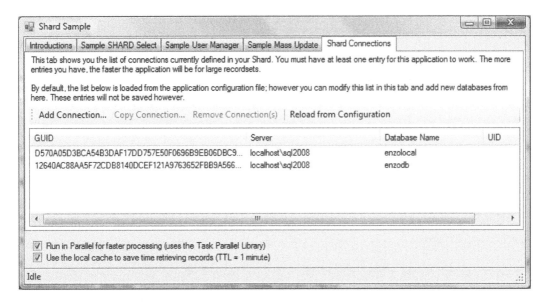

Figure 9-3. *Viewing shard connections*

Reading Using the Shard

Now that you've reviewed how connection strings are handled in the application and the library, you need to know how the shard handles a SELECT operation against multiple databases. In its simplest form, the library executes the SELECT operation against the list of connections defined previously.

The client application calls ExecuteShardQuery, which in turn loops over the list of SqlConnection objects (see Figure 9-4). If you look at the code, you can see that a copy of each connection object is made first; this is to avoid any potential collisions if the client code makes a call to this method multiple times (a connection can only make one call at a time). Then, for each connection, the code calls ExecuteSingleQuery, which is the method in the shard library that makes the call to the database.

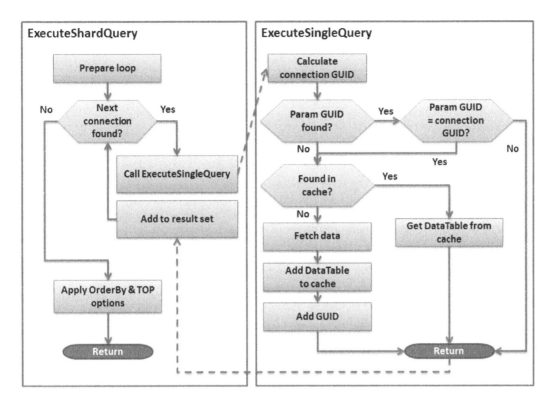

Figure 9-4. *Reading from the shard*

The ExecuteShardQuery method is designed to call the ExecuteSingleQuery method multiple times in parallel using the TPL. The TPL provides many useful methods to easily handle parallel processing without having to manage threads. The shard library uses Parallel.ForEach, which is a construct that allows the code to execute an anonymous method multiple times concurrently, and automatically adjusts the number of threads depending on your computer's hardware configuration. So, the more CPUs you have, the faster the following code executes, if you have enough connections to loop through. Note, however, that you need to lock the data object (line 5), which is a DataTable, because it could be accessed by other executing threads. Finally, the Merge method on the DataTable object concatenates resultsets from the various connections. After the loop has executed, the resulting data object has the list of records retrieved from the shard, in no guaranteed order:

```
1. Parallel.ForEach(connections,
2.    delegate(SqlConnection c)
3.    {
4.     DataTable dt = ExecuteSingleQuery(command, c, exceptions);
5.     lock (data)
6.        data.Merge(dt, true, MissingSchemaAction.Add);
7.    }
8. );
```

The following code is a simplified version of the actual sample application. (For clarity, some code that calculates execution time and performs exception handling has been removed.) Line 4 sets the command text to be executed, such as a SELECT statement, and line 5 executes it against the shard. Instead of calling ExecuteReader, the code calls ExecuteShardQuery to use the shard. Line 7 binds the resulting DataTable and displays the records returned by the shard:

```
1. SqlCommand cmd = new SqlCommand();
2. DataTable dataRes = new DataTable();
3.
4. cmd.CommandText = this.textBox1.Text;
5. dataRes = cmd.ExecuteShardQuery();
6.
7. dataGridView2.DataSource = dataRes;
```

Figure 9-5 shows the outcome of this code. The SELECT statement is designed to return database object names and types. Executing the statement against the shard performs as expected. However, notice that an extra column has been added to the display: __guidDB__. This is the name of the GUID column introduced previously. This column doesn't help much for reading, but it enables updates and deletes, as you will see later.

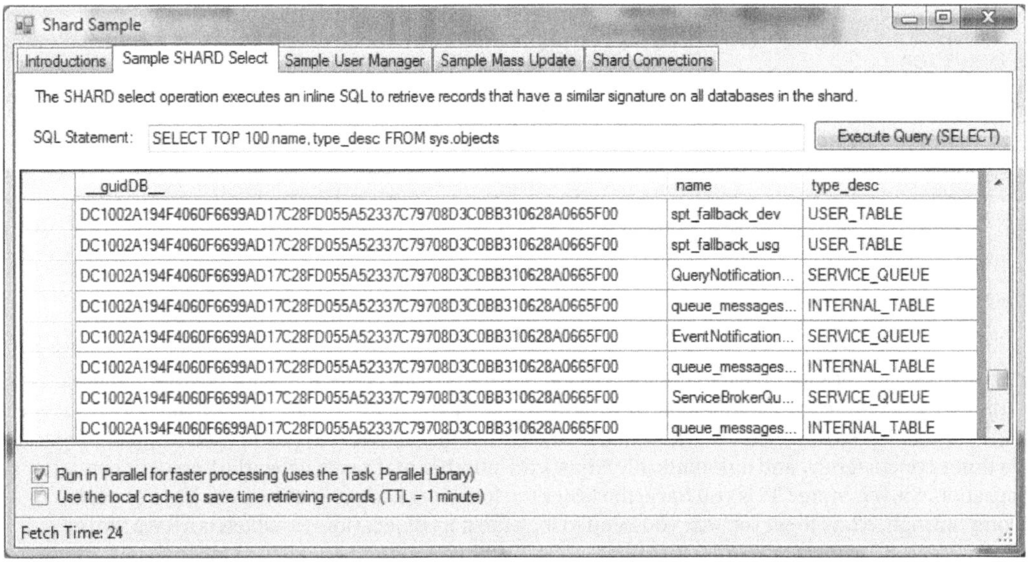

Figure 9-5. *Showing records returned by the shard*

The GUID provided is unique for each database connection, as long as one of the key parameters is different in the connection string of each connection. It's added by the ExecuteSingleQuery method described previously. Within this method, a column is added in front of all the others, which carries the GUID. In the following code extract, line 3 creates the data column of type string, and line 4 sets its default value to the connection's GUID. Line 7 fills the data table with the query's result, along with the added GUID column. The following is the logic used to add this GUID:

```
1.// Add the connection GUID to this set of records
2. // This helps us identify which row came from which connection
3. DataColumn col = dt.Columns.Add(_GUID_, typeof(string));
4. col.DefaultValue = connection.ConnectionGuid();
5.
6. // Get the data
7. da.Fill(dt);
```

Caching

To minimize roundtrips to the source databases, the shard library provides an optional caching mechanism. The caching technique used in this library offers basic capabilities and can be extended to address more complex scenarios. The objective of this library is to cache the entire DataTable of each database backend whenever requested. Figure 9-6 shows the logical decision tree of the caching approach. It's important to note that this library calculates a cache key based on each parameter, the parameter value, each SQL statement, and the database's GUID.

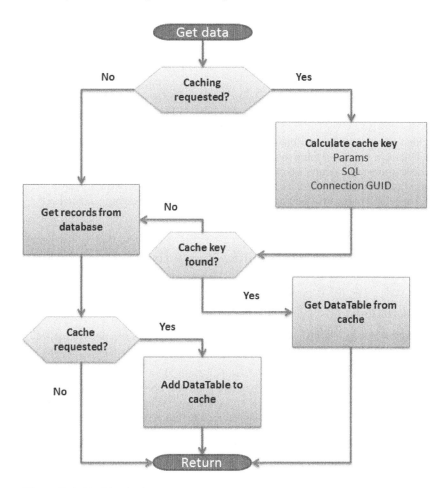

Figure 9-6. *Caching logic*

The effect of the cache is visible when you connect to SQL Database. Considering that connecting to a SQL Database instance takes up to 250 milliseconds the first time, memory access is significantly faster. The importance of the cache increases as the number of records increases and the number of databases increases in the shard.

The cache provided by this library also provides a time-to-live (TTL) mechanism that implements either an absolute expiration or a sliding expiration scheme. An absolute expiration resets the cache automatically at a specific time in the future, whereas the sliding setting moves the expiration time if the cache items are used before expiring. The following code shows how the caching is implemented. Line 1 creates a CacheItemPolicy used to define the behavior of the cache. Line 3 implements the sliding window cache, and line 5 implements the absolute approach:

```
1. CacheItemPolicy cip = new CacheItemPolicy();
2. if (UseSlidingWindow)
3.    cip.SlidingExpiration = defaultTTL;
4. else
5.    cip.AbsoluteExpiration = new DateTimeOffset(System.DateTime.Now.Add(defaultTTL));
6. MemoryCache.Default.Add(cacheKey, dt, cip);
```

You can enhance this caching technique in multiple ways. For example, the DataTable object stored in the cache can be compressed when it contains many rows. Compression algorithms tend to increase latency, but the overall performance benefits may be worth a slight delay.

Another way to enhance this caching storage is to create different cache containers, so you can control at a more granular level which container holds which kind of data. Doing so lets you control a different setting per container, for example; or you may decide to always compress one cache container but not another.

Finally, the cache provided in this library isn't distributed; it's local to the machine running the library. If you need to develop a more robust cache, consider looking into the Windows Server AppFabric; its caching technology provides enterprise-level capabilities.

■ **Note** For more information about the Windows Server AppFabric , visit http://msdn.microsoft.com/appfabric.

Updating and Deleting Records in the Shard

At this point, you're ready to see how updates and deletes take place through the shard. Updates and deletes against the databases in the shard can be performed either for records in a given database or against all databases. At a high level, here are some guidelines you can use to decide on an approach:

- **Update or delete records in a single database.** You update or delete one or more records in a database when you already know the database GUID to use. This is the case when you use the shard to retrieve records, because the database GUID is provided for all records returned.

- **Update or delete records across databases.** Generally speaking, you update or delete records across databases in the shard whenever you don't know which database a record is in, or when all records need to be evaluated.

To update or delete records in a single database, you must provide a command parameter that contains the database GUID to use. Here's the code that updates a single record in the shard. On lines 1 through 7, the code creates a command object that calls a stored procedure that requires two parameters. On line 9, the code adds the database GUID to use. This extra parameter is removed by the shard library before making the call to the requested database:

```
1. cmd.CommandText = "sproc_update_user";
2. cmd.CommandType = CommandType.StoredProcedure;
3.
4. cmd.Parameters.Add(new SqlParameter("@id", SqlDbType.Int));
5. cmd.Parameters["@id"].Value = int.Parse(labelIDVal.Text);
6. cmd.Parameters.Add(new SqlParameter("@name", SqlDbType.NVarChar, 20));
7. cmd.Parameters["@name"].Value = textBoxUser.Text;
```

```
8.
9. cmd.Parameters.Add(new SqlParameter(PYN.EnzoAzureLib.Shard._GUID_, labelGUID.Text));
10.
11. ExecuteShardNonQuery (cmd);
```

Note that calling a stored procedure isn't required for this code to run. All that is required is that a SqlCommand object be used; the SQL code may very well be inline SQL. There are pros and cons of using stored procedures and inline SQL in a sharding environment. As you may already know, using inline SQL can introduce security threats, such as SQL injection; and stored procedures are typically much faster because they are precompiled. However, keep in mind that using stored procedures introduces a new level of complexity because you will need to make sure your stored procedures are identical across all your shard databases.

Deleting a record from the shard is virtually identical. The command object is created with the required stored procedure parameters in lines 1 through 5. On line 7, the code adds the database GUID to use:

```
1. cmd.CommandText = "sproc_delete_user";
2. cmd.CommandType = CommandType.StoredProcedure;
3.
4. cmd.Parameters.Add(new SqlParameter("@id", SqlDbType.Int));
5. cmd.Parameters["@id"].Value = int.Parse(labelIDVal.Text);
6.
7. cmd.Parameters.Add(new SqlParameter(PYN.EnzoAzureLib.Shard._GUID_, labelGUID.Text));
8.
9. ExecuteShardNonQuery (cmd);
```

■ **Note**   The ExecuteShardNonQuery method behaves differently depending on its database GUID parameter. If it has no GUID parameter, it executes the query against all databases. If it has a database GUID parameter with a value, it executes the query against the specified database. If it contains a database GUID parameter with a NULL value, it executes the query against the next database in the shard using round-robin. You will see how to use round-robin calls when adding records in the shard shortly.

Figure 9-7 shows the sample application updating a record from the shard. When you click Reload Grid, a SELECT statement is issued against the shard, which returns the database GUID for each record. Then, when you select a specific record (by selecting the entire row), the record details are loaded in the right section of the screen, along with the record's database GUID. At this point, the record can be updated or deleted. If you run this sample program, make sure to follow the configuration steps found in the Introductions tab.

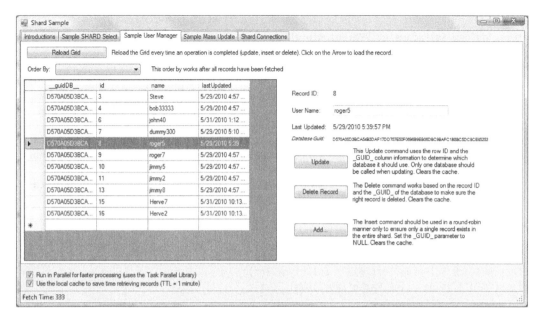

Figure 9-7. *Sample application updating a record in the shard*

Because records are being updated or deleted, the client code clears the cache to force future SELECT statements to fetch records from the databases in the shard. The shard library exposes a ResetCache method that does just that. You can improve this logic by also performing the same update or delete operation of records in the cache.

Updating or deleting records across databases in the shard is even simpler. The following code executes an inline SQL statement using a SqlCommand object. Because no database GUID is provided, this statement executes the statement across all databases in the shard. When you perform updates or deletes across databases, it's important to set the parallel flag correctly, as shown on line 1:

```
1. PYN.EnzoAzureLib.Shard.UseParallel = checkBoxParallel.Checked;
2. cmd.CommandText = "UPDATE TestUsers2 SET LastUpdated = GETDATE()";
3. cmd.CommandType = CommandType.Text;
4. ExecuteShardNonQuery (cmd);
```

Adding Records to the Shard

You see how easy it is to add records to the shard databases. This shard works best from a performance standpoint when all databases in the shard have a roughly equal number of records; this is because parallel processing is performed without any deterministic logic. As a result, the more spread out your records are in the shard, the faster it is. You can add records in the shard in two ways:

- **In a single database.** If you're loading the shard for the first time, you may decide to load certain records in specific databases. Or you may decide to load one database with more records than others, if the hardware is superior.

- **Across databases.** Usually, you load records in the shard without specifying a database. The shard library uses a round-robin mechanism to load records.

Adding a record in a specific database is no different than updating or deleting a record in a database; all you need to do is create a SqlCommand object, set the INSERT statement, and add a SqlParameter indicating the database GUID to use.

Adding one or more records across databases requires a slightly different approach. The round-robin logic stores the last database used to insert records in the shard. The shard library exposes two methods to perform inserts:

- ExecuteShardNonQuery. As you've seen previously, this method extends the SqlCommand object and executes statements against the next database in the shard (round-robin) if the GUID parameter is NULL. This convention is used to let the shard library know that it should move its internal database pointer to the next database in the shard for the next round-robin call.

- ExecuteParallelRoundRobinLoad. This method extends List<SqlCommand> and provides a mechanism to create a collection of SqlCommand objects. Each SqlCommand object contains an INSERT statement to execute. This method adds a NULL database GUID and calls ExecuteShardNonQuery to execute all the statements with round-robin support. This construct simplifies loading a shard quickly by spreading INSERT statements evenly across all databases.

The following code shows how the client prepares the call to ExecuteParallelRoundRobinLoad. Line 1 creates a collection of SqlCommand objects. Then, on line 3, an outer loop executes for each value found in the userName array (this is a list of names to add to the shard). From lines 5 to 16, a SqlCommand object is created for each name to INSERT and is added to the collection. Line 22 makes the actual call to ExecuteParallelRoundRobinLoad. Finally, on line 23, if all goes well, the library's cache is cleared:

```
1.  List<SqlCommand> commands = new List<SqlCommand>();
2.
3.  foreach (string name in userName)
4.  {
5.      if (name != null && name.Trim().Length > 0)
6.      {
7.          SqlCommand cmdToAdd = new SqlCommand();
8.          cmdToAdd.CommandText = "sproc_add_user";
9.          cmdToAdd.CommandType = CommandType.StoredProcedure;
10.
11.          cmdToAdd.Parameters.Add(
12.          new SqlParameter("name", SqlDbType.NVarChar, 20));
13.          cmdToAdd.Parameters["name"].Value = name;
14.
15.          commands.Add(cmdToAdd);
16.      }
17. }
18.
19. // Make the call!
20. if (commands.Count > 0)
21. {
22.     commands.ExecuteParallelRoundRobinLoad();
23.     Shard.ResetCache();
24. }
```

▪ **Note**   The call to ExecuteParallelRoundRobinLoad is different in two ways from all the other methods you've seen so far. First, there is no need to add the database GUID parameter; it creates this parameter automatically with a NULL value. Second, this method executes on a List<SqlCommand> object instead of SqlCommand.

Figure 9-8 shows the sample application screen that creates the array of names to load in the shard. Six names are added in the shard using round-robin, as previously described.

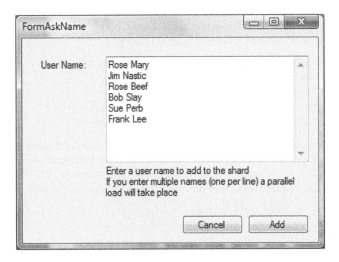

Figure 9-8. *Sample application adding records using round-robin*

Managing a Shard

Having created a shard and reached the point of being able to run queries and add data, you can begin to think about higher-level issues: how to handle exceptions, manage performance, control transactions, and more.

Managing Exceptions

So far, you've learned the basic principles of the sample shard library. You saw how to select, insert, update, and delete records in various ways through the methods provided by the library. Let's discuss how you can manage exceptions that the shard may throw at you.

The current library doesn't handle rollbacks, but it may throw exceptions that your code needs to capture. In the previous example (Figure 9-8), all the records were inserted except Jim Nastic: that name was too long for the SqlParameter object (hence it threw a "Value Would Be Truncated" exception).

The library handles exceptions through the AggregateException class provided by the TPL; this class holds a collection of exceptions. This is necessary because the library executes database calls in parallel. As a result, more than one exception may be taking place at the same time. You need to aggregate these exceptions and return them to the client for further processing.

For example, the shard library's ExecuteSingleNonQuery method takes a ConcurrentQueue<Exception> parameter, which represents an object that stores exceptions. This object is thread-safe, meaning that all running threads can add new exceptions to it safely without running into concurrency issues. The following code shows that if an exception is detected in the ExecuteSingleNonQuery method, the code adds the exception to the queue on line 14. Also, as a convention, the exception is rethrown if the queue isn't provided (line 16):

```
1. private static long ExecuteSingleNonQuery(
2.   SqlCommand command,
3.   SqlConnection connectionToUse,
4.   System.Collections.Concurrent.ConcurrentQueue<Exception> exceptions
```

```
5.  )
6.  {
7.        try
8.        {
9.        // ...
10.        }
11.        catch (Exception ex)
12.        {
13.        if (exceptions != null)
14.            exceptions.Enqueue(ex);
15.        else
16.            throw;
17.        }
18.   }
```

The following code shows the ExecuteShardNonQuery method, which calls the ExecuteSingleNonQuery method just described. Line 1 creates the exception queue (ConcurrentQueue), which is passed as a variable to ExecuteSingleNonQuery. After the parallel execution of the database calls is complete, the code checks whether the exception queue is empty. If it isn't empty, an AggregateException is thrown, which contains the collection of exceptions stored in the exception queue (lines 13 and 14):

```
1. var exceptions = new System.Collections.Concurrent.ConcurrentQueue<Exception>();
2.
3. Parallel.ForEach(connections, delegate(SqlConnection c)
4. {
5.    long rowsAffected = ExecuteSingleNonQuery(command, c, exceptions);
6.
7.    lock (alock.
8.        res += rowsAffected;
9.
10.    }
11. );
12.
13. if (!exceptions.IsEmpty)
14.    throw new AggregateException(exceptions);
```

As you can see, managing exceptions can be a bit tricky. However, these exception helper classes provide a good mechanism to store exceptions and return a collection of exceptions that the client code can consume.

Managing Performance

So far, you've seen how the shard library works and how you can use it in your code. But it's important to keep in mind why you go through all this trouble—after all, there is nothing trivial in creating a shard library. This shard library does something important: it allows a client application to grow parts (or all) of a database horizontally, with the intention of improving performance, scalability, or both.

What does this mean? It means the shard library can help an application keep its performance characteristics in a somewhat consistent manner as more users use the application (scalability), or it can help an application perform faster under a given load (performance). If you're lucky, the shard library may be able to achieve both. However, this won't happen without proper planning. The shard library by itself is only a splitter, in the sense that it spreads calls to multiple databases.

Shards don't necessarily help performance; in certain cases, a shard hurts both performance and scalability. The reason is that a shard imposes an overhead that wouldn't otherwise exist. Figure 9-9 shows the difference between a standard ADO.NET call selecting records and best-case and worst-case scenarios when fetching the same records from a shard. In the best case, all records are assumed to be split in three distinct databases; the shard is able to concurrently access all three databases, aggregate the three resultsets, and filter and/or sort the data. The shard must then manage all of the following, which consumes processing time:

- Loops for connecting to the underlying databases

- Loops for fetching the data

- Data aggregation, sorting and filtering

In the worst case, all these operations can't be executed in parallel and require serial execution. This may be the case if the TPL detects that only a single processor is available. Finally, you may end up in a situation that mixes worst- and best-case scenarios, where some of the calls can be made in parallel, but not all.

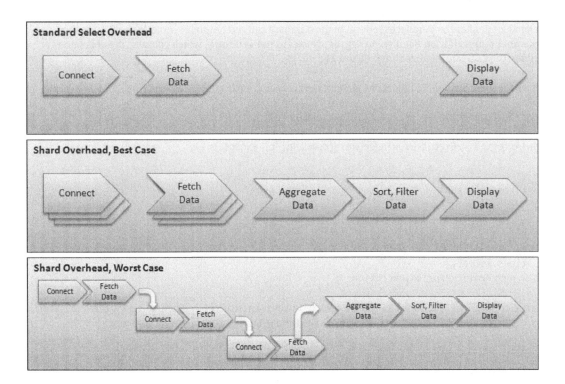

Figure 9-9. *Data access overhead comparison*

Now that all the warnings are laid out, let's look at a scenario for which a shard makes sense and probably improves both performance and scalability. Imagine a DOC table that contains only two records. The table contains a few fields that represent document metadata, such as Title and Author ID. However, this table also contains a large field: a varbinary column called Document that holds a PDF file. Each PDF file is a few megabytes in size. Figure 9-10 shows the output of the table. Because this database is loaded in SQL Database, the SELECT * FROM DOCS statement returns a few megabytes of data on an SSL encrypted link. The execution of this statement takes about 2.5 seconds on average, or roughly 1.25 seconds per record.

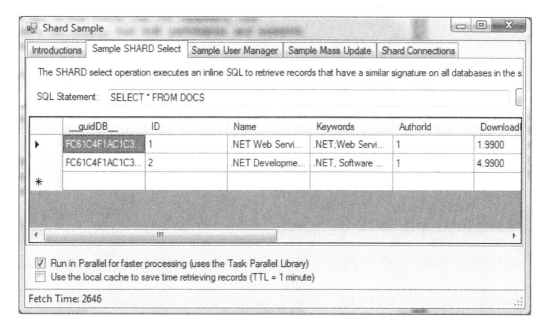

Figure 9-10. *Sample table containing documents in one database*

Both records come from the database; you can see this by looking at the database GUID, which is similar for both records. However, if you move the second record to another SQL Database instance, the average execution time drops to about 1.8 seconds. Figure 9-11 shows the result of the same statement that executed in 1.4 seconds (you can see that the database GUIDs are now different). This is half the execution time of the first result.

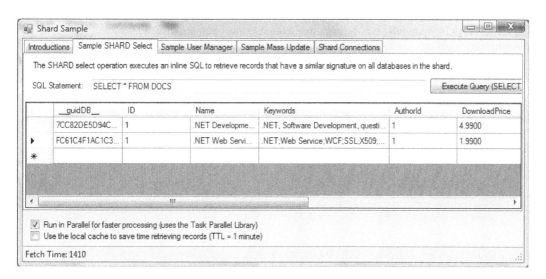

Figure 9-11. *Sample table containing documents in two databases*

You can execute this statement much more quickly because almost the entire time is spent returning the Document field. Figure 9-12 tells you that returning all the fields against both databases without the Document field takes only 103 milliseconds. This shows that using a shard can provide performance benefits even if there is a processing overhead; however, this may not always be the case. Be sure to carefully evaluate your database design to determine which tables, if any, can take advantage of parallel execution.

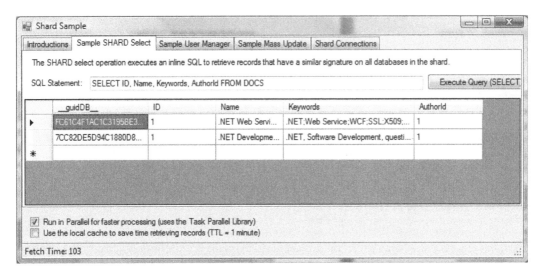

Figure 9-12. Excluding the Document field from the SELECT

Working with Partial Shards

Note that building a shard isn't an all-or-nothing approach. You can easily create a partial shard for a set of tables. Depending on how your code is structured, you may or may not need to build logic that understands sharding, depending on which tables you need to access. Sharding logic is best built in a data access layer (DAL), where the physical organization of tables is separated from the organization of business objects.

For example, you can design an application that consumes business objects directly. These business objects in turn consume command objects, which are specialized routines smart enough to load data in memory structures by calling execution objects. Figure 9-13 shows the Authors object calling two command objects that load data from two separate libraries: the standard ADO.NET library and the shard library built in this chapter. The complexity of determining which library to call is deferred to the lowest level possible, protecting the application and business objects from database structural changes.

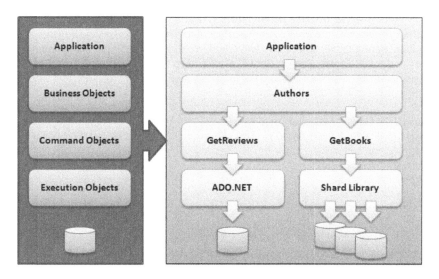

Figure 9-13. *Example application design implementing a partial shard*

Managing Transaction Consistency

Because distributed transactions aren't supported in SQL Database, shard libraries for SQL Database don't offer transactional consistency. But you should look carefully at your transactional needs and what this means to your application design.

You can add transactional capabilities in the shard library described in this chapter by changing the ExecuteShardNonQuery and ExecuteParallelRoundRobinLoad methods. To do so, you need to add a separate transaction context to all connection objects and commit them in a loop at the end of the last execution. If any exception occurs, you must roll back all the changes.

■ **Note**   As mentioned earlier, the shard library is an open-source project and is likely to evolve over time. Check for the latest release to see which features are supported.

Managing Foreign Key Constraints

Another interesting issue to consider in shard databases is related to foreign key constraints. You may quickly realize that maintaining referential integrity can be challenging regardless of the sharding approach you use.

To maintain relational integrity, the following concerns apply:

- **Data duplication.** Because you don't know which records are where in the shard, the parent tables need to be duplicated in every database. For example, a table that contains the list of states (Florida, Illinois, and so on) may need to be replicated across all databases.

- **Identity values.** Adding records in one database can't be easily replicated across to other databases. Thus, using an identity value as the primary key may be difficult because you aren't guaranteed to have the same value in all databases in the shard. For example, the StateID value for Florida may be 10 in one database and 11 in another.

When it comes to data duplication, you can either treat the parent tables as overhead and duplicate them across databases, allowing you to maintain strong referential integrity (RI), or sacrifice RI in the database by sharding the parent tables as well. If you decide to shard parent tables, you can no longer enforce RI in the database; but you may still be able to enforce RI in your code by adding RI constraints to your DataTable objects. You can do so by creating a DataRelation object in the DataTable's ParentRelations collection. For example, the following code adds RI to the DOCS and AUTHORS DataTable objects:

```
1. SqlCommand cmd1 = new SqlCommand("SELECT * FROM Authors");
2. SqlCommand cmd2 = new SqlCommand("SELECT * FROM Docs");
3. DataTable authors = ExecuteShardQuery(cmd1);
4. DataTable docs = ExecuteShardQuery(cmd2);
5. DataRelation dr = new DataRelation("RI",
6. authors.Columns["authorId"],
7. docs.Columns["authorId"]);
8. docs.ParentRelations.Add(dr);
```

The issue with identity values lies in the fact that an automatic identity is created for each record. But because the tables are split across databases, you aren't guaranteed to have the same values over time. To solve this issue, you need to create RI rules that depend not on identity values, but on codes. In the case of the table that stores states, you create a StateCode column (which stores FL for Florida, for example) and use that column as your primary key and in your RI rules. This ensures that all databases in the shard use the same values to maintain integrity.

Designing a Multitenant System

The shard library built in this chapter is designed to access data using a round-robin mechanism. New data could be stored in any underlying database and a breadcrumb is used to temporarily remember which database contains which data. This works well for certain applications but may prove difficult to use for business applications where customer records need to be isolated. Let's review another HPS: a schema-separation architecture for customer data in a multitenant system.

Schema-based security and data isolation were described in Chapter 3. You learned that schema-based isolation provides a good security model to protect customer data from other tenants in the same database and how to properly configure access control for this model.

To design this system we must consider the following points:

- **Service Account.** In order to leverage connection pooling for each customer you will need to make sure your connection strings use service accounts. A service account is a login that users do not know about and is used only by the system. Each customer will have its own service account.

- **Login Database.** You will also need to create a central database containing the connection string each customer should use. Alternatively, you could store customer connection strings in a configuration file; however, keeping this setting in a database makes it easier for maintenance.

- **Customer ID.** A customer ID needs to be created for each customer; the customer ID then needs to be stored in memory (usually in the Session state) so that the system can retrieve the connection string given the Customer ID.

Figure 9-14 shows how the system can process a request for a specific customer when reading or changing data. This workflow assumes that the customer has already logged in and is authenticated with the application; the authentication process is responsible for storing the Customer ID in memory (the Customer ID could be stored in the application cache or the session state for an ASP.NET application).

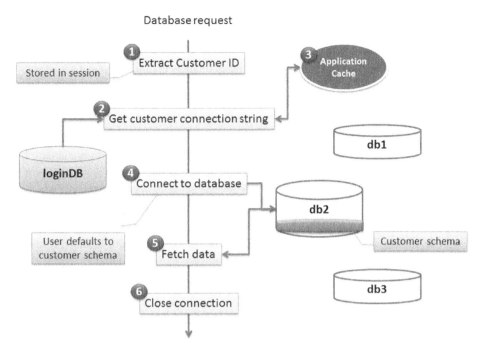

Figure 9-14. *Logic used to fetch data in a multitenant, schema-based architecture*

When the database request is issued, the cost fetches the Customer ID from the local cache (1) and uses the Customer ID to retrieve the customer connection string from the login database (2). The system then saves the connection string for the customer in its internal cache (3) for future requests. The database connection string contains the service account to use along with the database assigned to the customer. The system then connects to the database (4). Because the service account has a default schema pointing to the customer schema the system issues the T-SQL command against the correct schema automatically (5). The system can then return the customer data and close the connection (6).

You should know that a multitenant system distributed over multiple databases with a service account for each customer can create a Connection Pooling Fragmentation problem for large systems. That's because a connection pool will be created for each customer. In addition if you use multiple load-balanced middle-tier servers, each server will hold its own set of connection pools. As a result you should carefully test your system across multiple customers by monitoring your database connections to avoid possible throttling conditions when too many connections are established against a SQL Database instance. If you use SQL Database Federations instead of the schema container approach, you will not experience the Connection Pooling Fragmentation issue because all database connections are established against a single database (the root database) using the same service account, regardless of the Customer ID.

Performing maintenance operations on a customer schema can be a challenge. Your application will need to prevent customers from connecting until the schema maintenance task is completed. For example, if you want to move a customer to another database you can follow these steps:

1. Place the customer in maintenance mode to avoid data changes (through your application).

2. Create a backup copy of the customer schema (you can use the free Enzo Backup tool to back up a specific schema at `http://www.bluesyntax.net/`); alternatively you can create a complete copy of the database using the `CREATE DATABASE ... AS COPY OF...`; however, this method requires removing all the other customers' schema containers that are not supposed to move to the new database.

3. Restore the schema container to a new database if you used a tool to back up the schema.

4. Change the connection string in the login database to point to the new database.

As you will see in Chapter 10, Federations solve this issue by providing an inline SPLIT operation that allows you to reconfigure your shard without any downtime.

Creating Vertical Partition Shards

The majority of this chapter discussed the HPS, but it's important to also be familiar with vertical partition shards (VPSs). A VPS stores an application database schema across multiple databases; in essence, the application database is split in such a way that no database in the shard holds the complete schema.

Let's consider a simple application database that is made of two tables: Users and Sales. The Users table contains a few thousand records, and the Sales table contains a few million records. You can design a VPS with two databases: the first contains the Users table, and the second contains the Sales table.

This type of shard makes it easy to isolate the processing power needs of certain tasks without affecting the other database. For example, you can use the Users table to process login requests from users while at the same time using the Sales table for a CPU-intensive calculation process or to run long reports.

You can also build a VPS by splitting a table across multiple databases. For example, the Sales table may store large binary fields (such as documents). In this case, you can split the Sales table such that common fields are stored in one database, and the field containing documents is stored in another database.

A VPS does bring it own set of challenges, such as the difficulty of keeping strong RI between databases and, in the case of SQL Database, ensuring transaction consistency. These considerations are only meant to bring certain design issues to the surface when you're thinking about a VPS. Depending on your database design, a VPS may work very well and may be simpler to implement than an HPS.

Big Data with Hadoop for Windows Azure

Although this book is about SQL Database, you should know that Microsoft is introducing Hadoop for Windows Azure, a big data initiative that offers the Apache Hadoop framework on the Azure cloud.

Hadoop is a distributed computing model allowing you to scale your processing needs to a very large number of machines reliably for both structured and unstructured data. When working with Hadoop, you implement software logic to distribute your computing needs using open source subprojects, such as the Hadoop Distributed File System and the Hadoop MapReduce. Each machine in the Hadoop network offers local compute and storage for massively distributed computational needs.

At the time of this writing, Hadoop for Windows Azure is only available by invitation, and limited information is available. If you have large amounts of data to analyze and need a massively scaled out environment, take a look at Microsoft's offering for Hadoop.

Summary

As you've seen, building databases with SQL Database can be complex if you need to scale your database design or if you're looking to develop a high-performance system. This chapter introduced you to the design and implementation of a shard library that gives you the necessary building blocks to experiment with a flexible and scalable architecture.

You saw how to use caching in a data access layer and how parallel processing of SQL statements can increase performance of your applications. You also explored more advanced topics, such as referential integrity and exception management. This chapter provides you with the necessary background to create your own shard and create high-performing applications against SQL Database.

Federations

One of the major tenets of any cloud computing platform is elasticity, allowing systems to scale beyond certain limits of their current designs. With Federations, SQL Database delivers on that promise; it is a technology your SQL Database instances can use to scale over time based on size or performance bottlenecks.

You may have certain expectations about how this technology should work, one of which is likely to be transparency to your applications. You may expect that no code changes should be necessary to your existing applications if you were to use Federations. Like anything else, radical features like Federations come with certain compromises. Considering that this is the first incarnation of Microsoft's answer to scaling out the database tier, you will need to account for certain limitations before you can reap the benefits. This chapter will help you understand what problems Federations answer and how to best leverage this feature.

Introducing Federations

Until now, the only practical way developers and administrators could improve the performance and scalability of a database that needs both read and write access, without introducing significant code changes, was to add more memory, more CPU, or more disks on the same server. This is referred to as "scaling up." The Federation feature was introduced on the SQL Database platform with the intent of solving the scalability issues of traditional database servers; it provides a way to "scale out" a database by adding more servers to your database.

Federations versus Sharding

In the database world, sharding is a general term describing the distribution of highly related data across multiple physical machines. As a result, sharding is the implementation of a scale-out architecture used by large databases in order to harness the computing power of multiple machines. Federations are SQL Database's implementation of the sharding concept. To explain where Federation fits in the big picture, I'll outline the various scaling models available. The scaling models described below are architected around the concept of a *data domain*, which is the primary unit of data segregation used in a shard. For example, in most commercial applications the data domain is the customer. In astronomy the data domain could be a galaxy, or a planet. In finance, it could be the fiscal year.

- **Scale Up**. As described previously, scale-up architecture involves adding more resources to a machine holding data. The fundamental issue with scale-up architecture is that at some point adding more resources on a server doesn't yield better performance, because the application is not designed to account for all the available resources, and the law of diminishing returns applies. All the data domain instances are stored in the same database, and every query needs to include the data domain it is using (such as a WHERE clause when searching for a specific customer ID). This is the architecture used by most systems.

- **Linear Shard**. In a linear shard architecture, the application is designed to split every data domain instance into its own database. So in the case of a customer-driven data domain, each customer has its own database. In this model, queries do not need to filter on the data domain, since the connection string already points the query to the correct customer data. The major drawback of this approach is that administrators are managing as many databases as there are customers. In SQL Database, this can also mean additional operating expenses.

- **Compressed Shard**. A compressed shard is similar to a linear shard in the sense that data domain instances are isolated. However, the isolation is performed by schema containers in the database, instead of the database itself. In this model, each data domain is a database schema, and multiple databases could be used to store the schemas. Typically this model reduces the number of physical databases used and could reduce some operating expenses as a result.

- **Federation**. A federation is a form of shard compression. At first the data is stored in a single database (scale up); however, administrators can split the data into two or more databases (compressed shard) in which each database contains a collection of data domain instances. One could in theory achieve a linear shard with Federations by splitting each data domain instance into its own database, although in practice this would probably not be practical. As a result, Federation is a sharding architecture allowing administrators to implement degrees of compression based on actual usage patterns of their database and achieve an optimum cost/benefit implementation. As you will see later, Federations are also more flexible because an administrator can implement multiple data domains, which is not possible with the other models. In summary, a federated database can implement one or more data domains, each of which is its own shard with its own compression.

Why Use Federations?

Let's start by understanding why some applications are designed (or redesigned) to use Federations. As hinted previously, Federations solve two common problems: storage space in SQL Database and performance over time.

As you know, SQL Database is limited in size to 150GB of data. What do you do if your database grows beyond this space limitation? Your choices are simple: truncate some of the data (or archive old records) or use Federations. Because Federations allows you to split tables across multiple databases, you could spread your data across multiple 150GB databases, giving you terabytes of storage capacity in SQL Database. For example, your database may have a table called PurchaseHistory with hundreds of millions of records in it and representing 90% of all storage needs. You could federate this table across multiple servers, and leave all the other tables unchanged. If your PurchaseHistory table were to grow to 1TB in size, you would need seven SQL Database instances of 150GB each to store that table (called federation members), plus the original database containing all the other tables (called the root database). A great feature of Federations is that you can add more databases over time as your storage needs increase. So if your table grows to 1.1TB, just add another 150GB database.

Another important driver for adoption of Federations is database performance. When the number of users grows in your application, the database workload typically increases. There are more records to process over time, and because you have more users, the database will typically experience an increase in requests. At some point, the workload increases so much that your application may experience slowdowns, and even throttling from SQL Database. Federations can help you achieve higher performance, in certain cases, because instead of processing all the requests in a single database, you are essentially distributing certain requests to multiple databases, each with its own allocation of CPU, memory, I/O, and TempDB. In other words, Federations increase your computational resources naturally because your data is stored on servers that share virtually nothing in common.

Federations Overview

Let's dive a little deeper into Federations and explore how this technology works. The first thing you need to do is learn the terminology that describes the components of Federations.

- **Federation Root**. The federation root is the SQL Database instance from which all federations are created. It is the original database you created. This database will hold the tables that are not federated, which could be your configuration tables, or other tables that do not need to be federated.

- **Federation.** A federation is a logical group of tables that share a common subset of data: the data domain. For example, your database may be storing customer records, purchase history records, addresses, customer leads, and so on. Each one of these data sets could be a candidate for federation. A federation is created in the federation root.

- **Federation Member**. A federation member is a physical database holding all or some of the records of a federation. A federation has one or more federation members. For example, if you created a PurchaseHistory federation, you may have your purchase history records stored across two databases; these two databases would be called federation members. Your first federation members will be the same size as your root database initially, or the size of the federation member being split during a SPLIT operation. The size of a federation member can be changed on an individual basis. Although you can enforce referential integrity between tables within a federation member, you cannot enforce referential integrity outside of a federation member.

- **Federation Key**. The federation key is the data domain of a federation used to partition your data; for example, it could be the customer ID. Each federation has a federation key, and each federation member holds a set of values of the key. For example, all customer IDs less than 500 are stored by the first federation member, and customer IDs greater than or equal to 500 in another one. The federation key is used to split records across different databases. The federation key has special requirements: it can only be an int, bigint, uniqueidentifier, or a varbinary(n).

- **Atomic Unit**. An atomic unit (AU) represents a data domain instance (the value of a federation key). For example, if your federation key is customerId, each set of records for a given customer ID is an AU. When you issue database requests, you can specify to execute the statement across the entire federation member, or limit the scope of the statement to a given AU (for example, customerId=10), which automatically filters the records to a single customer.

- **Reference Table**. Although a federation contains tables that are split across multiple federation members, it can also contain tables that are used as reference tables. These tables are stored in federation members, but they are not federated. Reference tables are not maintained automatically across federation members. Developers are responsible for making sure these tables are kept in sync across federation members.

Let's walk through an example of how you would create your first federation. Figure 10-1 shows the process taking place when you create your first federation.

209

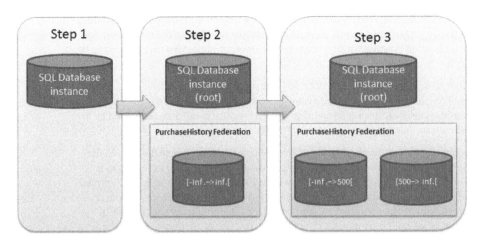

Figure 10-1. *Process to create the first federation*

In Step 1, you create a database using the regular CREATE DATABASE statement from the master database in SQL Database:

```
// Create a 1GB database. This will become our root database shortly.
// Make sure you connect to master before running this statement.
CREATE DATABASE EnzoLog2
```

In Step 2, you create your first federation. Let's call this federation PurchaseHistory and pick a BigInt for the partition key, which will be partitioned on purchaseId. Connect to your new database and run the CREATE FEDERATION statement as follows:

```
// Connect to your new database before running this statement
CREATE FEDERATION PurchaseHistory (purchaseId BigInt RANGE)
```

■ **Note**   Keep in mind that you will be charged for every new federation member you create, in addition to the root database.

The CREATE FEDERATION statement creates another database; it is your first federation member. Federation members have random database names. The only way to connect to the federation is to issue the USE command. Now that we have our first federation member, we need to build the schema (tables, stored procedures, and so on) of the federation. This is important because the schema of this federation member will be used when we create additional federation members.

If you are trying to federate an existing table, you will need to treat this operation as a data migration effort; indeed you cannot simply federate a table that already exists in the root database. You would first need to create the federation member, the table itself, and then use another tool (like SQL Server Integration Services) to migrate the data from the root database to the federation member. At that point, you can start splitting the table located in the federation member.

So let's connect to the first federation member and create a Purchase table. Notice that the USE FEDERATION command requires a value for the federation key; it uses this value as a hint to find the correct federation member. Because this is our first federation member, you can use any value for purchaseId; all possible values for purchaseId currently point to the same federation member.

```
// Connect to the federation member
// FILTERING=OFF means that we are working with all the atomic units in
// this federation member
USE FEDERATION PurchaseHistory (purchaseId = 0) WITH FILTERING=OFF, RESET

// Create a federated table on the purchaseId federation key
CREATE TABLE Purchases (
  pid bigint NOT NULL primary key, -- unique identifier for this record
  amount decimal(10, 2) NOT NULL,  -- the amount of the purchase
  storeId int NOT NULL             -- the store where the purchase was made
  )
  FEDERATED ON (purchaseId = pid)
```

Let's create additional objects in this federation member. First let's create a reference table, which contains the list of stores, and a stored procedure that returns the total sales amount for a given store:

```
// Create a reference table called StoreLocations
CREATE TABLE StoreLocations (
  storeId int NOT NULL primary key,
  storeName nvarchar(20) NOT NULL,
  zipCode nvarchar(10) NOT NULL
  )
```

Let's also add a stored procedure and a foreign key reference:

```
// Create a stored procedure that returns purchases made in a zip code
CREATE PROC GetPurchasesByZipCode(@zipCode nvarchar(10))
AS
SELECT * FROM Purchases P JOIN StoreLocations S
  ON P.storeId = S.storeId
WHERE S.zipCode = @zipCode

// Let's add the foreign key now.
ALTER TABLE Purchases
  ADD CONSTRAINT fk_storeId
  FOREIGN KEY (storeId) REFERENCES StoreLocations (storeId)
```

Last, but not least, let's add a few records in our tables. You will see how the split operation will redistribute our records shortly.

```
INSERT INTO StoreLocations VALUES (1, 'Boca Raton', '33498' )
INSERT INTO StoreLocations VALUES (2, 'Orlando', '32801' )

INSERT INTO Purchases VALUES (100, 25.0, 1)
INSERT INTO Purchases VALUES (200, 75.0, 2)
INSERT INTO Purchases VALUES (300, 50.0, 1)
INSERT INTO Purchases VALUES (500, 100.0, 2)
INSERT INTO Purchases VALUES (600, 12.0, 1)
```

At this point, the PurchaseHistory is a shard with a single database in it (a scale-up shard in some ways). Federations allow you to manage the degree of compression by splitting shards further. Imagine that we need to split our records so that the Purchases table is split over two databases, as illustrated in Step 3 of Figure 10-1. You split the federation by connecting to the ROOT database and using the ALTER FEDERATION command as shown here:

```
// Connect to the root database
USE FEDERATION ROOT WITH RESET

// Alter the federation to issue the split command
ALTER FEDERATION PurchaseHistory SPLIT AT (purchaseId = 500)
```

The ALTER FEDERATION statement takes place asynchronously and is an online operation. While the split is taking place you can access your federation members normally. Once the split is completed your federation will contain two federation members and will be transactionally consistent. Because the split creates two new federation members, copies all the objects and records, and drops the original federation member, your application may experience a connection drop at the end of the split operation. If this is the case you simply need to reconnect. To obtain the status of any operation performed on the federation, check out the dm_federation_operations view in the root database. If no records are returned, the split operation you started earlier is completed:

```
// Query the status of the split operation
SELECT * FROM sys.dm_federation_operations
```

The split operation copied all the objects from the original federation member, including the stored procedure, the reference table and its data, and the foreign key.

Let's take a look at our data in both federation members, one at a time.

```
// Connect to the first federation member
USE FEDERATION PurchaseHistory (purchaseId = 0) WITH FILTERING=OFF, RESET

// Get some data; three records will come back
SELECT * FROM Purchases P JOIN StoreLocations S ON P.storeId = S.storeId

// Now let's connect to the second federation member
USE FEDERATION PurchaseHistory (purchaseId = 500) WITH FILTERING=OFF, RESET

// Get some data; two records will come back
SELECT * FROM Purchases P JOIN StoreLocations S ON P.storeId = S.storeId

// You can also execute the stored procedure
EXEC GetPurchasesByZipCode '33498'
```

Now that we have two federation members, you may need to update a record. But which federation contains your record? Your application does not need to know about the low-level implementation details. It just needs to know the value of the atomic unit you want to update. Let's update purchaseId=100 to another amount:

```
// Connect to the federation member containing purchaseId=100
USE FEDERATION PurchaseHistory (purchaseId = 100) WITH FILTERING=OFF, RESET

// Get some data; three records will come back
UPDATE Purchases SET amount = 17.25 WHERE pid = 100
```

The WHERE clause used here may give you the impression that you are dealing with scale-up architecture, since it is the only scalability model requiring such a clause. That's because we specified the connection with FILTERING=OFF, which allows the query to access all the atomic units in the current federation member. Alternatively, you can tell SQL

Database that you want to work with a specific atomic unit, giving you the impression you have no other record than the one you want to change. The following statements are the preferred approach to update your records. Note the use of FILTERING=ON.

```
// Connect to the first federation member
// FILTERING=ON is optional; it is the default setting.
USE FEDERATION PurchaseHistory (purchaseId = 100) WITH FILTERING=ON, RESET

// Get some data; three records will come back
UPDATE Purchases SET amount = 17.25
```

You can apply the same logic to add or delete records in the federation member. If you want to delete multiple atomic units you need to use the FILTERING=OFF option so that your statement can affect multiple records. Also, the INSERT statement will fail if you are trying to insert an atomic unit for which the key falls outside of the current federation member partition key range.

Creating More Federations

So far we have created a single federation and split the records in two in order to create two federation members. However, the federation we created only makes sense for historical purchases because its partition key is on purchaseId. As discussed in the introduction to this chapter, one of the major benefits of Federations is the ability to define multiple data domains and manage the compression of each domain separately. What if we also have a large table that tracks customer visits?

No problem! We can create as many federations as we need and place a collection of tables inside them. Let's create another federation called CustomerVisits:

```
// Connect back to the root database
USE FEDERATION ROOT WITH RESET

// Create a new federation
CREATE FEDERATION CustomerVisits (visitId BigInt RANGE)

// Connect to our first federation member
USE FEDERATION CustomerVisits (visitId=0) WITH FILTERING=OFF, RESET

// And let's create a table with a few records
CREATE TABLE CustomerVisits (
  vId bigint NOT NULL PRIMARY KEY,
  dateOfVisit dateTime NOT NULL,
  storeId int NOT NULL)
FEDERATED ON (visitId = vid)

INSERT INTO CustomerVisits VALUES (1, getdate(), 1)
INSERT INTO CustomerVisits VALUES (2, getdate(), 2)
INSERT INTO CustomerVisits VALUES (3, getdate(), 2)
INSERT INTO CustomerVisits VALUES (4, getdate(), 1)
INSERT INTO CustomerVisits VALUES (5, getdate(), 1)
```

We now have two federations and three federation members in total, as shown in Figure 10-2.

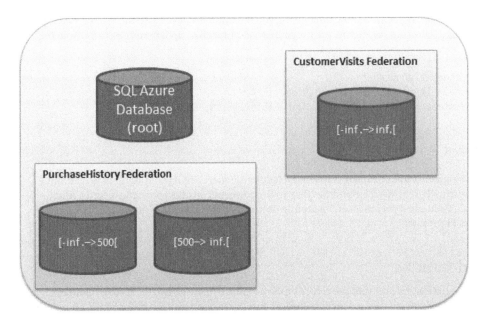

Figure 10-2. *Creating multiple federations*

■ **Note**   So far you have created federation keys with a BigInt value. However, you cannot use an IDENTITY column on a federated table, so your application will need to generate the next primary key value for your federated tables. Although the use of a UniqueIdentifier is a bit more cumbersome, it is popular because no logic needs to be maintained to create the next identifier.

Managing Federations

So far you have seen how to create federations, split federation members, and add records to federated tables. You may wonder what tools exist to view your federations and their members, and how to tell whether your federations are ready for a split.

To manage your federations, turn to the SQL Database Management Portal. You access this portal by first logging into your usual Windows Azure Management Portal (http://manage.windowsazure.com). Find your newly created database under SQL Database and click the Manage button at the bottom of the screen as seen in Figure 10-3.

Figure 10-3. *Managing your SQL Database instance*

Clicking on the Manage icon brings up another window, asking you to log in to the database server you selected. On that screen you can also specify the name of your database (EnzoLog2 in my example). Once logged in, you are in the SQL Database Management Portal, as shown in Figure 10-4.

Figure 10-4. *Viewing the properties of your database*

You will notice that your federations are showing up on the right; both CustomerVisits and PurchaseHistory can be seen in Figure 10-4. Let's click on PurchaseHistory. The Drop Federation button right underneath it becomes enabled, allowing you to drop the entire federation with a single click. Dropping a federation will drop all the federation members. From this screen you can also create a new federation by clicking the New button on top, or you can also view the performance of your queries by clicking Query Performance. Note, however, that the performance information shown will only apply to the root database because that's what we are looking at right now.

To view the details of a federation, click the arrow to its right. If you click to view the details of PurchaseHistory, for example, the screen will look like Figure 10-5. You can browse on top of each federation member, or click on them to see a window showing additional options. For example, you can resize individual federation members from this screen easily by clicking on Resize and specifying a target size. You can also perform a split operation from this screen easily by selecting Split and providing a value for the federation key at which the federation member will be split.

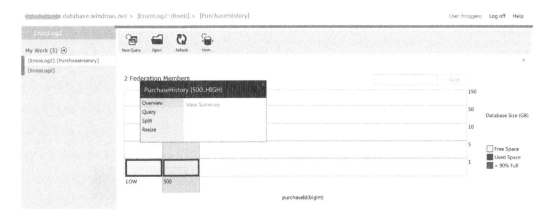

Figure 10-5. *Viewing a federation and its federation members*

Advanced Considerations

As you can see from the previous examples, Federations offer an important scalability model for cloud applications that need to scale beyond the capabilities of a single SQL Database instance. There are, however, certain challenges and considerations that are worth discussing before you decide to adopt this feature.

Limitations

Let's review some of the most important limitations you should be aware of before adopting Federations.

- **No Merging.** You may have noticed the lack of merging capability. Once you split a federation member, you cannot merge it back in the current version of SQL Database. Although this is a shortcoming, future versions of Federations will likely support this capability.

- **Independent Schemas.** As hinted previously, once a federation member has been created, its schema definition is independent from all the others in the same federation. In our previous example, you could connect to one of the federation members and drop a table, or add a column, or even change a stored procedure. Because there are no safeguards at this time, it is relatively easy to have federation members that have slightly different schemas. This could have some implications in your code, for example. So if you make an update to the schema of a federation member, remember to make the same changes to all the other federation members.

- **Limited Tool Support.** For the time being, most tools available on the market do not support federated databases, including some of the tools provided by Microsoft. Although this is very likely to change over time, you cannot use Data Sync services, Azure Reporting Services, or the database COPY operation with a federated member.

- **No Fan-Out.** Another important limitation is the lack of support for cross-federation member queries. In other words, you cannot issue a request that will span, or fan-out, multiple federation members, let alone multiple federations. If you want to obtain the total sum of your sales, you would normally run this simple statement:

  ```
  SELECT SUM(amount) FROM purchases
  ```

- Because this statement cannot be executed against multiple federation members by SQL Database, you will need to run this query on every federation member, and perform the final sum operation in your code.

■ **Note**   Executing the same query across multiple databases is called a fan-out operation. Fan-out operations are not hard to implement in your code, although you should execute fan-out queries using multiple threads to improve the performance of your fetch operation.

There are many more limitations that apply to Federations that may impact your design or your ability to adopt Federations, such as no support for indexed views, lack of support for the timestamp and rowversion data types, and more.

■ **Note**   If you are planning to use Federations for your application, you should spend some time reviewing all the documented limitations on MSDN. Search for Federation Guidelines and Limitations using Bing.

Sharding Library

Some of the limitations discussed previously related to fan-out queries can be resolved by coding the logic yourself, or by using open source libraries that have solved this problem for you.

Of importance is that you can use the Enzo Sharding library discussed in previous chapters. The latest release supports Federations and allows you to execute statements across multiple federation members easily, using multithreaded operations for faster results. You can use the built-in fan-out operation of the library to perform schema changes across your databases, return a single result set, or execute simple aggregations across federation members.

With the latest library you can execute a distributed query, called D-SQL, using a syntax that extends T-SQL. The library detects the syntax automatically and executes the inner query across the federation members specified. Because this is a .NET library, you cannot use this command structure outside of your code. Here is an example of a D-SQL query that fetches all the PurchaseHistory records, regardless of the number of federation members:

```
SELECT * USING (SELECT * FROM Purchases) FEDERATED ON (PurchaseHistory)
```

The inner statement is the query being executed across the PurchaseHistory federation; a single data set is returned to the calling code. Here are a few other variations of D-SQL that perform other requests:

```
// finds the maximum amount across all federation members
SELECT MAX(amount) USING (SELECT MAX(amount) FROM Purchases)
  FEDERATED ON (PurchaseHistory)

// finds the sum of all sales for zipcode 33498
SELECT SUM(amount) USING (SELECT SUM(amount) FROM Purchases P
```

```
INNER JOIN StoreLocations S ON P.storeid = S.storeid
WHERE S.zipcode = '33498' )
FEDERATED ON (PurchaseHistory)

// Executes a stored procedure across all federation members and returns all the records
SELECT * USING (EXEC GetPurchasesByZipCode '33498' ) FEDERATED ON (PurchaseHistory)

// Performs a JOIN across the same federation to exclude certain records
SELECT * USING (SELECT * FROM CustomerVisits) FEDERATED ON (CustomerVisits)
WHERE storeid IN (SELECT DISTINCT storeid FROM Purchases WHERE amount >= 100)
FEDERATED ON (PurchaseHistory)
```

The library offers additional features, like caching, sorting, and filtering records based on atomic unit values. Because it's an open source project, you are welcome to dissect the code and implement your own version of the library for your own needs.

■ **Note**   To learn more about the Enzo Sharding library, visit `http://enzosqlshard.codeplex.com`. You will be able to download the open-source library and a sample application to get you started.

Summary

SQL Database offers a unique feature, called Federations, that promises elasticity at the database layer, giving you the option to scale your database tier quickly and efficiently. While the first release of this feature has a few limitations it is clear that many developers will be compelled to evaluate this feature and possibly adopt it to address their scalability needs.

◼ ◼ ◼

Performance Tuning

Designing for high performance becomes more important with a database that runs in the cloud because development objectives tend to minimize roundtrips and the amount of data being returned. This chapter provides an overview of some of the most common tuning and troubleshooting techniques available in SQL Database. Keep in mind that performance tuning is a very complex topic; as a result, this chapter can introduce only selected techniques.

The techniques presented are similar to the ones available in SQL Server, although some of the tools aren't supported in SQL Database. Along the way, you will walk through a few examples of how to improve the performance of a SQL statement and the steps required to tune it.

What's Different with SQL Database

Before diving into the specifics, let's review some of the things you need to remember when tuning your Azure databases. Some of the techniques you may be using today are available, but others may not be.

Methods and Tools

Because a SQL Database runs on a hosted and shared infrastructure, it's important to understand which tuning methods are available and which aren't. Table 11-1 outlines some of the key methods traditionally used by developers and DBAs in tuning a database system. The term *system* is appropriate here because at times you need to tune the database server, and in other instances you need to tune the actual database code or even address database design issues.

Table 11-1. *Typical tuning methods and tools*

Method or Tool	Available?	Comments
SQL Profiler	No	Tools using server-side traces, such as most auditing tools, SQL Profiler, and the Database Engine Tuning Advisor, aren't supported.
Execution plan	Yes	SQL Server Management Studio (SSMS) can display actual execution plans against a SQL Database. You'll review this later in the chapter.
Perfmon	No	Any Windows monitoring tool that is typically used for performance tuning is unavailable.
DMVs	Limited	A few dynamic management views (DMVs) are available and provide insightful information about running sessions and statements previously executed.
Library metrics	Yes	ADO.NET provides library-level statistics that offer additional insight to developers, such as the total processing time from the consumer standpoint and bytes transferred.

The table lists some tuning methods and tools that you may be familiar with. It also indicates which are available for use with SQL Database. The unsupported tools listed in the table (such as SQL Profiler and Perfmon) are typically those that are—say, in a SQL Server environment—used by DBAs and system administrators.

Coding Implications

Because you have no access to the server-side configuration settings of SQL Database, such as disk configuration, memory allocation, CPU affinity, and so forth, you need to place more emphasis on the quality of your SQL statements—and, now more than ever, your network traffic. Indeed, the number of network roundtrips your code generates and the number of packets returned have an impact on performance because the connection to SQL Database is a far link (meaning that it's far away) when connecting directly with client applications, and the communication is encrypted.

Your performance-tuning exercise should include the following areas:

- **Connection pooling.** Because establishing a new connection requires multiple network roundtrips by itself and can affect your application's performance, you should ensure that your connections are pooled properly by using a service layer when possible and a service account so that your connection string doesn't change. In addition, SQL Database will throttle you if you establish too many connections. This behavior is controlled by the denial of service (DoS) feature briefly discussed in Chapter 3.

- **Packet count.** Because the time spent to return data is greater than you may be used to, you need to pay attention to SQL code that generates too many packets. For example, Print statements generate more network traffic than necessary and should be removed from your T-SQL if at all possible.

- **Indexing.** You may remember from Chapter 2 that SQL Database may throttle your connection if it detects that your statement is consuming too many resources. As a result, proper indexing becomes critical when tuning for performance.

- **Database design.** Of course, certain database designs are better than others for performance. A heavily normalized design improves data quality, but a loosely normalized database typically improves performance. Understanding this tradeoff is also important when you're developing against SQL Database.

- **Parallel Data Access.** If your code accesses multiple databases, in a shard environment, for example, you may need to introduce multithreading to your code or tune your current parallelism approach to avoid unnecessary locks.

Tuning Techniques

Let's dive into the specifics of performance tuning, keeping in mind what you've learned so far. This section starts by looking at database tuning capabilities and then moves up the stack, all the way to the client library making the actual SQL call.

Dynamic Management Views

SQL Database provides a few handy system views called dynamic management views (DMVs) that are also available in SQL Server. SQL Database exposes a subset of the DMVs, but all those related to query execution are available. SQL Database supports the DMVs listed in Table 11-2.

Table 11-2. *Dynamic management views used for performance tuning*

DMV	Comments
sys.dm_exec_connections	Partially supported. Returns the list of connections established in SQL Database. Note that some of the interesting columns, such as client_net_address (returning the client machine's MAC address), aren't available.
sys.dm_exec_query_plan	Fully supported. Returns the XML execution plan of a SQL query or a batch.
sys.dm_exec_query_stats	Fully supported. Returns aggregate performance information for cached query plans.
sys.dm_exec_requests	Fully supported. Returns information about the statements being executed by SQL Database.
sys.dm_exec_sessions	Partially supported. Returns the current session opened along with performance information about that session. However, it doesn't return last-login information, such as the last_successful_logon column.
sys.dm_exec_sql_text	Fully supported. Returns the text of a SQL batch.
sys.dm_exec_text_query_plan	Fully supported. Returns the execution plan in text format for a SQL query or batch.

■ **Note** Although queries against some of these views can run when you're connected to the master database, they don't return the information you're looking for unless you connect to the database that your application is running against. Also, a user must have VIEW DATABASE STATE permission to see all executing sessions on the database; otherwise, the user sees only the current session.

If you're looking for performance metrics for a SQL statement and you can isolate the statement to a unique database connection, or the statement is no longer executing, the dm_exec_sessions DMV is for you. This is one of the system views that provides performance metrics such as CPU time and duration. However, this DMV accumulates the performance metrics over all the statements executed through the same connection. So, in order to test a database query and retrieve performance metrics of that query alone, you need to establish two connections: one to execute the query, and another to read the performance metrics so as not to interfere with the performance data that SQL Database has collected.

■ **Note** You need to establish two connections using the same login name, or you can't retrieve the performance metrics of the SQL statement you're trying to tune.

For example, establish a connection to SQL Database, and run the following SQL query:

```
SELECT TOP 50 * FROM sys.indexes
```

Note your session ID; it's found on the status bar in Microsoft SQL Server Management Studio. You can also find it on the Query tab, in parentheses. For example, in Figure 11-1, the session ID is 144: you can see it both on the selected tab and in the status bar at the bottom.

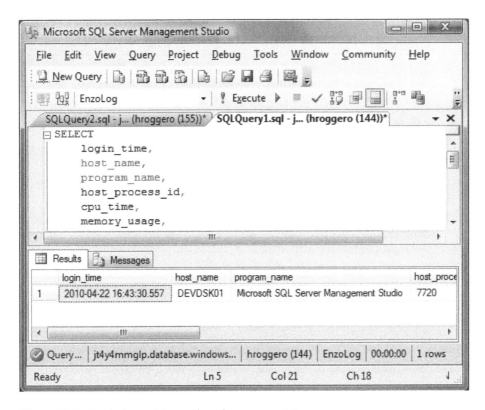

Figure 11-1. *Capturing a statement's performance metrics*

Next, open another query window, which opens a new connection in SQL Database. Run the following query (see Figure 11-1), and make sure to specify the session ID being investigated:

```
SELECT
    login_time,
    host_name,
    program_name,
    host_process_id,
    cpu_time,
    memory_usage,
    total_elapsed_time,
    reads,
    writes,
    logical_reads,
    row_count,
    original_login_name
FROM sys.dm_exec_sessions
WHERE session_id = 176          // replace with your session_id
```

This statement returns important performance metrics for your previous SQL statement, as explained in Table 11-3.

Table 11-3. *Selected columns from* `sys.dm_exec_sessions`

Metric	Value	Comment
login_time	2010-04-22 16:43:30.557	The login time of the session. Note that sessions can be reused over time, through connection pooling. This time represents the last successful login.
host_name	DEVDSK01	The machine name that made the connection to SQL Database.
program_name	SSMS	The application name that is executing the statement on the client workstation.
host_process_id	7720	The Windows Process ID (PID) that is executing the statement on the client workstation. You can view the PID of your applications in Task Manager in Windows.
cpu_time	15	The CPU time, in milliseconds, consumed by the SQL statements since the connection was established.
memory_usage	2	Number of 8KB bytes consumed by the connection so far.
total_elapsed_time	32	The duration of the statement in milliseconds. This includes the time to execute the statement and the time it takes to return the data to the client machine.
reads	1	Number of physical reads.
writes	1	Number of physical writes.
logical_reads	322	Number of logical reads.
row_count	50	Number of rows returned.
original_login_name	MyTestLogin	The login name of the user who successfully connected.

At this point, you need to be aware of a point that is very important for performance tuning. The `cpu_time` is perhaps the best metric you can use to determine how long a statement takes to execute in SQL Database. The `total_elapsed_time` can be misleading. Elapsed time represents the time it takes for SQL Database (or SQL Server) to fetch the data and return all the data to the client. So, if your client is slow at displaying data, SQL Database slows down to match the speed of the client; the slowdown is a function of TCP (Transmission Control Protocol) programming and has nothing to do with SQL Database. As a result, `total_elapsed_time` shows the entire time it takes to execute the statement and the client time necessary to finish fetching the data. The `total_elapsed_time` is the same as the Duration measure returned by SQL Profiler; note that if you are sending a batch with multiple requests, the `total_elapsed_time` is the summation of all individual execution times.

Connection Pooling

Earlier, this chapter mentioned that connection pooling is an important consideration for performance. Although this statement is generally accurate in the world of database programming, it becomes critical for SQL Database. A poorly designed application may create too many connection requests, which can end up flooding SQL Database. If too many connection requests are established, your connections may be *throttled*, meaning that you can no longer connect for a period of time.

You should know that connection pooling is affected if any part of the connection string is changed (even slightly), such as the application name or the login ID (UID). A new connection pool is created even if you change the order of the parameters of a connection string. For example, if you have an application that performs three database operations, and the operations use the following connection strings, respectively, three pools are created, and hence three distinct database connections are established in SQL Database on the same database:

```
Server=XYZ;Initial Catalog=DB1;UID=hroggero;PWD=123456
Server=XYZ;Initial Catalog=DB1;PWD=123456;UID=hroggero
Server=XYZ;Initial Catalog=DB1;UID=hroggero;PWD=123456;Application Name=MyApp
```

To ensure that the same database connection is used, you must ensure that the three operations use the exact same connection string:

```
Server=XYZ;Initial Catalog=DB1;UID=hroggero;PWD=123456
Server=XYZ;Initial Catalog=DB1;UID=hroggero;PWD=123456
Server=XYZ;Initial Catalog=DB1;UID=hroggero;PWD=123456
```

To measure the number of database connections open on a given database, you can use the sys.dm_exec_connections management view. A row is returned for each distinct database connection; the fewer rows, the better!

Execution Plans with SSMS

Sometimes you need to dig deeper and understand how SQL Database fetches data, and then use that information to improve performance. In SQL Server, you can also use execution plans to observe the impact of changes to the underlying hardware, such as changing memory configuration. Although you have no control over configuration settings with SQL Database, execution plans can still be very useful to see the impact of your indexes and to view which physical operators are being used.

Whereas logical operators are used in a SQL statement, such as LEFT JOIN, *physical operators* tell you which technique SQL Database is using to solve a given logical operation or to fetch additional data. The most common physical operators SQL Database uses to represent JOIN operations are listed in Table 11-4.

Table 11-4. *Physical* JOIN *operators*

Operator	SSMS Symbol	Comment
Nested loop		A loop is performed in SQL Database to retrieve data. For each record in Table 1 matching the WHERE clause, find the matching records in Table 2. On large recordsets, loops can be costly.
Hash match		A hash is calculated for each record in each table participating in a JOIN, and the hashes are compared for equality.
Merge		Merge operators are usually the fastest operators because they perform a single pass of the tables involved by taking advantage of the order in which the data is stored or retrieved.

You can give SQL Database certain hints to use a specific physical operator, but using them isn't generally recommended. You have three proper ways to influence SQL Database to select an effective physical operator:

- **Review your WHERE clause.** This is perhaps the most overlooked aspect of performance tuning. When you have the choice, applying the WHERE clause on the tables that have the most rows gives you new opportunities for indexing.

- **Optimize your database design.** Highly normalized databases force you to create more JOIN statements. And of course, the more JOIN statements, the more tuning you need to do. While you shouldn't necessarily plan to have tables at first normal form, denormalizing certain tables can offer performance benefits.

- **Create better indexes.** Having a good indexing strategy is important. The order of your columns and the number of columns can make a world of difference for SQL Database. This chapter reviews indexing shortly.

■ **Note**   To run the following examples, you need to execute the `tuning.sql` script available on the book's download page. It creates a few sample tables with test data. Make sure to select a user database when running this script.

To show which physical JOIN operators have been selected, execution plans provide insights into the volume of data being worked on and the relative cost of certain operations. For example, execute the following SQL statement (after running the `tuning.sql` script):

```
SELECT T.Name, T.UserType
FROM TestUsers T INNER JOIN TestUserType UT
   ON T.UserType = UT.UserType
WHERE T.AgeGroup > 0 AND UT.UserTypeKey = 'Manager'
```

This statement returns 25 rows. To view the execution plan, you need to request it before running the statement. Either press Ctrl + M or choose Query ➤ Include Actual Execution Plan from the menu in SQL Server Management Studio, and re-run the SQL statement. You should now see an Execution Plan tab. Click the tab to see output similar to that shown in Figure 11-2.

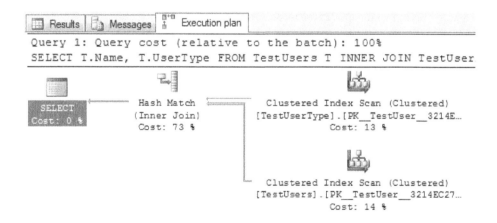

Figure 11-2. Sample execution plan, not tuned

In order to fully understand the previous execution plan, let's review additional symbols often seen in execution plans. Table 11-5 shows a few symbols provided by SSMS that have clear performance implications.

Table 11-5. *Lookup, index scan, and index seek operators*

Operator	SSMS Symbols	Comment
Lookup		Lookups can be costly when the statement returns thousands of rows and a lookup is needed for every row. If you determine that the lookup is costly, consider creating a covering index.
Index scan		An index or clustered index scan may or may not be a bad thing. *Scanning* means that SQL Database reads all the records sequentially in the index. Scanning isn't good for performance if you return a fraction of the records being scanned, in which case an index is needed. But if you want to return all the records from a table, a scan is necessary.
Index seek		An index or clustered index *seek* means the first record matching the query is found quickly, without scanning.

Execution plans can show many other symbols that have very specific meanings, including hints that a query is using multiple processors, and so on.

Because no indexes are defined on the underlying tables (outside of the required clustered index) and the execution plan in Figure 11-2 shows two clustered index scans (which are equivalent to table scans in this case), you have a potential performance problem. The INNER JOIN logical operator is executed with a hash match physical operator. You can see a thicker line coming into the hash match; hovering your cursor on this line shows you that 50 records are being consumed by the JOIN operation (see Figure 11-3). Also, you can see that a clustered index scan is being used to fetch data for both tables. Finally, note that the hash match operation consumes 73% of resources of the entire statement; this means it takes more time to JOIN the records than to read the data.

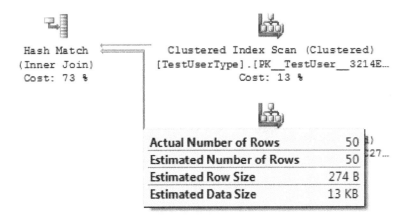

Figure 11-3. *Verifying how many records are being consumed by a JOIN operator*

In summary, the statement you've been working with has three potential issues:

- **Index scans.** An index scan is performed on both tables, likely causing more reads than necessary.

- **Heavy operator processing.** The hash match operation is consuming most of the processing time.

- **More reads than records returned.** As you can see from Figure 11-3, the statement is processing 50 records but returning only 25. This may be a hint that you're reading more records than necessary. However, this isn't always a problem in itself—just something to keep an eye on.

■ **Note** For those familiar with heap tables, SQL Database doesn't allow them. If you intend to insert records into a table, a clustered index must be defined on the table.

You'll see shortly how indexing can help you tune this statement. But before leaving the topic of execution plans, it's important to be familiar with a few more points:

- **Relative query cost.** Notice in Figure 11-2, shown earlier, that near the top of the window, a query cost is displayed. This is a relative measure compared to all the other statements being executed as a batch. In this example, the value is 100% because it's the only statement. You should know, however, that this value can be misleading. It's calculated dynamically by SQL Server Management Studio based on estimated costs, not actual costs. As a result, this value is rarely accurate.

- **Advanced calls.** Certain operations, such as XML calls and using functions in your SQL statements, are usually misrepresented in an execution plan; as such, SQL Database (and even SQL Server) may return 1% as a cost for those operations, when the actual cost can be much higher. This may lead you down the wrong path when tuning your SQL statements.

- **Discarding output.** As discussed previously, the duration (as measured by sys.dm_exec_sessions) includes display time, and that applies to SQL Server Management Studio. To minimize the time it takes to display the data, you can disable the output by checking the necessary settings in Query ➤ Query Options. The same option appears in two places: in the Grid Results and Text Results. Figure 11-4 shows how to disable the output from the Grid display.

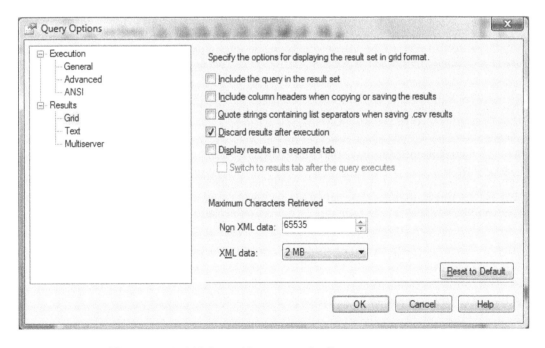

Figure 11-4. *Disabling output in SQL Server Management Studio*

Execution Plans with the Management Portal

You should also note that the SQL Database Management Portal allows you to view execution plans; however, the symbols representing the logical operations and the functionality provided are different.

For example, the display area changes depending on the zoom level, showing a simplified view when zooming out and allowing you to see problem areas very quickly. Figure 11-5 shows that the T-SQL statement consumes the most resources (total cost) on its Index Seek operation.

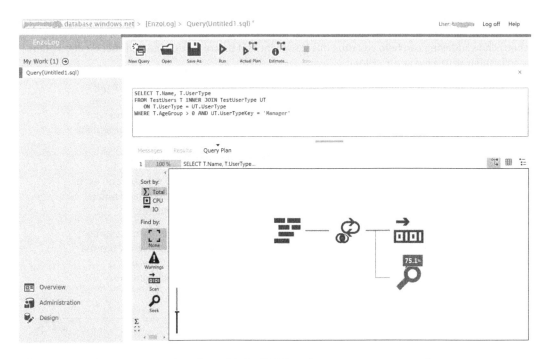

Figure 11-5. *Viewing an execution plan with the SQL Database management portal*

You probably realized that the Index Seek symbol is different from the one shown by SSMS. Although the symbols are very sleek and largely self-describing, you may find it a bit more difficult to tune certain T-SQL operations, because some of the symbols are simplified. For example the Non-Clustered Index Seek and the Clustered Index Seek operations are combined into a single symbol in the management portal. Nevertheless, if you zoom enough you will see a description of the operation under the symbol, clearly identifying which operation is being represented as will be seen in Figure 11-7.

Clicking on one of the symbols will give you additional details, as shown in Figure 11-6, similar to what you can see in SSMS. Clicking on the View More button will display extensive information about the operation. To close the detailed window, simply click in an empty area in the execution plan area.

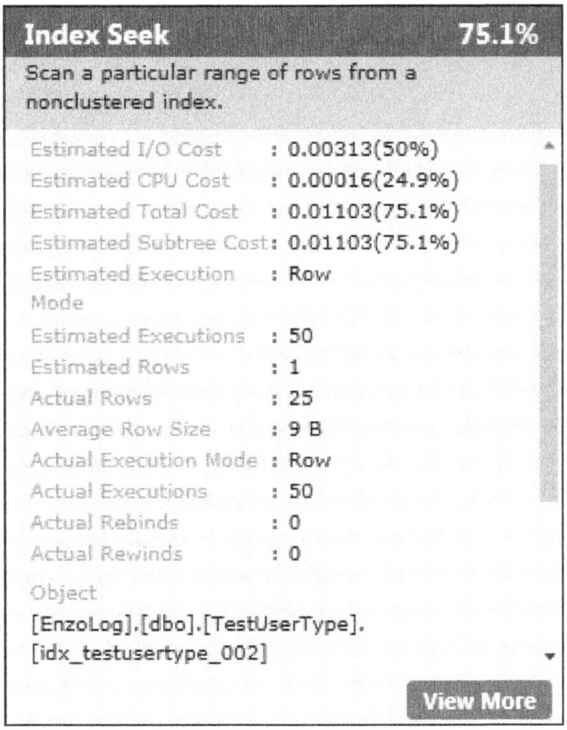

Figure 11-6. *Viewing operation details*

You will find that the management portal for SQL Database includes some interesting options, such as the ability to sort batch statements by total resource consumption, CPU, or I/O. You can also quickly locate certain operations, such as warnings and scans, by selecting the appropriate icon on the left side. And you can also switch the display of the execution plan to a simple list or a nested list by clicking on the top right icons without rerunning the T-SQL statement. Figure 11-7 shows the same execution plan as shown in Figure 11-5, sorted by CPU and zoomed in all the way; it shows that the Clustered Index Scan is the operation consuming the most CPU resources on the server.

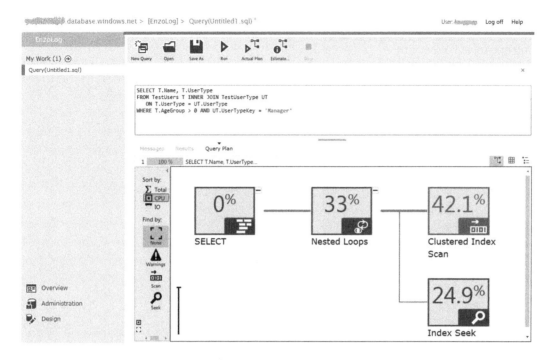

Figure 11-7. *Sorting the execution plan by CPU*

Query Performance with the Management Portal

Another handy screen available on the management portal is the Query Performance summary page. To access this page, simply click on the database and choose Query Performance. You will see a list of queries with a few important metrics such as CPU ms/sec, Duration ms/sec and more, as shown in Figure 11-8. You can sort the list by clicking on a column title.

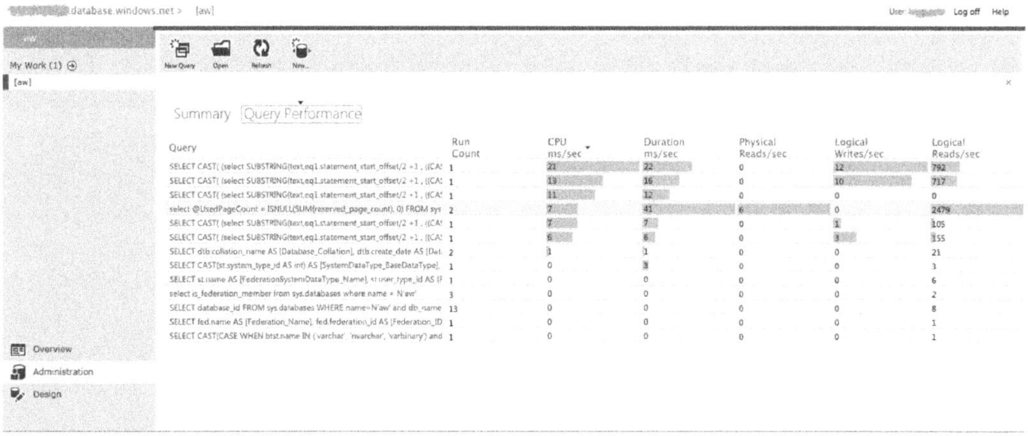

Figure 11-8. *Query Performance summary screen*

If you click on a query, another screen will appear with further details, as shown in Figure 11-9; these metrics come primarily from the sys.dm_exec_query_stats dynamic management view.

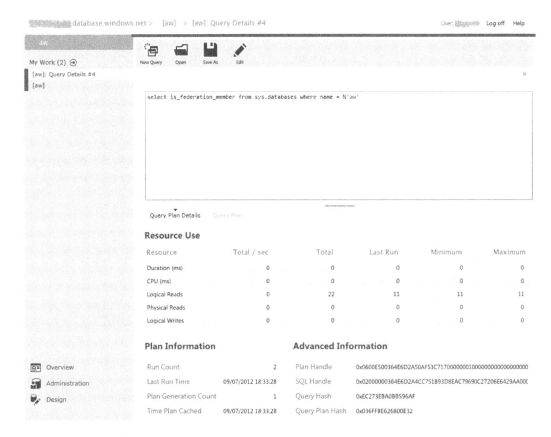

Figure 11-9. *Query Performance detail screen*

If you have used the sys.dm_exec_query_stats view before, you know that it contains important performance metrics but will not store this information for you; this view displays current information only. So make sure to check the Query Performance screens shortly (within a few minutes) after you experience a performance issue.

Indexing

Creating the right indexes can be complex; it can take a long time to fully understand indexing and fine-tune database queries. One of the most important things to remember with indexing is that its primary purpose is to help SQL Database find the data it needs quickly. Like SSMS, the SQL Database Management Portal offers hints when a missing index is detected. While these hints can be useful, it is still important to understand the logic behind indexing so that you can optimize the performance of your database.

Indexes are like smaller tables that contain a subset of the primary table. The tradeoff is that indexes consume space and must be maintained by the SQL Database engine as the primary data changes, which can impact performance under certain scenarios.

Let's quickly review a simplified syntax to create an index:

```
CREATE INDEX [index_name] ON [table_name]
   (col1, col2...)
   INCLUDE (col3, col4...)
```

Although creating an index is simple, it's important to verify that it's being used by SQL Database and that it has the desired effect. To continue the previous example (from Figure 11-2), you can create an index on the TestUsers table. But first, let's back up and review a few things about the table and the statement you wish to optimize.

It's important to realize that the columns included in the first part of the index are used as a key when searching for data in the index and when joining tables. And because it's acceptable to have multiple columns as part of the key, their order is absolutely critical! At times, you pick the columns that are included in the WHERE clause first and then those that are part of the JOIN. You may find, however, that sometimes it's best to start with the JOIN columns; this depends on your statement and the data at hand. You will need to try both approaches to determine which one works for you. Next come the columns in the INCLUDE section of the CREATE INDEX command; these columns are here for only one reason: they help avoid a lookup into the primary table for data that is needed by the SELECT clause. Performing lookups isn't always a performance issue, but it can become an issue if you have a lookup operation in a large batch of records.

■ **Note**   An index that contains all the columns needed to serve a query is called a *covering index*.

If you dissect the previous SELECT query, you obtain the columns in the following list (in order of placement in the index) that belong to the TestUsers table:

- WHERE. Contains the AgeGroup field from TestUsers.

- JOIN. Contains the UserType field from TestUsers.

- SELECT. Contains the Name and UserType fields. The UserType column is already part of the JOIN clause; there is no need to count it twice.

Let's begin by creating an index that looks like this:

```
CREATE INDEX idx_testusers_001 ON TestUsers
   (AgeGroup, UserType)
INCLUDE (Name)
```

Running the statement now yields the execution plan shown in Figure 11-10. This is a better plan than the one in Figure 11-2 because SQL Database is performing an index seek instead of an index scan. Using an index seek means SQL Database is able to locate the first record needed by the statement very quickly. However, you still have an index scan on the TestUserType table. Let's fix that.

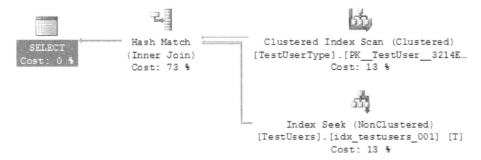

Figure 11-10. *Effect of adding an index on the TestUsers table*

To remove the index scan on TestUserType, you add another index following the previous guidelines. Because no columns are needed in the SELECT clause, you can leave the INCLUDE section alone. Here's the index:

```
CREATE INDEX idx_testusertype_001 ON TestUserType
(UserTypeKey, UserType)
```

■ **Note** Although it's minimal, there is a risk associated with adding new indexes in production systems. Certain routines, especially batch programs, typically depend on data being properly ordered to calculate running sums or carry out specific tasks. If an index is favored over another to run a query, it's possible for the new index to be used, which has the potential to change the order in which the data is returned. If all your statements include an ORDER BY clause , this problem won't affect you. But if some of your programs rely on the natural order of records, beware! Also, keep in mind that adding indexes can negatively impact performance by increasing overhead.

Your execution plan should now look like that in Figure 11-11. Notice that the physical operator has been changed to a loop. Also notice that the cost of the query has shifted away from the JOIN operator: the highest relative cost (76%) of the plan is spent reading the data from the TestUserType index.

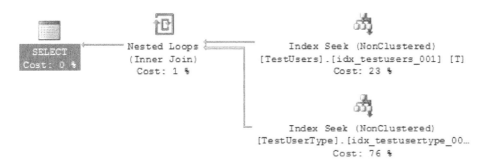

Figure 11-11. *Effect of indexing on the physical operators*

But the tuning exercise isn't over just yet. If you hover your cursor on the TestUserType_001 index, you see that the loop performed a lookup (index seek) on that index 50 times (look for Number of Executions in Figure 11-12)! This isn't great, but it's probably better than without the index, because SQL Database picked this new execution plan.

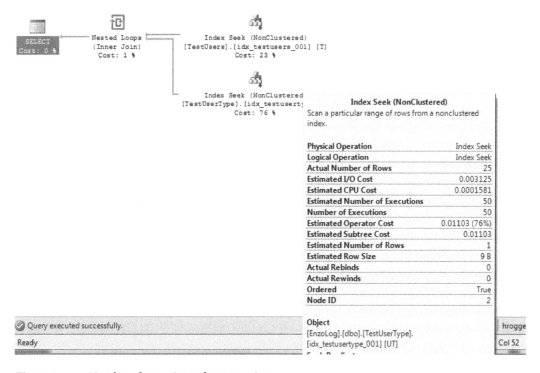

Figure 11-12. Number of executions of an operation

To reduce the number of lookups, you can change the order of the fields by creating a new index. Let's run this statement:

```
CREATE INDEX idx_testusers_002 ON TestUsers
    (UserType, AgeGroup) INCLUDE (Name)
```

■ **Note** Instead of creating a new index, you could change the one previously created. However, when troubleshooting database performance issues, it's important to see how the SQL Database query engine behaves; SQL Database chooses the index it deems the most effective. So go ahead—create as many indexes as you want until you have a good execution plan, and then clean up the unnecessary indexes when you're finished.

If you run the statement again, you see a result close to Figure 11-13. The execution plan is now well balanced. The data search is virtually equal on both tables (49%), with seek operations on both; the number of executions is 1 for both; and the cost of the loop operation is minimal (2%) because there is no real looping taking place.

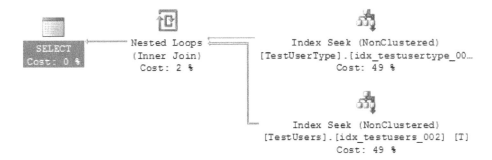

Figure 11-13. Well-balanced execution plan

If you pay attention to the Actual Number of Rows value, you see that this statement fetches only 25 records from the underlying table, instead of 50; this reduces disk reads over time.

Last but not least, if you were to look at the SELECT statement from a design standpoint, you could ask whether the UserTypeKey value should be unique. The table schema doesn't carry a unique index on that field, but should it? Can there be only one Manager user type? If the answer is yes, then you know the TestUserType table will always return a single record for a Manager user type, in which case you may be able to remove the JOIN entirely and apply the WHERE clause on the TestUsers table directly:

```
SELECT T.Name, T.UserType
    FROM TestUsers T
    WHERE T.AgeGroup > 0 AND T.UserType = 1
```

Not only is this statement much simpler, but the execution plan becomes trivial, meaning that SQL Database can serve this request without spending much time optimizing it. This change means you're moving the filter from a table with few records (only 3 in TestUserType) to a table with many records (100 in TestUsers). And whenever you have the option to make such a move, you should. SQL Database spends far fewer resources this way. Of course, such a move isn't always possible, but you need to know the importance of having a proper database design before you begin tuning.

■ **Note** Performance tuning can be fun. However, you may end up tuning forever if you don't set yourself performance objectives.

Indexed Views

Indexed views are an excellent alternative when you absolutely need to JOIN data, and traditional indexing doesn't yield the performance you're looking for. Indexed views behave like tables; the data covered is materialized to disk so it can be retrieved quickly. Before jumping on indexed views, understand that they have certain limitations and that due to their nature, you may incur a performance hit through the usual Insert, Delete, and Update statements. Taking the previous statement as an example, let's see how to create an indexed view to support the JOIN operation.

First, create a view that contains the statement you want to tune. Make sure you include all the columns you need in the SELECT clause:

```
CREATE VIEW vTestUsersType WITH SCHEMABINDING AS
    SELECT T.Name, T.UserType, T.AgeGroup, UT.UserTypeKey
    FROM dbo.TestUsers T INNER JOIN dbo.TestUserType UT ON
    T.UserType = UT.UserType
```

Next, create a unique clustered index on the view:

```
CREATE UNIQUE CLUSTERED INDEX IDX_VIEW_TestUsers
ON vTestUsersType
(UserTypeKey, AgeGroup, Name, UserType)
```

Et voilà. When you run the statement again, you see a beautiful execution plan like the one in Figure 11-14. Because the view contains all the necessary columns, and the clustered index contains all the columns of the view, you obtain the fastest possible data-retrieval technique, next to caching.

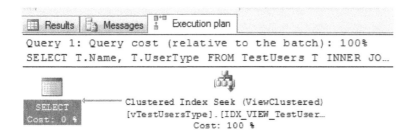

Figure 11-14. *Indexed view example*

Stored Procedures

You've seen various ways to tune your statements and improve execution plans. However, keep in mind that you also have stored procedures at your disposal.

Stored procedures can give you an edge if you need to execute logic that requires a large volume of data. Because you know that returning lots of data turns into a performance problem in SQL Database, you can place the business logic that needs the data in a stored procedure, and have the procedure return a status code. Because you aren't charged for CPU time, this becomes an affordable option.

Stored procedures can also be a security tool, allowing you to proxy the calls to underlying tables through a procedure and never allowing direct access to the tables.

Imagine that you need to calculate the cost of an item; however, in order to calculate the cost, you must loop to obtain certain values and perform advanced operations. You can make a call from your application and calculate the cost in the application code as follows:

```
float cost = 0.0;  // the total cost
int id = 15;       // the product category

string sql = "SELECT * FROM category WHERE catergoryId = " + id.ToString();
SqlConnection conn = new SqlConnection(connString);
SqlCommand cmd = new SqlCommand(sql, conn);
cmd.CommandType = CommandType.Text;
conn.Open();
SqlDataReader dr = cmd.ExecuteReader();

try
{
   while (dr.Read())
```

```
   {
       cost += 0.25 * ...; // calculation logic goes here
   }
}
finally
{
   dr.Close();
   conn.Close();
}
```

Or you can calculate the cost in a stored procedure and change the previous code to call the stored procedure instead:

```
float cost = 0.0;    // the total cost
int id = 15;         // the product category

string sql = "proc_CalculateCost";
SqlConnection conn = new SqlConnection(connString);
SqlCommand cmd = new SqlCommand(sql, conn);
cmd.Parameters.Add(new SqlParameter("categoryId", SqlDbType.Float);
cmd.Parameters[0].Value = id;
cmd.CommandType = CommandType.StoredProcedure;
conn.Open();
SqlDataReader dr = cmd.ExecuteReader();

try
{
   if (dr.Read())
       cost = (float)dr[0];
}
finally
{
   dr.Close();
   conn.Close();
}
```

The code for the stored procedure looks something like this:

```
CREATE PROC proc_CalculateCost
 @categoryId int
AS

DECLARE @i intDECLARE @cost float
SET @cost = 0.0

SET @i = (SELECT count(*) FROM category WHERE ID = @categoryId)
WHILE (@i > 0)
BEGIN
   SET @cost = @cost + 0.25*(SELECT Min(dollars) FROM ...)
   SET @i = @i - 1
END

SELECT @cost
```

The advantage of calling a stored procedure is that you don't need to fetch the necessary records across the Internet to calculate the cost figure. The stored procedure runs where the data is located and returns only a single value in this case.

Provider Statistics

Let's look at the ADO.NET library's performance metrics to obtain the library's point of view from a performance standpoint. The library doesn't return CPU metrics or any other SQL Database metric; however, it can provide additional insights when you're tuning applications, such as giving you the number of roundtrips performed to the database and the number of packets transferred.

As previously mentioned, the number of packets returned by a database call is becoming more important because it can affect the overall response time of your application. If you compare the number of packets returned by a SQL statement against a regular SQL Server installation to the number of packets returned when running the same statement against SQL Database, chances are that you see more packets returned against SQL Database because the data is encrypted using SSL. This may not be a big deal most of the time, but it can seriously affect your application's performance if you're returning large recordsets, or if each record contains large columns (such as a varbinary column storing a PDF document).

Taking the performance metrics of an ADO.NET library is fairly simple, but it requires coding. The methods to use on the SqlConnection object are ResetStatistics() and RetrieveStatistics(). Also, keep in mind that the EnableStatistics property needs to be set to true. Some of the most interesting metrics to look for are BuffersReceived and BytesReceived; they indicate how much network traffic has been generated.

You can also download from CodePlex an open source project called Enzo SQL Baseline that provides both SQL Database and provider statistics metrics (http://EnzoSQLBaseline.CodePlex.Com). This tool allows you to compare multiple executions side by side and review which run was the most efficient. Figure 11-15 shows that the latest execution returned 624 bytes over the network.

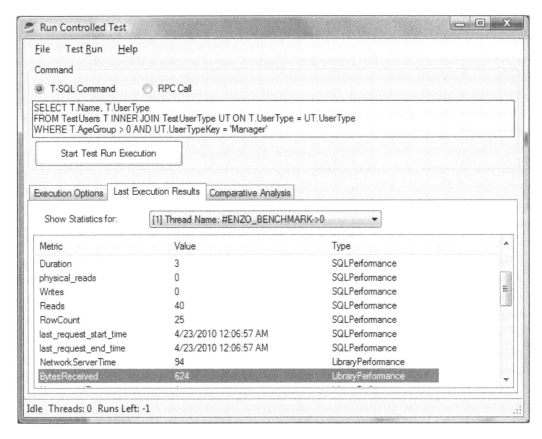

Figure 11-15. *Viewing performance metrics in Enzo SQL Baseline*

■ **Note**   If you'd like to see a code sample using the ADO.NET provider statistics, go to
http://msdn.microsoft.com/en-us/library/7h2ahss8.aspx.

Application Design

Last, but certainly not least, design choices can have a significant impact on application response time. Certain coding techniques can negatively affect performance, such as excessive roundtrips. Although this may not be noticeable when you're running the application against a local database, it may turn out to be unacceptable when you're running against SQL Database.

The following coding choices may impact your application's performance:

- **Chatty design.** As previously mentioned, a chatty application uses excessive roundtrips to the database and creates a significant slowdown. An example of a chatty design includes creating a programmatic loop that makes a call to a database to execute a SQL statement over and over again.

- **Normalization.** It's widely accepted that although a highly normalized database reduces data duplication, it also generally decreases performance due to the number of JOINs that must be included. As a result, excessive normalization can become a performance issue.

- **Connection release.** Generally speaking, you should open a database connection as late as possible and close it explicitly as soon as possible. Doing so improves your chances of quickly reusing a database connection from the pool when you have a large number of connections being made. Indeed, connections are released in the pool when they are closed. If you do not release your connections quickly enough, you could create a condition in which connection requests are queued until connections become available in the pool, or connection requests time out if the wait is too long.

- **Shared database account.** Because SQL Database requires a database login, you need to use a shared database account to retrieve data instead of using a per-user login. Using a per-user login prohibits the use of connection pooling and can degrade performance significantly, or even render your database unusable due to throttling.

There are many other application design considerations, but the ones listed here apply the most to programming against SQL Database. For more information, read the following chapter from Microsoft's Patterns and Practices: http://msdn.microsoft.com/en-us/library/ff647768.aspx.

Summary

This chapter provided an overview of some of the most important tuning techniques that are available to help you address SQL Database performance issues. As you've seen, troubleshooting and tuning statements can be complex and require various tools and methods to obtain the desired outcome. You saw a few dynamic management views and execution plans, took a quick tour of indexing, and briefly touched on the statistics provided by the ADO.NET library. You also learned about some design considerations that can affect application performance.

You can discover additional techniques and concepts on Microsoft's web site at http://msdn.microsoft.com/en-us/library/ms190610(v=sql.105).aspx.

CHAPTER 12

Windows Azure Mobile Services

Since the release of the first edition of this book 2010 the SQL Azure OData service has been removed. That's not a bad thing. OData is still around, and you can still prop up a WCF data service and communicate via the OData protocol. In fact, if you use WCF Data Services, you might very well be using OData. WCF Data Services supports the OData protocol, which allows you to expose your data as a feed with resources that are addressable by URIs. OData allows you to expose data from a variety of sources, ranging from Microsoft Excel to websites, not just relational databases. Creating a data service that exposes an OData feed really boils down to three simple and basic steps:

> **Define the model:** WCF Data Services natively supports models that are based on the ADO.NET Entity Framework.

> **Create the data service:** Define a data service which exposes a class that inherits from the DataService class.

> **Configure the data service:** Configure access to resources (such as tables) and service operations, and define service-wide behavior. WCF Data Services disables access to resources that are exposed by the entity container by default.

However, this chapter is not about WCF Data Services or OData. Windows Azure SQL Database (AKA SQL Azure) doesn't natively support OData, as it did during the SQL Azure lab days of the OData service. Instead, in late August 2012, Microsoft released (in Preview) the Windows Azure Mobile Services.

Windows Azure Mobile Services is designed specifically to allow developers to quickly and easily connect their client applications to a cloud-based backend running on Windows Azure, regardless of the platform the client is running on (such as Windows 8 device, Android table, or iOS).

The beauty of Windows Azure Mobile Services is that it enables you to get up and running extremely quickly by providing a foundation for building a rich client experience. As you will see in this chapter, Windows Azure Mobile Services allows you to connect your application very quickly.

Note   Keep in mind that the description here is based on Windows Azure Mobile Services in Preview, meaning that it is not in production at the time of this writing, and some details may change when it is actually released.

Getting Started

To use Windows Azure Mobile Services, you will need a Windows Azure account. Chapter 1 explains how to sign up for an account, so that process won't be explained here. Working with Windows Azure Mobile Services is as simple as navigating to the Windows Azure Portal at https://manage.WindowsAzure.com. Once you log in with your Live ID, you'll notice a new tab on the Navigation pane called Mobile Services, as shown in Figure 12-1.

Figure 12-1. *The Mobile Services option on the Navigation pane*

Creating a new Windows Azure Mobile Services service is as simple as selecting the Mobile Services tab in the Navigation pane, selecting the New button at the bottom of the portal, and finally selecting Create to bring up the New Mobile Service wizard, shown in Figure 12-2.

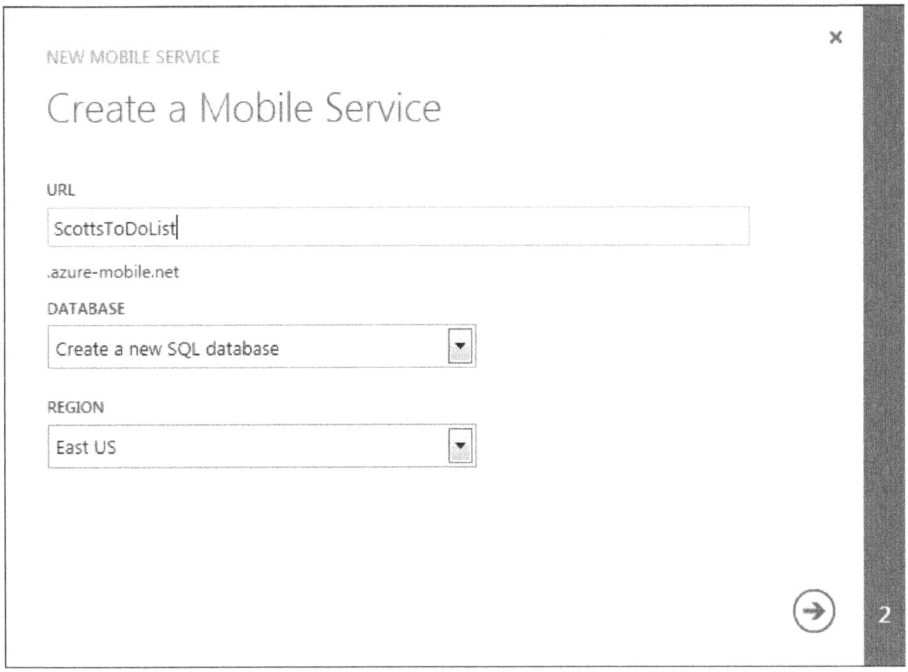

Figure 12-2. Page 1 of the New Mobile Service wizard

The first page of the New Mobile Service wizard asks you to provide a name for the service. The service name, as you can see, is actually a URL that the application will access. You don't need to specify the entire URL, just the name. As you can see in Figure 12-2, I simply supplied a name. The service will append the remainder of the URL for me.

Next you need to select either to use an existing Windows Azure SQL Database instance or create a new database instance. In this example, I selected to create a new database. Thus, I selected the option Create a New SQL Database and specified the region in which I want the database created.

The second page or the New Mobile Service wizard asks you to name the new database. In this case, because I selected to create my database in the East US region, the dialog searched and found that I have a SQL Database server in that region and listed it in the Server drop down for me. I simply need to fill in the login name and password, as shown in Figure 12-3.

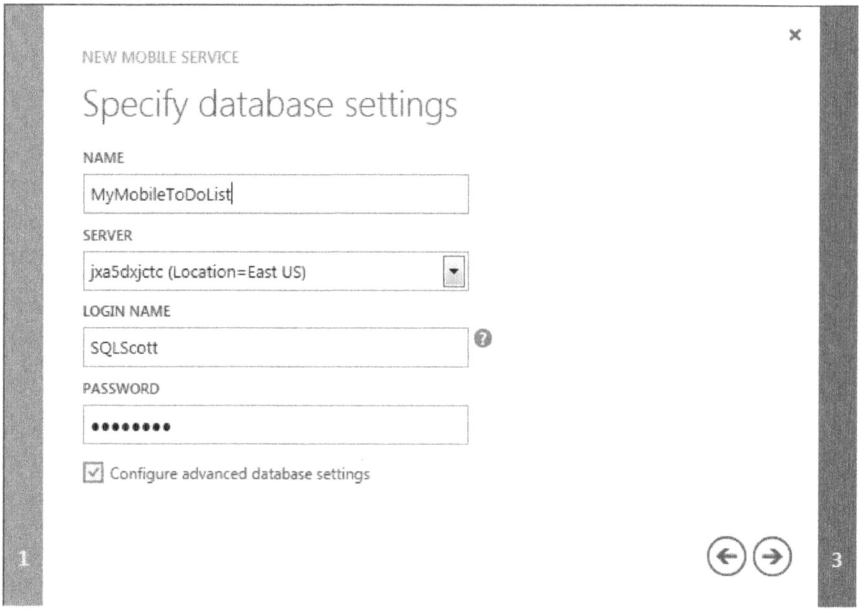

Figure 12-3. *Page 2 of the New Mobile Service wizard*

You can optionally select the Configure Advanced Database Settings option (as shown in Figure 12-3), which displays the Advanced Database Settings page where you can select the database Edition (Web or Business), database size, and collation. If you prefer to accept the default advanced settings, namely a 1GB Web Edition database with the SQL_Latin1_General_CP1_CI_AS collation setting, simply click OK (the check mark) on the Advanced Database Settings page.

Once the information is filled in on the Specify Database Settings page, click OK. A new Windows Azure Mobile Service is then provisioned on Windows Azure, creating a new data store in Windows Azure SQL Database (thus the need to enter database information in the wizard), which allows you to save any type of data you need for your application. Next it will create a number of REST service endpoints that the application can call to perform tasks such as saving data, performing push notifications, and securely logging in.

The Mobile Services creation process takes only a moment, and once it is complete the new service will be listed in the portal, as shown in Figure 12-4. The service is now running in Windows Azure and is ready for use. Figure 12-4 shows the mobile service name and the status columns, but off to the right in the fourth column is the URL to the service. Clicking this URL opens a new browser tab with a page stating that the Windows Azure Mobile Service is up and running.

Figure 12-4. *Selecting the new Mobile Service in the portal*

Creating the service is just the beginning, but as was mentioned earlier, it really doesn't get much more difficult. The next step is to create an application to communicate with this service, and luckily, we don't need to do much for that, either.

Back in the Windows Azure Management Portal, click the service Name, highlighted in Figure 12-4, which will take us to the familiar Dashboard that is common in the Preview portal. This Dashboard provides a quick-start experience that you also see when working with the other Windows Azure services such as Web sites and Database.

Clicking the service Name link takes you to the quick-start Get Started page, shown in Figure 12-5. On this page are provided two easy walkthrough examples; one which shows you how to connect an existing application to the mobile service, and another which walks you through how to create a new application from scratch. As shown in Figure 12-5, this example will be using the Create a New Windows Store App option.

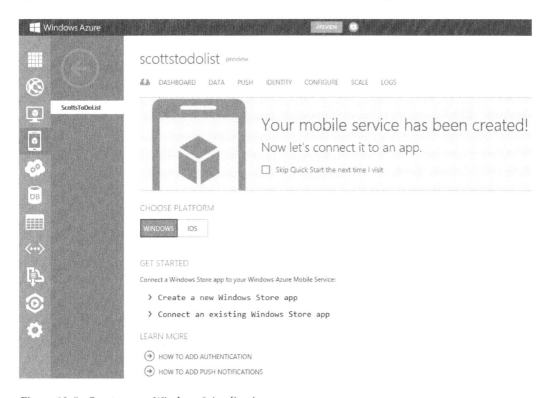

Figure 12-5. *Create a new Windows 8 Application*

If you already have an existing application, connecting to it really isn't that difficult. Selecting the Connect an Existing Windows Store App option simply asks you to select your development language, and you then just copy and paste a few lines of code into the existing application; doing this provides access to the Mobile Services SDK to perform the tasks mentioned above (save data, push notifications, and so on).

For this exercise, select Create a new Windows Store App, which provides a three-step walkthrough of building a new application. Step 1 asks you to download Visual Studio and the Mobile Services SDK. If you haven't downloaded Visual Studio yet, the link will take you to the appropriate page to download Visual Studio 2012 Express. If you already have Visual Studio 2012 installed, click the second link, which will install the Mobile Services SDK.

Once all the appropriate tools are installed, the next step is to create the necessary tables. Tables can be added at any time, and this chapter will cover that later on. Tables are used to store data that your Mobile Services application needs. You can create any number of tables, which will be stored in Windows Azure SQL Database in the database instance specified during the provisioning of the mobile service (in our ScottsToDoList example, this is the MyMobileToDoList database instance shown in Figure 12-3). Even though SQL Database is used as the data store, the schema that these tables can have is really quite flexible.

In this tutorial the new application will create the appropriate table and schema for us, so simply click the Create TodoItem Table button. Within a matter of seconds the table will be created and, as shown in Figure 12-6, the page will let us know that the table is indeed created.

Figure 12-6. *Creating the supporting table*

The third step is to Download the application. Yes, you read it right, download the app. This tutorial will download an entire ready-to-go sample application that will work with the mobile service just created and with no code modifications.

Select the language (as shown in Figure 12-7, in this example we're choosing C#) and click the Download button, which will download a zip file containing a starter project.

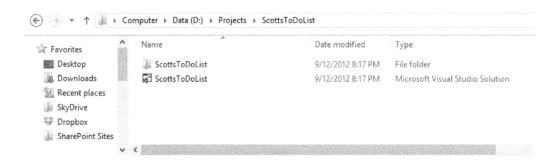

Figure 12-7. *Downloading the Visual Studio solution for C#*

Save the zip file to your local hard drive and then unzip it. As shown in Figure 12-8, the zip file that was downloaded contains an entire Visual Studio Solution.

		Computer ▸ Data (D:) ▸ Projects ▸ ScottsToDoList			
		Name	Date modified	Type	
☆ Favorites		📁 ScottsToDoList	9/12/2012 8:17 PM	File folder	
🖥 Desktop		🗗 ScottsToDoList	9/12/2012 8:17 PM	Microsoft Visual Studio Solution	
📥 Downloads					
📄 Recent places					
🗂 SkyDrive					
📦 Dropbox					
📁 SharePoint Sites					

Figure 12-8. *The downloaded and extracted C# project directory*

Open the solution by double-clicking the solution file and open the Solution Explorer window. In Solution Explorer (Figure 12-9) you should notice two files: App.xaml and MainPage.xaml. Both of these pages contain stub code automatically provided for the developer.

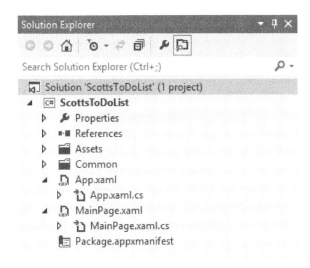

Figure 12-9. *The sample solution*

Open the `App.xml.cs` file and notice at about line 25 the reference to the Mobile Services service created earlier. This was automatically injected into the application prior to downloading the zip file, so that you can run the application as is without any code modifications.

The `MainPage.xaml` file contains the UI of the project which, as you will see when the project is run, provides the means to enter and save To Do items. If you open the `MainPage.xaml` file you will see that the `ToDoItem` is a simple class that contains three properties. Later in the chapter you will see that those properties match the columns in the table created in step 2 in Figure 12-6.

Scrolling down in the `MainPage.xaml` file you will see all the necessary code to insert a new ToDo item into the table as well as to query and retrieve all the items in the table.

Go ahead and run the application by pressing F5. When the application loads, you will see Insert a TodoItem on the left and Query and Update Data on the right. Enter a ToDo item and choose Save. Within a matter of seconds the item will appear on the right side of the page (no need to click Refresh), as shown in Figure 12-10.

Figure 12-10. *Running the project*

What happened when the Save button was clicked? A simple REST call was sent to Windows Azure; it accessed the Windows Azure Mobile Service (via the Mobile Services reference in the `App.xml.cs` file) and saved the data to the SQL Database instance.

If you are running this on Windows 8, you will need to go back to the start menu in Windows 8 to return to Visual Studio to stop debugging.

Data

The Data tab in the portal simply lists the tables that the available Windows Azure Mobile Services are using. Figure 12-11 shows the table used in the example earlier in the chapter. The three columns show the table name, the number of indexes on the table, and the number of records in each table.

Figure 12-11. *Running the project*

Mobile Services tables are quite flexible, so much so that you can simply define a table without any columns (although when the table is created, an id column is automatically created for you). When data is initially inserted into the table the service creates the appropriate columns automatically. However, for this functionality to work, the Enable Dynamic Schema option must be set to On. This option can be found on the Configure tab (see Figure 12-11), three tabs to the right of the Data tab.

While on the surface the Data page is simple, there is much, much more that is available when working with tables. Clicking the table name in the portal will take you to a series of pages that allow you to browse the data, work with the columns, define security permissions on the table, and perform additional operations during any CRUD (Create, Read, Update, and Delete) operations. The following sections detail each of the four tabs.

Browse

The Browse tab (Figure 12-12) simply lets you browse data in the selected tables. You can switch between tables by selecting the table in the left navigation bar. If the amount of data exceeds the size of the page, you can use the forward and back arrows to navigate between multiple data pages.

Figure 12-12. *The Browse tab*

Columns

The Columns tab (Figure 12-13) allows you to manage columns in the table. Columns can be added or deleted. Once a column is created, its data type cannot be changed. To delete a column, select any column other than the indexed column and click the Delete button at the bottom of the portal. Columns can be added in either of two ways—first, by dropping and re-creating the table (not recommended, because of the loss of data), or second, by sending from the application an insert request that includes the new property. To do this, Dynamic Schema must be enabled.

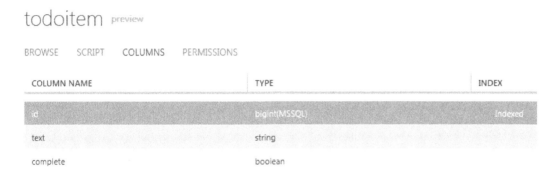

Figure 12-13. *The Columns tab*

This tab also allows you to define indexes on the table. By default, an index is placed on the id column, but columns can be added to the index to improve query performance. To add a column to the index, select the column and click Set as Index. Columns used regularly in queries for sorting or filtering should be included in the index. Be careful not to add too many columns to the index; this can be detrimental to performance. There are many tools available, including SQL Server Management Studio, that allow you to examine queries that are hitting the database to help determine which columns in the table would be beneficial to add to the index.

Permissions

The Permissions tab provides the ability to define who has Insert, Update, and Delete permissions. As shown in Figure 12-14, there are four options:

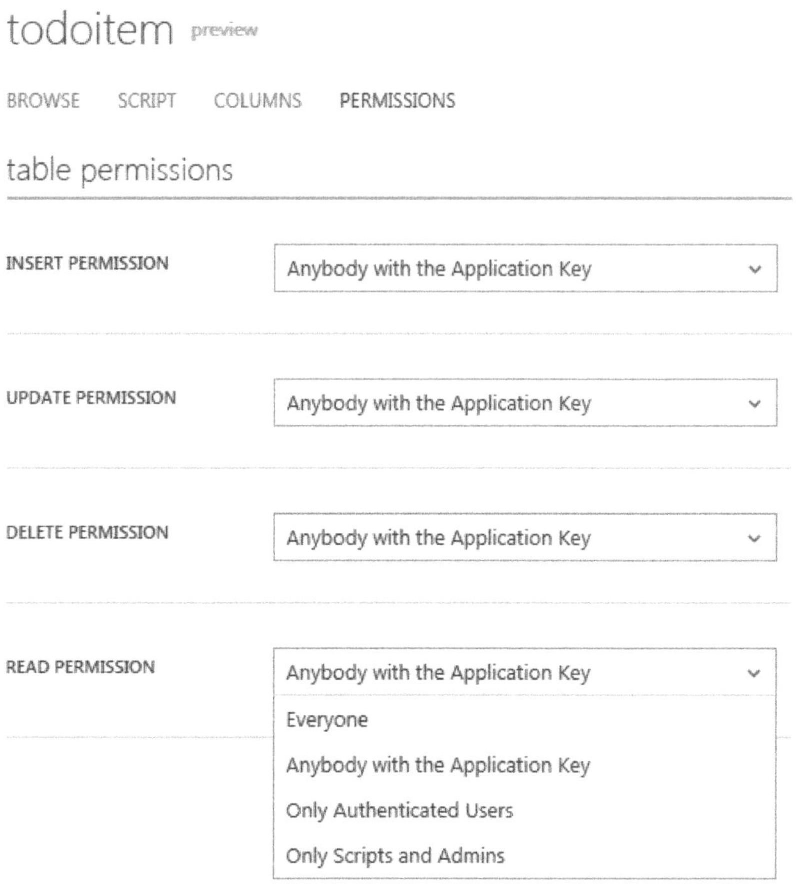

todoitem preview

BROWSE   SCRIPT   COLUMNS   **PERMISSIONS**

table permissions

INSERT PERMISSION

Anybody with the Application Key	⌄

UPDATE PERMISSION

Anybody with the Application Key	⌄

DELETE PERMISSION

Anybody with the Application Key	⌄

READ PERMISSION

Anybody with the Application Key	⌄
Everyone	
Anybody with the Application Key	
Only Authenticated Users	
Only Scripts and Admins	

Figure 12-14. *The Permissions tab*

Everyone: Any request for the operation against the table is accepted. With this option, your data is wide open to everyone.

Anybody with the Application Key: The application key is required to perform the operation. The application key is distributed with the application. Because this key is not securely distributed, it cannot be considered a security token. To secure access to your mobile service data, you must instead authenticate users before accessing.

Only Authenticated Users: Only authenticated users are permitted to perform the operation. In this preview release, Windows 8 app clients are authenticated by Live Connect. Scripts can be used to further restrict access to tables based on an authenticated user.

Only Scripts and Admins: The operation requires the service master key, which limits the operation only to registered scripts or to administrator accounts.

Depending on the type and sensitivity of the data , it is recommended that the Everyone option be used sparingly. If there is data that needs protecting and is of sensitive nature, the second or third option should be used as a best practice. Authenticating users should be a practice to prevent access to sensitive data.

Script

The Script tab (Figure 12-15) provides the ability to create *scriptlets*, server-side custom logic that will run on each operation (Insert, Update, Delete, and Read). Scriptlets are pieces of JavaScript code you can register to be executed. The name of the function must match the operation selected, except for Delete operations, which must be named del.

Figure 12-15. *The Script tab*

These scripts allow the injection of business logic into table operations. For example, client authentication can take place here based on the userIdvalue of the supplied userobject.

Advanced Settings

We have talked about Mobile Services from the Data point of view, but there are a few other items that need to be highlighted to give Windows Azure Mobile Services a complete preview. The three settings tabs that we will highlight in this section come from the main page of the Mobile Service and can be seen in Figure 12-16: Push, Identity, and Scale.

Figure 12-16. *Mobile Services tabs*

Push

With Windows Azure Mobile Services you can send push notifications to your Windows Store application by using the Windows Push Notification Service (WNS). Sending push notifications to your application requires that you first configure your mobile service to work with WNS. This is accomplished by simply entering the Client Secret and Package SID values in the Push tab, as shown in Figure 12-17.

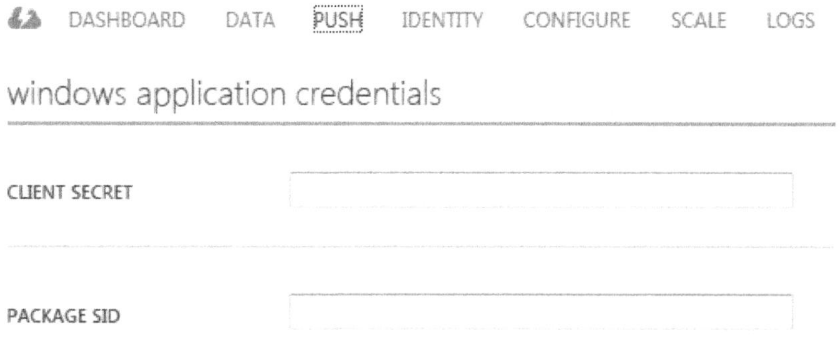

DASHBOARD   DATA   PUSH   IDENTITY   CONFIGURE   SCALE   LOGS

windows application credentials

CLIENT SECRET

PACKAGE SID

Figure 12-17. *Push notification settings*

These values are provided by WNS when you register your app on the Windows Push Notification & Live Connect page at

```
https://appdev.microsoft.com/StorePortals/en-us/
```

Enabling Push notifications requires first that you register your application for the Windows Store, at which point during the registration process you will be given the Client Secret and Package SID. At that point your application is now configured to work with WNS.

Identity

Windows Azure Mobile Services integrates with a number of different social media, third-party, and Microsoft applications to make it easy to authenticate users from within your application. The integration is supported through a number of identity providers. Currently, Mobile Services supports the following identity providers:

- Microsoft
- Facebook
- Twitter
- Google

Figure 12-18 shows the information necessary to configure a Microsoft account, Facebook, and Twitter for Windows Azure Mobile Services. To enable authentication, you will first need to register your application with one of the above-mentioned identity providers to obtain the necessary ID or key and secret and then use that information in this settings window to configure the application to work with that provider.

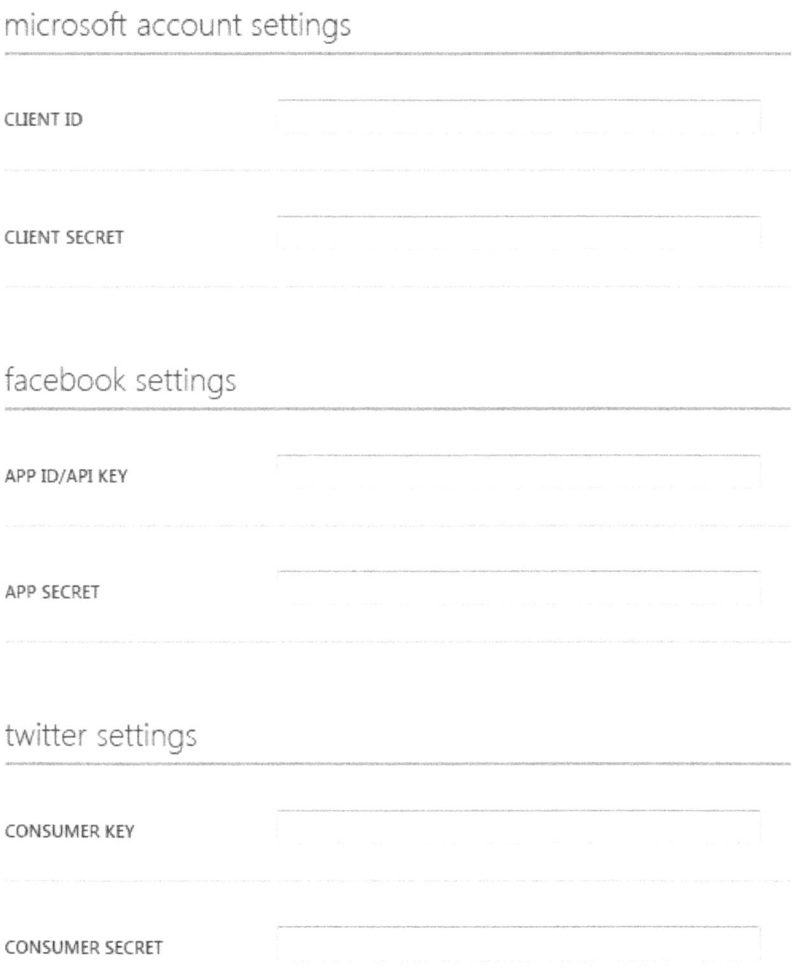

microsoft account settings

CLIENT ID

CLIENT SECRET

facebook settings

APP ID/API KEY

APP SECRET

twitter settings

CONSUMER KEY

CONSUMER SECRET

Figure 12-18. *Identity Provider settings*

You will also need to add authentication code to your application to handle the process of users logging in. When a user login is authenticated by Mobile Services, the value of the userid property on the user object is set to a value that uniquely identifies the user. This value can then be used to authorize access to data.

Scale

The Scale tab is where you define the resources available to your application. Scaling your mobile service is as simple as switching between Shared and Reserved resource mode and setting the number of instances of the mobile service and the size of those instances, as shown in Figure 12-19.

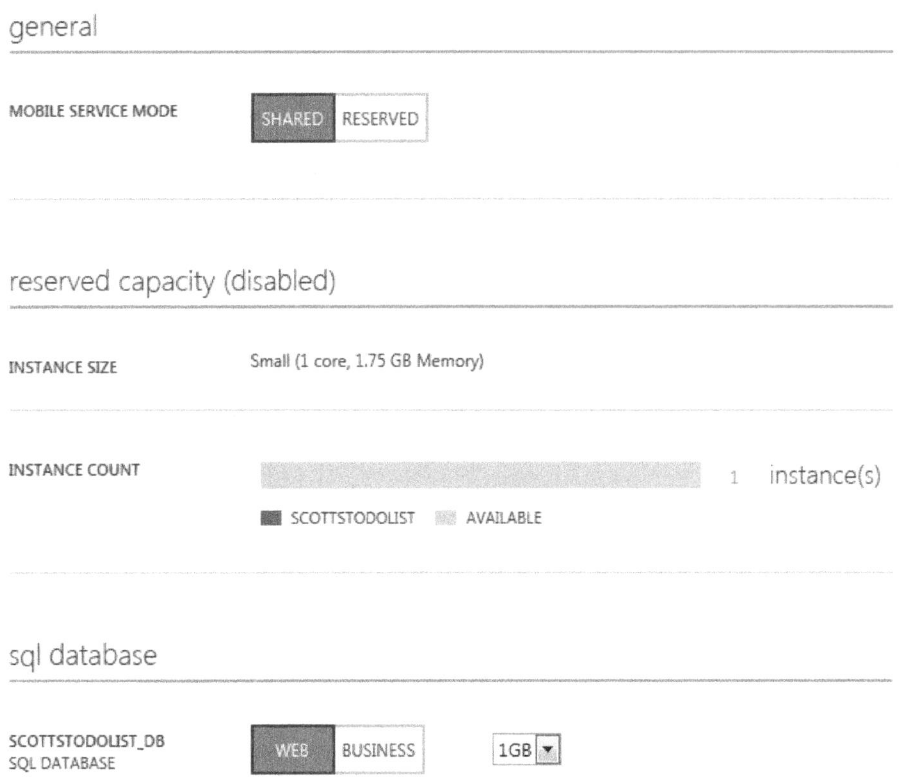

general

MOBILE SERVICE MODE	SHARED	RESERVED

reserved capacity (disabled)

INSTANCE SIZE   Small (1 core, 1.75 GB Memory)

INSTANCE COUNT   [_____]   1   instance(s)

■ SCOTTSTODOLIST   ▨ AVAILABLE

sql database

SCOTTSTODOLIST_DB   [WEB   BUSINESS]   [1GB ▼]
SQL DATABASE

Figure 12-19. *Mobile Service Scale settings*

By default, the mobile service is set to Shared mode, which means that all of your instances are running in a shared environment, co-located with other mobile services. Resources such as memory and CPU are shared among the mobile services.

Switching to Reserved mode means that your mobile services have dedicated resources available to your mobile service, including memory, CPU, and bandwidth. Other mobile services cannot use the resources dedicated to your mobile service.

In Windows Azure Mobile Services, you can also scale the Windows Azure SQL Database instances used by the service. Setting the Mobile Service Mode to Reserved means that all of your mobile services in the same region run in Reserved mode.

■ **Note**   This chapter has touched on the configuration tabs lightly simply because its focus was on SQL Database used as a data store for Windows Azure Mobile Services. For further information on how to configure push notifications or provider integration, visit www.windowsazure.com/en-us/develop/mobile/.

Summary

While Windows Azure Mobile Services is still in Preview as this book goes to press, it should be obvious that this feature is quite exciting and really puts the "cherry on top" for Windows Azure. This chapter illustrated how easy it is to store and retrieve data in a Windows Azure SQL Database from a Windows Store application.

We began this chapter by creating a Windows Azure mobile service and then configured that service to use a Windows Azure SQL Database as the data store. We then downloaded the sample application, and you saw how easy it is to read and write data using Windows Azure Mobile Services, as well as to create an application for the Windows Store.

Lastly, we took a brief look at some of the configuration settings that can be used within your application, such as social media integration with Facebook and Twitter, and with applications from other providers, such as Microsoft and Google. We also looked at the all-important aspect of scaling your mobile service and how easy it is to do that.

SQL Database Management Portal

This appendix introduces you to the online SQL Database Management Portal built by Microsoft. It is a web-based application that allows you to design, manage, and monitor your SQL Database instances. Although the current version of the portal does not support all the functions of SQL Server Management Studio, the portal offers some interesting capabilities unique to SQL Database.

Launching the Management Portal

You can launch the SQL Database Management Portal (SDMP) from the Windows Azure Management Portal. Open a browser and navigate to https://manage.windowsazure.com, and then login with your Live ID. Once logged in, click SQL Databases on the left and click on your database from the list of available databases. This brings up the database dashboard, as seen in Figure A-1. To launch the management portal, click the Manage icon at the bottom.

Figure A-1. *SQL Database dashboard in Windows Azure Management Portal*

■ **Note**   You can also access the SDMP directly from a browser by typing `https://`*`sqldatabasename`*`.database.windows.net`, where `sqldatabasename` is the server name of your SQL Database.

A new web page opens up that prompts you to log in to your SQL Database server. If you clicked through the Windows Azure Management Portal, the database name will be automatically filled and read-only. If you typed the URL directly in a browser, you will need to enter the database name manually. Enter a user name and password; then click Log on (Figure A-2).

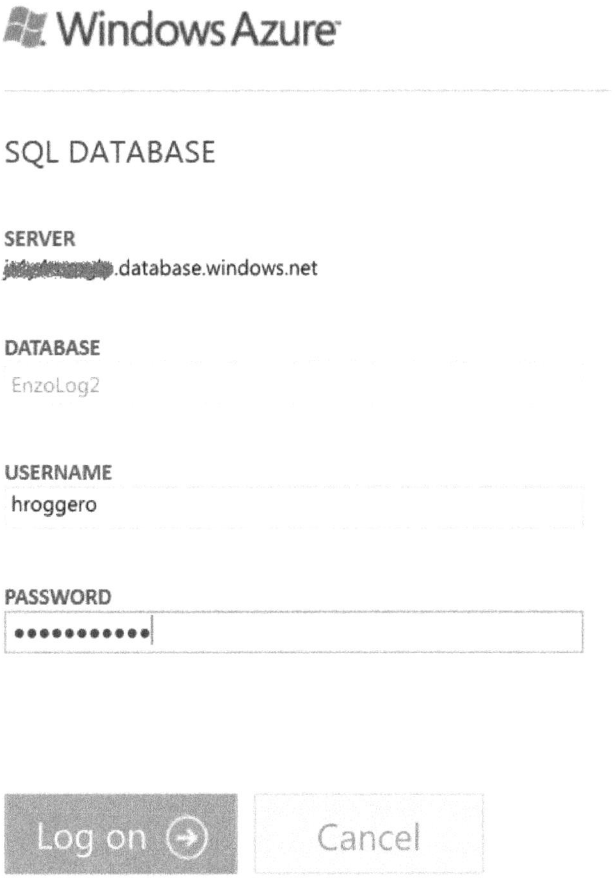

Windows Azure

SQL DATABASE

SERVER
.database.windows.net

DATABASE
EnzoLog2

USERNAME
hroggero

PASSWORD
●●●●●●●●●●●

Log on ⊕   Cancel

Figure A-2. *SQL Database Manage Portal login screen*

Once logged on, you will see a page similar to Figure A-3, which defaults to the administration summary page of the database instance, giving you general information about your database instance such as its free space, current connections, and more. You can also access the design page, a section of the portal that allows you to manage tables, views, and stored procedures. The administration and design features are explained next.

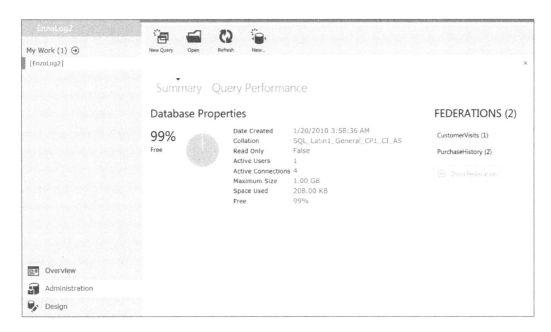

Figure A-3. *Administration Summary screen*

Administration Features

The administration section of the portal allows you to manage your federations, monitor current query performance, and run T-SQL queries and optionally view their execution plans. Chapter 10 covered federations at length, so this appendix will focus on the other administration features.

Run T-SQL Statements

Let's first run a T-SQL statement and look at the options available to us. From the administration Summary page, click the New Query icon on top of the page. This opens up a new query window. You can open as many windows as needed to run multiple queries as you would in SQL Server Management Studio. Type and execute the following statement (click the Run icon to execute it):

```
SELECT * FROM sys.tables
```

Running this query returns the list of tables currently found in your database. The query window and its result are shown in Figure A-4. The output shows you a grid containing the fields as columns and a row for each table. A scrollbar shows up on the right if needed. Between the query window and results area, two links are provided: Messages and Results. The Results link is selected by default (it has a little downward arrow on top of it). Clicking on Messages will shows you any associated message for the query, including any error messages. As in the SQL Server Management Studio, if an error is found, the Messages window would be shown by default instead of the Results window.

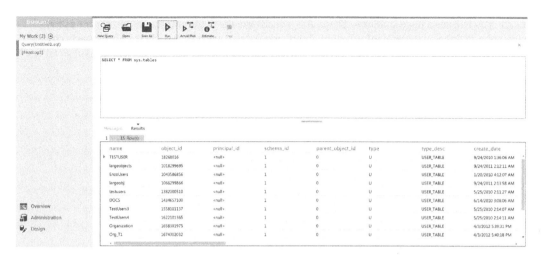

Figure A-4. *The Query window and results area*

▓ **Note**   You can use the splitter in the middle of the screen, between the query window and the results area, to adjust the visible area as desired.

Note that you can run multiple queries from the same window as well. For example, execute the following batch:

```
SELECT * FROM sys.tables
SELECT * FROM sys.procedures
```

You may notice that the results area of the page only shows the list of tables, just as in Figure A-4. However if you click on the Rows summary (Figure A-5), you'll see a drop-down list with the complete list of result sets, one for each statement in the batch. If you click the second item, assuming your database has stored procedures, you will see the result set for the second statement in the batch. You may also notice a visual cue in the drop-down list, indicating the relative number of records returned by each statement in the batch. Because the second statement returned 6 rows out of a total of 21 in the batch, the second item in the list contains a bar filled at about 25% of the length of the item.

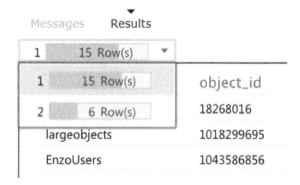

Figure A-5. *Switching the Results view*

View Execution Plans

You can also view either an estimated execution plan or the actual plan from the same query window. The Actual Plan and Estimated Plan icons are next to the Run icon you clicked previously. With the same two T-SQL statements entered previously, click the Actual Plan icon. When the execution is finished, you will notice a Query Plan link next to Results. Click on this link; you will see the execution plan shown in Figure A-6.

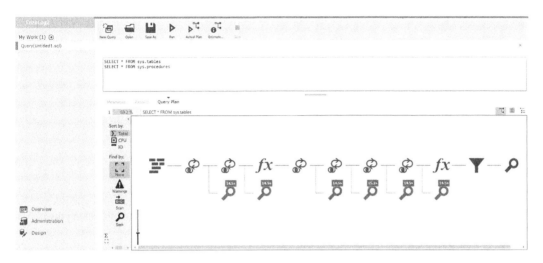

Figure A-6. *Viewing the actual execution plan*

The Sort By icons on the left allow you to pinpoint which operators consume the most resources. By default, the execution plan shows a graphical display highlighting the operators that consume the most CPU and I/O resources. You can click on the CPU or IO icon on the left to show the operators that consume the most CPU or I/O resources, respectively.

The Find By icons on the left allow you to highlight execution warnings, index scans, or index seeks. Note that table scans cannot exist, because SQL Database does not support heap tables. You can also zoom in or out easily using the vertical bar on the bottom left. Doing so changes the display of the icons when you zoom in enough, as shown in Figure A-7.

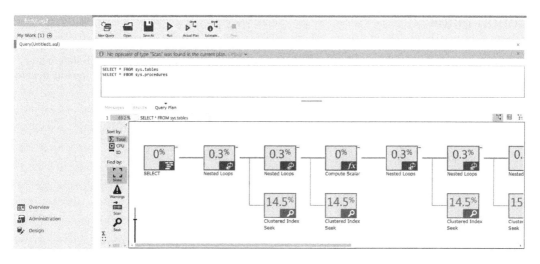

Figure A-7. *Zooming in on the Actual execution plan*

If you switch the active statement from the batch (as previously shown in Figure A-5), the execution plan for the second statement will be displayed. You can also display the execution plan in a grid or a tree by clicking the appropriate icon on the top right of the execution plan window.

Monitor Current Query Performance

To view the statements recently executed on your database, select the database name on the left panel (EnzoLog2 in my example). This will bring you back to a page similar to Figure A-3., where you choose Query Performance on the top. A page similar to Figure A-8 will appear, showing the list of recent statements that were executed against the database with summary performance metrics. Note that these metrics show averages, not the current values. For example, the second column displays CPU ms/sec, which is an average of CPU consumption in millisecond over the duration of the session, expressed in seconds.

Query	Run Count	CPU ms/sec	Duration ms/sec	Physical Reads/sec	Logical Writes/sec	Logical Reads/sec
SELECT CAST((select SUBSTRING(text.eq1.statement_start_offset/2 +1 .	1	51	58	8	0	94
SELECT * FROM sys.tables	5	0	0	0	0	36
SELECT * FROM sys.tables	1	0	0	0	0	0
SELECT * FROM sys.procedures	1	0	0	0	0	0
SELECT database_id FROM sys.databases WHERE name=N'EnzoLog2' .	14	0	0	0	0	0
SELECT CAST((select SUBSTRING(text.eq1.statement_start_offset/2 +1 .	1	0	0	0	0	0
select is_federation_member from sys.databases where name = N'Enzo .	2	0	0	0	0	0
SELECT CAST((select SUBSTRING(text.eq1.statement_start_offset/2 +1 .	1	0	0	0	0	0
SELECT CAST((select SUBSTRING(text.eq1.statment_start_offset/2 +1 .	1	0	0	0	0	0
select @UsedPageCount = ISNULL(SUM(reserved_page_count), 0) FROM .	1	0	0	0	0	0
SELECT dtb.collation_name AS [Database_Collation], dtb.create_date AS .	1	0	0	0	0	0
SELECT CAST((select SUBSTRING(text.eq1.statement_start_offset/2 +1 .	1	0	0	0	0	0

Figure A-8. *Recent T-SQL statements executed against your database*

If you click on one of the statements, you will see detailed performance metrics. By default the page shows you the Query Plan Details, including duration, CPU, read, write and plan metrics (see Figure A-9). You can also view the graphical execution plan by clicking on Query Plan.

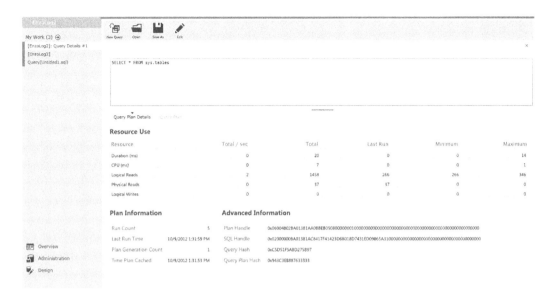

Figure A-9. *Performance details for a specific T-SQL statement*

Design Features

The design section of the portal allows you to manage database objects, including tables, views, and stored procedures. As you will see, the design section offers many advanced graphical options, including the ability to create indexes and foreign keys.

Designing Tables

To access the design section, click Design at the bottom left of the portal. Notice that the top section of the resulting page shows you three headers: Tables, Views, and Stored Procedures. By default the Tables header is selected, and the page shows you the list of existing tables, as seen in Figure A-10. Using the icons on the bottom of this page you can create a new table or drop a selected existing table. You can also filter the list of tables by typing characters in the search box.

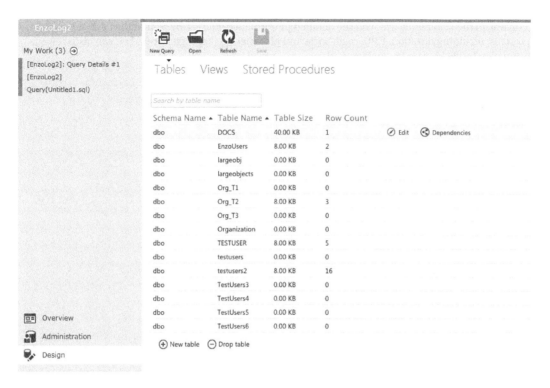

Figure A-10. *List of tables in a SQL Database instance*

The page used to create a new table is identical to the one used to edit an existing table. You'll see how to edit a table shortly, but let's look at the Dependencies feature first.

Two icons (Edit and Dependencies) automatically appear if you move your mouse over the list of tables. The Edit icon looks like a small pencil. The other icon is the Dependencies icon.

If you click on the Dependencies icon for a table, a new page will be displayed, showing its object dependencies in a graphical format, as seen for my DOCS table in Figure A-11. The graph shows me that a view called v_Documents depends on my DOCS table. From this view I can directly edit these objects by clicking on their Edit icons.

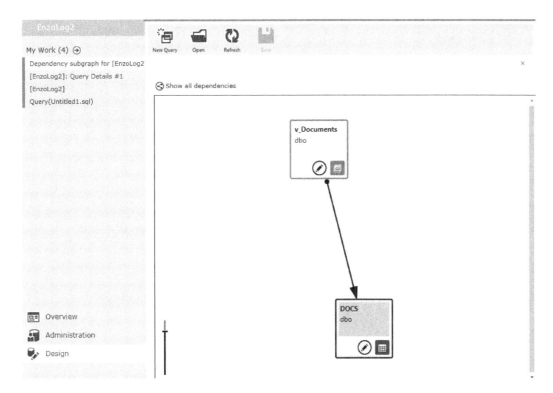

Figure A-11. *A dependencies graph*

Clicking on the Edit icon on the DOCS table opens the table-editing page, which offers a graphical interface for changing the table definition, as shown in Figure A-12. From this page you can add, edit, and delete table columns. You can also change which fields are part of the Primary Key and whether fields are required. After making changes, click the Save icon on top.

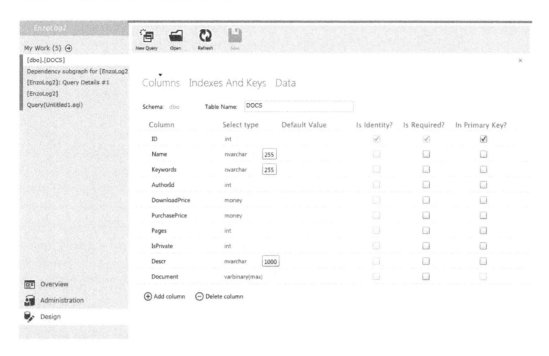

Figure A-12. *The table design page*

Click on the Indexes and Keys header to view, add, and delete indexes and foreign keys associated with the table. The page does not allow you to edit existing Indexes. Figure A-13 shows you the clustered index on the DOCS table, which has no foreign key defined.

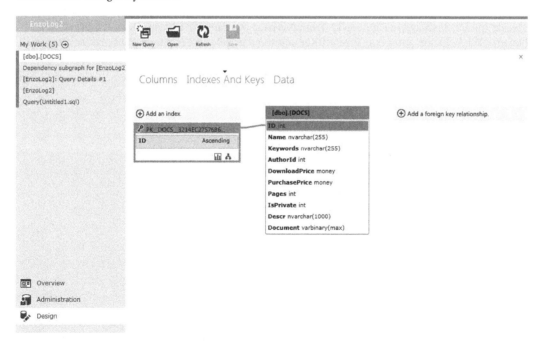

Figure A-13. *Editing indexes and foreign keys*

To add an index, click the Add an Index icon. A panel will be displayed, and check boxes will become available next to each column in the table. Specify the name of the index and select the table columns that belong to it. You can also choose Advanced Options, which will show index settings to automatically rebuild indexes. Choose the ONLINE option, specify a filter for the index (as shown in Figure A-14), and then click the Save button in the panel to create the index.

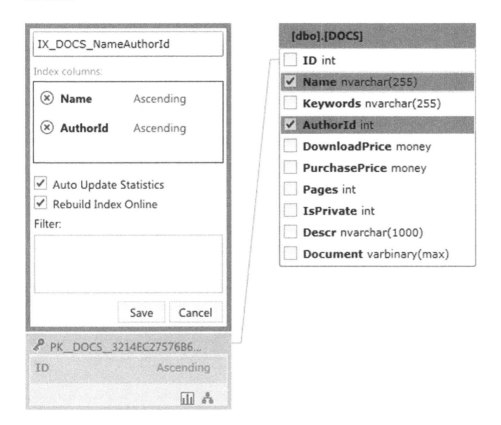

Figure A-14. *Creating an Index*

To add a foreign key, click Add a Foreign Key Relationship, which is the icon you see toward the right in Figure A-13. A new panel will be displayed, allowing you to select specific operations, including On Delete and On Update settings, as shown in Figure A-15. Click on Select a Reference Table to display the list of available tables. Then select the reference table by clicking on its name. Next click the Select a Reference column to choose which column is used as a reference. Once the reference table and the column have been selected, the available columns to choose from in the source table (DOCS) are adjusted to those that match the data type of the reference column. Select the source columns that will be used (as shown in Figure A-16), and then click the Save button in the panel.

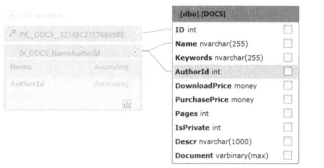
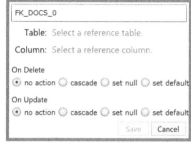

Figure A-15. *Creating a foreign key*

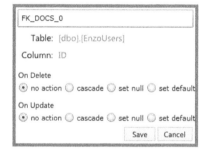

Figure A-16. *Selecting the source and reference fields*

To delete an index or a foreign key constraint, click the Delete icon (shown as an X) on the right side of the object.

You can also view and edit the data stored in a selected table by clicking the Data header (see Figure A-17). This page shows you the top 200 records of the table by default. Clicking the All Rows link will display all the rows in the table. You can add a row (by choosing Add Row) or delete the selected row (using Delete Row).

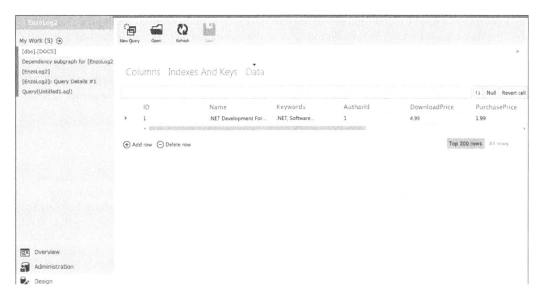

Figure A-17. *Viewing table data*

Clicking a specific column value will also allow you to edit the column. For example, Figure A-18 shows you that I am editing the DownloadPrice value of the first row to $19.99.

Figure A-18. *Editing a Column*

A new icon—it resembles a pencil—on the left side of the row allows me to undo my edits, and the box on top of the table list shows the new value entered (you can edit the value in the column field directly, or in the text box area on top).

Clicking the up/down arrow on the right of the text box expands or collapses the text area (see Figure A-18). Clicking the Null icon sets the value to Null. Clicking the Revert Cell icon resets your changes back to the original value. To save your changes, click the Save icon at the top of the screen. Note that you will not be able to edit all data types; for example, binary columns cannot be edited.

Designing Views

To manage your views, click the Views header from the default design page (shown earlier in Figure A-10). You will see a list of existing views. You can delete a view by selecting the view and then clicking Drop View at the bottom. Browsing the list with the mouse will also display the Edit and Dependencies icons discussed previously. You can also filter the list of views by typing characters in the Search box on top.

Let's create a view. Click the New view icon at the bottom of the list. A new page allows you to specify the name of the view, its schema (you can change the default schema by clicking on it and selecting from a list of available schemas, if any are available in the database), and the T-SQL of the view in the middle of the page. Figure A-19 shows you that I am creating a view called v_DBO_Tables in the dbo schema. Click the Save icon on top to create the view.

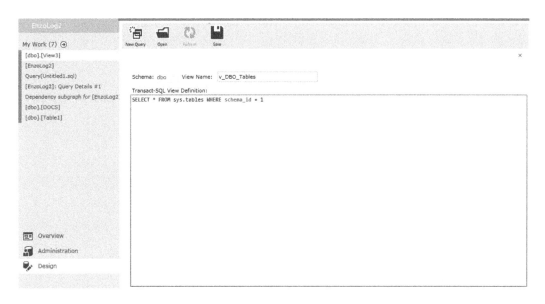

Figure A-19. *Creating a view*

Once the view has been created, the page will display two new headers: Design and Data. The Design header allows you to edit the current view, and the Data header displays the list of records returned by the view, similar to the Data page for tables shown in Figure A-17. The difference, however, is that the output of the view is read-only, so you cannot change the data returned by the view.

Designing Stored Procedures

To manage your stored procedures, choose Stored Procedures from the design page shown in Figure A-10. The list of stored procedures is displayed, and the features available on this page are identical to those explained for the views.

To create a new stored procedure, choose New Stored Procedure at the bottom of the list. A new page allows you to select the schema of the stored procedure, specify its name, add parameters, and enter the T-SQL of the stored procedure. To add a parameter, click the Add Parameter icon and specify the parameter name, its type (and size), its default value, and whether the parameter is an output (see Figure A-20). Click the Save icon to create the stored procedure.

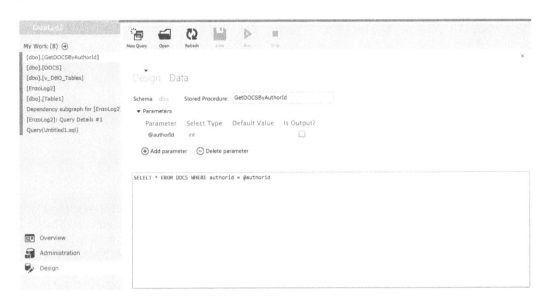

Figure A-20. *Creating a stored procedure*

If an error occurs, a panel will appear on top of the area you are currently working on; you can expand the message to view the details of the error, as shown in Figure A-21. In this example the field author_id referenced in the T-SQL code does not exist, preventing the T-SQL from compiling.

Figure A-21. *An error message in the portal*

Once the stored procedure has been created, you can execute it to view the output. Click the Data header to view the page where you can execute the stored procedure. If your stored procedure has parameters, a list of input parameters will be displayed, and you can specify an input (in the In Value column). The other columns in the list of input parameters are for informational purposes only and cannot be modified. These additional columns show you which parameters are output parameters, what their default values are, and their data types. Once you have specified the input parameters click the Run button on top. The output of the stored procedure, along with the input parameters specified, will look like Figure A-22. If multiple result sets are returned by the stored procedure you can select one using the drop-down immediately below the Results link as shown in Figure A-5 earlier.

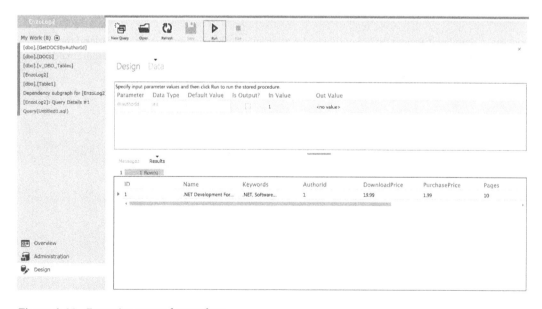

Figure A-22. *Executing a stored procedure*

Summary

As you surely noticed while reading this appendix, the management portal is designed with simplicity and expansion in mind. You saw how easy it is to manage tables, views, and stored procedures, and how to execute statements while monitoring performance metrics from recently executed statements in your database instance. The SMDP will continue to evolve rapidly; as a result, you can expect differences in behavior and additional features over time.

■ ■ ■

Windows Azure SQL Database Quick Reference

SQL Azure supports T-SQL. Chances are that you're already familiar with SQL Server T-SQL syntax if you're reading this book. However, not everything you know and love about SQL Server is supported yet in Windows Azure SQL Database. For example, many of the T-SQL statements are hardware-related or OS/server-related, such as creating certificates or creating backup devices. This appendix provides a quick reference to the syntax that is currently supported in Windows Azure SQL Database as of Service Update 4.

■ **Note**   You can find a complete list and reference that describes T-SQL features supported in Windows Azure SQL Database at http://msdn.microsoft.com/en-us/library/ee336281.aspx.

Supported T-SQL Statements

Table B-1 lists the supported T-SQL statements that you can use in Windows Azure SQL Database. These statements can be used as exactly as you currently know them without any limitations.

Table B-1. *Fully Supported T-SQL Statements*

ALTER ROLE	DENY *Object Permissions*	ORDER BY *Clause*
ALTER SCHEMA	DENY *Schema Permissions*	OUTPUT *Clause*
ALTER VIEW	DROP LOGIN	OVER *Clause*
APPLOCK_MODE	DROP PROCEDURE	PRINT
APPLOCK_TEST	DROP ROLE	RAISERROR
BEGIN_TRANSACTION	DROP SCHEMA	RETURN
BEGIN...END	DROP STATISTICS	REVERT
BINARY_CHECKSUM	DROP SYNONYM	REVOKE *Object Permissions*
BREAK	DROP TYPE	REVOKE *Schema Permissions*
CAST and CONVERT	DROP USER	ROLLBACK TRANSACTION

(continued)

Table B-1. (*continued*)

CATCH (TRY...CATCH)	DROP VIEW	ROLLBACK WORK
CEILING	END (BEGIN...END)	SAVE TRANSACTION
CHECKSUM	EXCEPT and INTERSECT	SELECT @*local_variable*
CLOSE	FETCH	SELECT Clause
COALESCE	FOR *Clause* (XML and BROWSE)	SET @*local_variable*
COLUMNPROPERTY	FROM	SWITCHOFFSET
COMMIT TRANSACTION	GO	TERTIARY_WEIGHTS
COMMIT WORK	GOTO	THROW
CONTEXT_INFO	GRANT *Object Permissions*	TODATETIMEOFFSET
CONTINUE	GRANT *Schema Permissions*	TOP
CONVERT	GROUP BY	TRIGGER_NESTLEVEL
CREATE ROLE	GROUPING_ID	TRUNCATE TABLE
CREATE SCHEMA	HashBytes	TRY...CATCH
CREATE STATISTICS	HAVING	UNION
CREATE VIEW	Hints (Query, Table, Join, etc.)	UPDATE
CRYPT_GEN_RANDOM	IDENTITY (*Property*)	UPDATE STATISTICS
CURRENT_REQUEST_ID	IF...ELSE	USER
CURSOR_STATUS	INSERT BULK	SWITCHOFFSET
DBCC SHOW_STATISTICS	IS [NOT] NULL	WAITFOR
DEALLOCATE	MERGE	WHERE
DECLARE @local_variable	MIN_ACTIVE_ROWVERSION	WHILE
DECLARE CURSOR	OPEN	WITH (*Common Table Expression*)
DELETE	OPTION Clause	

Partially Supported T-SQL Statements

Table B-2 lists the partially supported T-SQL statements that you can use in Windows Azure SQL Database. "Partially supported" means you can use these statements, but with some variations (or limitations) to the syntax. Examples are provided following the table.

Table B-2. *Partially Supported T-SQL Statements*

ALTER AUTHORIZATION	CREATE SPATIAL INDEX	DROP TRIGGER
ALTER DATABASE	CREATE SYNONYM	DISABLE TRIGGER
ALTER FUNCTION	CREATE TABLE	ENABLE TRIGGER
ALTER INDEX	CREATE TRIGGER	EXECUTE
ALTER LOGIN	CREATE TYPE	EXECUTE AS
ALTER PROCEDURE	CREATE USER	EXECUTE AS *Clause*
ALTER TABLE	CREATE VIEW	GRANT *Database Permissions*
ALTER TRIGGER	DENY *Database Permissions*	GRANT *Database Principal Permission*
ALTER USER	DENY *Database Principal Permission*	GRANT *Type Permissions*
ALTER VIEW	DENY *Type Permissions*	INSERT
CREATE DATABASE	DISABLE TRIGGER	REVOKE *Database Permissions*
CREATE FUNCTION	DROP DATABASE	REVOKE *Database Principal Permission*
CREATE INDEX	DROP INDEX	REVOKE *Type Permissions*
CREATE LOGIN	DROP TABLE	USE
CREATE PROCEDURE		

For example, when you're creating or altering a stored procedure in Windows Azure SQL Database, the FOR REPLICATION and ENCRYPTION options aren't supported. Thus, the following isn't valid:

```
CREATE PROCEDURE GetUsers
WITH ENCRYPTION
FOR REPLICATION
AS
    SET NOCOUNT ON;
    SELECT Title, Name, Intro
    FROM Users
GO
```

However, the following is valid:

```
CREATE PROCEDURE GetUsers
WITH RECOMPILE, EXECUTE AS CALLER
AS
    SET NOCOUNT ON;
    SELECT Title, Name, Intro
    FROM Users
GO
```

The CREATE/ALTER table syntax for Windows Azure SQL Database is a bit trickier, because there are several unsupported options:

- ON *keyword* {*partition_schema* | *filegroup*} (such as ON PRIMARY)
- TEXTIMAGE_ON
- FILESTREAM_ON
- *<column_definition>*
  - FILESTREAM
  - NOT FOR REPLICATION
  - ROWGUIDCOL
  - SPARSE
- *<data_type>*
  - CONTENT
  - DOCUMENT
  - xml_schema_collection
- *<column_constraint>*
  - FILLFACTOR
  - ON
  - NOT FOR REPLICATION
- *<column_set_definition>*
- *<table_constraint>*
  - FILLFACTOR
  - ON
  - NOT FOR REPLICATION
- *<index_option>*
  - PAD_INDEX
  - FILLFACTOR
  - ON PARTITIONS
  - DATA_COMPRESSION
  - ALLOW_ROW_LOCKS
  - ALLOW_PAGE_LOCKS
- *<table_option>*

Although this list may give the impression that much functionality is missing, keep in mind that most of the items in the list are there because they're related to operating system or hardware, and they don't apply in the Windows Azure SQL Database environment. As an example, the following CREATE TABLE statement is invalid:

```
CREATE TABLE [dbo].[Users](
        [ID] [int] IDENTITY(1,1) NOT FOR REPLICATION NOT NULL,
    [Name] [nvarchar](50) NULL,
    [NTUserName] [nvarchar](128) NULL,
    [Domain] [nvarchar](50) NOT NULL,
    [Intro] [nvarchar](100) NULL,
    [Title] [nvarchar](50) NOT NULL,
    [State] [nvarchar](10) NOT NULL,
    [Country] [nvarchar](100) NULL,
    [PWD] [varbinary](100) NULL,
    [rowguid] [uniqueidentifier] NULL,
PRIMARY KEY CLUSTERED
(
        [ID] ASC
)WITH (PAD_INDEX  = OFF, STATISTICS_NORECOMPUTE  = OFF,
IGNORE_DUP_KEY = OFF, ALLOW_ROW_LOCKS  = ON, ALLOW_PAGE_LOCKS  = ON)
ON [PRIMARY]
) ON [PRIMARY]
```

This syntax is invalid for several reasons. The NOT FOR REPLICATION clause on the IDENTITY column isn't supported. Nor are the two ON PRIMARY clauses, the ALLOW_ROW_LOCKS clause, or the ALLOW_PAGE_LOCKS clause. For example, the ON PRIMARY clause specifies which filegroup the table and the index for the primary key are placed on. Since it is not possible to create filegroups in Windows Azure SQL Database due to no drive system access, it makes no sense to support this statement.

However, the following syntax *is* valid:

```
CREATE TABLE [dbo].[Users](
    [ID] [int] IDENTITY(1,1) NOT NULL,
    [Name] [nvarchar](50) NULL,
    [NTUserName] [nvarchar](128) NULL,
    [Domain] [nvarchar](50) NOT NULL,
    [Intro] [nvarchar](100) NULL,
    [Title] [nvarchar](50) NOT NULL,
    [State] [nvarchar](10) NOT NULL,
    [Country] [nvarchar](100) NULL,
    [PWD] [varbinary](100) NULL,
    [rowguid] [uniqueidentifier] NULL,
PRIMARY KEY CLUSTERED
(
    [ID] ASC
)WITH (STATISTICS_NORECOMPUTE  = OFF, IGNORE_DUP_KEY = OFF))
```

For detailed information about exactly what is supported and what isn't, visit http://msdn.microsoft.com/en-us/library/ee336267.aspx.

Unsupported T-SQL Statements

The list of unsupported T-SQL statements is long, but that isn't as negative a thing as it may appear. In most cases, unsupported statements are operating-system or hardware-related, and they don't apply in the Windows Azure SQL Database environment.

Because there are so many unsupported statements, this appendix doesn't list them all. You can find a complete list at http://msdn.microsoft.com/en-us/library/ee336253.aspx. Table B-3 provides a shorter list, highlighting some unsupported statements that you should particularly be aware of.

Table B-3. *Unsupported T-SQL Statements*

BACKUP CERTIFICATE	DBCC CHECKTABLE
BACKUP MASTER KEY	DBCC DBREINDEX
BACKUP SERVICE MASTER KEY	DBCC DROPCLEANBUFFERS
CHECKPOINT	DBCC FREEPROCCACHE
CONTAINS	DBCC HELP
CREATE/DROP AGGREGATE	DBCC PROCCACHE
CREATE/DROP RULE	DBCC SHOWCONTIG
CREATE/DROP XML INDEX	DBCC SQLPERF
CREATE/DROP/ALTER APPLICATION ROLE	DBCC USEROPTIONS
CREATE/DROP/ALTER ASSEMBLY	KILL
CREATE/DROP/ALTER CERTIFICATE	NEWSEQUENTIALID
CREATE/DROP/ALTER DEFAULT	OPENQUERY
CREATE/DROP/ALTER FULLTEXT (CATALOG, INDEX, STOPLIST)	OPENXML
CREATE/DROP/ALTER PARTITION FUNCTION	RECONFIGURE
CREATE/DROP/ALTER QUEUE	RESTORE
CREATE/DROP/ALTER RESOURCE POOL	SELECT INTO *Clause*
CREATE/DROP/ALTER SERVICE	SET ANSI_DEFAULTS
CREATE/DROP/ALTER XML SCHEMA COLLECTION	SET ANSI_NULLS
DBCC CHECKALLOC	SET ANSI_PADDING_OFF
DBCC CHECKDB	SET OFFSETS
DBCC CHECKIDENT	WITH XML NAMESPACES

Supported Data Types

If you've been following Windows Azure SQL Database since its initial release to the public, you realize that Microsoft has come a long way in supporting much of the functionality and many of the data types found in your local, on-premises instance of SQL Server. Table B-4 lists those data types currently supported in Windows Azure SQL Database as of Service Update 4.

Table B-4. *Windows Azure SQL Database Supported Data Types*

Numeric	Date and Time	Character String	Unicode Character String	Binary String	Spatial	Other
bigint	date	char	nchar	binary	geography	cursor
bit	datetime2	varchar	nvarchar	varbinary	geometry	hierarchyid
decimal	datetime	text	ntext	image		sql_variant
int	datetimeoffset					table
money	smalldatetime					timestamp
numeric	time					uniqueidentifier
smallint						xml
smallmoney						
tinyint						
float						
real						

For a complete list of supported methods for the geography, geometry, hierarchyid, and xml data types, go to http://msdn.microsoft.com/en-us/library/ee336233.aspx.

Index

A

Advanced encryption standard (AES), 49
ASP.NET
    deployment in Windows Azure
        dialog box, 180
        management interface, 180
        package fields, 179
        steps, 179
        web application, 181
    roles, 171
AUTHN process, 59

B

Backup strategies, SQL Azure, 67, 95
    automation, copy, 97
    blue syntax, 97
    cloud services, 98
    copy, complete, 96
    database copy, 95
    DMV, 96
    Enzo backup, 97
    maintain history, 97
    status, copy, 96
    third party products, 97
    using export import, 97
Business Intelligence Development
            Studio (BIDS), 130

C

Community Technology Preview, 143

D

Data access layer (DAL), 30
Data management view (DMV), 96

Data migration, 67
    bcp utility, 92
        bcp import, 94
        data export, 93
        import data, 94
        invoking, 92
        output, bcp export, 93
        uniqueidentifier, 94
    database and data to SQL Azure, 67
        bacpac, 68
        DAC deployment, 70
        DAC Fx, 68
        data-tier application framework, 68
        deploy to SQL Azure, 69
            BACPAC import operation, 78
            DAC execution results, 71
            DAC export, 72
            DAC import, 75
            export and import, 72
            menu, DAC import, 75
            results, DAC export, 74
            settings, DAC export, 73
            settings, DAC import, 76
            specifying database instance, 77
        SQL Azure via BACPAC, 68
    import/export service, 68, 79
        AWMini BACPAC, 79
        BLOB storage, 79
        buttons in WAMP, 80
        cloud storage, 81
        completed database dialog, 82
        dialog, export, 83
        export, 82
        import, 79
    script wizards, 83
        additional errors, 89
        advanced options, 87
        against Azure database, 91

Data migration (*cont.*)
    DB engine type property, 84
    initiating, 84
    objects to migrate, 85
    options, 86
    reviewing, 88
    script fixing, 89
    settings, 86
    settings change, 90
    SQL script, 90
    SSMS, 84
    target objects, 84
    T-SQL, 88
Data Sync
  configuring
    add hub, 151
    apply filter, 157
    bi-directional, 152
    client install, 153
    client wins, 157
    completed group, 158
    conflict resolution, 157
    creation, 149
    database, 149
    data validation, 162
    debug and log, 160
    deploying group, 159
    dialog lists, 153
    direction from hub, 152
    table_dss_tracking, 160
    edit and resynchronize, 162
    error message, 160
    group template, 155
    to the hub, 152
    hub and member database, 150–156
    hub wins, 157
    information display, 161
    installation, client, 153
    management portal, 154
    navigation pane, 148
    on-premise database, 152
    provisioning, 148
    provision_marker, 160
    query, 162
    registering on server, 154
    resolution policies, 157
    row filtering, 157
    schema_info, 160
    scope_config, 160
    scope_info, 160
    selected tables, database, 159
    selecting on-premises, 155
    selecting, tables and columns, 156
    setting schedule, 158
    SQL data sync server, 147–149

    sync client, 154
    sync directions, 151
    sync group, 149–150
    tables to be synchronized, 156
    template, 150
    testing conflicts, 162
    triggers, 160
    validate, 161
  limitations, 163
  practices
    designs, 163
    initial synchronization, 164
    schedule, 164
    security, 164
  understanding SQL
    architecture, 145–147
    categories, 145
    cloud based application, 145
    common requirements, 145
    components, 146
    database synchronization, 144
    data sync architecture, 146
    foreign keys, 145
    hub and member, 144
    initial process, 144
    needs of, 143–144
    schema synchronization, 144
    server replication, 144
    Windows Azure Blob storage, 146
Design considerations, 23
  added features, 41
    Blob data stores, 42
    data encryption, 43
    Edge data caching, 42
    federations, 43
    SaaS applications, 43
    shared edge data, 42
  combining patterns, 37
    cascading, 38
    transparent and RWS, 37
  factors, 23
    application design, 26
    availability, 23
    caching performance, 28
    connection, direct *vs.* serviced, 27
    database instance, 24
    data connections, 27
    data privacy, 29
    encryption, 29
    fault handling application, 26
    instance cost, 28
    limitations, 29
    offsite storage, 23
    performance, 24
    pricing, 28

resource throttling, 28
retrieve data, 27
security, 29
SQL DB topology, 24
synchronizing data, 27
terminating database, 25
throttling performance, 24–26
transient errors, 25
patterns, 29
access techniques, shard, 33
aggregate, 36
data access layer, 30
direct connection, 29
methods and concepts, shard, 32
mirroring, 37
offload, 35
read-only shards, 34
read-write shards, 35
SaaS application, 30
shard, 31
smart branching, 30
transparent branching, 31
SLA monitoring, 39
Azure implementation, 40
implementing Azure, 41
onsite implementation, 40
Pre-Azure architecture, 39
Desktop as a service (DaaS), 2

E

Elastic Compute Cloud (EC2) services, 2

F, G

Federation
components, 208
atomic unit, 209
define, 209
key, 209
member, 209
reference table, 209
root, 209
considerations, 216
limitations, 216–217
shard library, 217–218
creation, split operation, 211
introduction, 207
management, 214
database instance, 215
details, 215
drop, 215
properties, 215
SQL DB portal, 214
view, members, 216

problems, 208
vs. sharding
compressed, 208
linear, 208
scale up, 207
scaling models, 207
usage
database instance, 208
limitation, 208
members, 208
root database, 208
First federation, 210
ALTER FEDERATION, 212
CREATE FEDERATION, 210
database, 210
FILTERING, 213
foreign key, 211
increasing, 213
members, 211–212
and members, 213
multiples, 214
stored procedure, 211
update record, 212
USE FEDERATION, 210

H

Hardware as a service (HaaS), 2
Health Insurance Portability and Accountability
Act (HIPAA), 66

I, J, K, L

Infrastructure as a service (IaaS), 2

M, N, O

Microsoft Systems Architecture (MSA), 2
Migrating databases, 67
data-tier application framework, 68
deploy to SQL Azure via
a BACPAC, 68
BACPAC import operation, 78
DAC deployment, 70
DAC execution, 71
DAC export, 72
DAC import, 75
database instance, 77
database to Azure menu options, 69
directly to SQL Azure, 69
export and import, 72
menu, DAC import, 75
results, DAC export, 74
settings, DAC export, 73
settings, DAC import, 76
import/export service, 68

■ P, Q

Performance designing
  general concept
    asynchronous UI, 184
    caching, 184
    chatty *vs.* chunky, 183
    coding strategies, 185–186
    data access layer, 183
    in disk, caching, 184
    horizontal partition shard, 185
    lazy loading, 183–184
    OnPassCompleted, 185
    parallel processing, 185
    read-write shard, 185
    shards, 185
    task parallel library, 185
    UI thread, 184
  hadoop for Windows Azure, 206
  managing shard, 198
    data access, 200
    database, table, 201
    data duplication, 203
    document field, 202
    exceptions, 198–199
    foreign key constraints, 203
    identity values, 203
    performance, 199
    processing time, 200
    referential integrity, 204
    table, database, 201
    transaction consistency, 203
    varbinary column, 200
    working with partial, 202
  multitenant system
    access control, 204
    database transfer, 205
    data isolation, 204
    schema-based architecture, 205
    schema security, 204
  shard, 186
    adding records, 196
    application design, 187
    caching, 193
    ConfigurationStrings, 189
    custom connection, 189
    DB connection management, 188
    deleting, virtually, 195
    ExecuteParallelRounRobinLoad, 197
    ExecuteShardQuery, 190
    ExecuteSingleQuery, 190
    extra parameter, 194
    GetHashCode method, 188
    GUID, 192
    library object, 187
    logic, caching, 193
    new connection to DB, 189
    reading applications, 190
    reading from, 191
    retrieved objects, 191
    returned records, 192
    round robin logic, 197–198
    sample application, 192, 196
    SQLCommand class, 187
    SQL server, 188
    technology to build, 187
    time-to-live, 194
    updata and delete records, 194
    view connections, 190
  Vertical Partition Shards, 206
Performance tuning
  with SQL database, 219
    implications, code, 220
    methods, 219
    tools, 219
    typical tuning, 219
  techniques, 220, 226
    adding index, 233
    application code, 236
    application performance, 239
    balanced plan, 235
    chatty design, 239
    clustered views, 236
    connection pooling, 223
    connection release, 240
    cost calculation, 237
    covering index, 232
    design, application, 239
    disable, SSMS, 227
    dynamic management views, 220
    Enzo SQL baseline, 239
    execution counts, 234
    execution, SSMS, 224
    indexed views, 235
    indexing, 227, 231
    index operators, 226
    INNER JOIN operator, 226
    JOIN operators, 224
    loop operation, 234
    management portal, execution, 228
    metrics for SQL statement, 221
    normalization, 239
    operation details, 229
    performance metrics, 222, 238
    physical operator, index, 233
    physical operators, 224
    potentials, 226
    query performance, 230
    record counts, 226
    session ID, 222

sorting execution, 230
SQL DB account, 240
SQL script, 225
statistics, 238
stored procedures, 236
sys.dm_exec_query_stats, 231
sys.dm_exec_sessions, 223
TCP programming, 223
TestUSers, 232
view, management portal, 228
Platform as a service (PaaS), 2
Project creation, Azure
    environment configuring, 168
    Visual Studio cloud, 169
        in 2008, 170
        in 2010, 171
        changed role name, 172
        editing roles, 172
        elevated mode, 169
        error message, 170
        project layout, 173
        roles, 171
        Silverlight business application, 172
        steps, 169

■ R

Representational state transfer (REST) call, 6
Research as a service (Raas), 2

■ S

Security, 45
    access control, 59
        authentication, 59
        AUTHN, SQL, 59
        authorization, 60
        AUTHZ model, 60
        compliance, 65
        container, schema, 64
        database connection, 61
        database roles, 60
        error object, 62
        HIPAA, 66
        internal firewall, 65
        Kerberos authentication, 59
        login and user creation, 60
        login, schema, 63
        MyTestLogin account, 60
        new schema owner, 62
        object's schema, 61
        schemas, 61–64
        security model, 64
        security, schema model, 64
        separation, schema, 64

SQL database firewall, 65
        SSPI, 59
        TCP 1433 out, 65
    certificates, 55
        BlueSyntaxTest, 56
        CipherText, 57
        common name, 56
        creation commands, 55
        line creation, 55
        private key, 55
        public key, 55
        RSA algorithm, 57
        thumbprint property, 57
        unique identifier, 56
        viewing, 56
        X 509, 55
    CIA triad, 45
    data, 48
        AES algorithm, 49
        byte array, 49
        CipherText, 50
        connection string, 48
        cryptographic methods, 50
        3DES, 49
        encryption, 48–50
        object model, 48
        secret key, 50
        SSL encryption, 48
        T-SQL statement, 49
    framework, 45
        availability, 46
        confidentiality, 45
        database architecture, 47
        data integrity, 46
        requirements, availability, 47
        TDE, 45
    hashing, 50
        access-control, 53
        algorithms, 54
        byte array, 51
        database, 51, 53
        data types, 51
        extension methods, 51
        HASHBYTES, 54
        MD5, 54
        N converter, 55
        parameter, 52
        records, 54
        Save() method, 54
        SHA-1, 54
        UserProperties, 51
        utility class, 51
        variable, 54
    Security.sql, 48
Security support provider interface (SSPI), 59

Software as a service (SaaS), 2, 30
SQL Azure Data Sync Services, 143
SQL Database, 1
    cloud computing, 1
        deployment, 1
        desktop as a service (DaaS), 2
        elastic compute cloud (EC2) services, 2
        failover, 1
        hardware as a service (HaaS), 2
        infrastructure as a service (IaaS), 2
        Microsoft system architecture, 2
        platform as a service (PaaS), 2
        research as a service (RaaS), 2
        resource usage, 1
        scalability, 1
        software as a service (SaaS), 2
        switching, 1
        typical services, 2
        Windows data center edition, 2
    limitations, 19
        backup/restore operation, 20
        backups, 20
        clone operation, 20
        CLR, 21
        drivers and protocols, 22
        heap tables, 21
        log files, 20
        miscellaneous, 21
        objects, 21
        procedures, 21
        restore, 21
        security, 20
        system functions, 21
        tables and views, 21
    Microsoft Azure platform, 3
        access for storage, 5
        affinity group, 5
        bulletin board systems (BBBs), 3
        business scenarios, 4
        cloud services, 3
        corporate environment services, 3
        data storage options, 6
        decoupling, 3
        geographic locations, 4
        geolocation, 4
        need of, 3
        REST call, 6
        SQL database, 3
        storing data, 5
        tabular data stream, 5
        types of storage, 6
        Windows Azure, 3
        Windows Azure geolocation, 4

    primer, 6, 15
        access rights, 18
        Azure plan, 7
        bandwidth consumption, 19
        billing for database, 18
        connecting with SSMS, 11–15
        connect to field, database, 14
        database instances, WAMP, 8
        error in firewall, 10
        firewall configure, 10
        instance creation, 7, 9
        logging to a server, 13
        login and user creation, 15
        login error, 16
        master database, viewing, 16
        new login, 15
        new user, 17
        obtain server name, 12
        output, statement, 18
        password error, 17
        register for Azure, 6
        server, 10
        settings, firewall, 10
        T-SQL command, 9
        user error, 17
    security
        connection constraints, 20
        disallowed user names, 20
        encryption, 20
        login name, 20
        SSPI authentication, 20
        TCP port 1433, 20
SQL Database Management Portal (SDMP)
    administration
        actual execution plan, 261
        monitoring performance, 262
        performance report, 263
        query window and results area, 260
        switching, results view, 260
        T-SQl statements, 259
        T-SQl *vs.* database, 262
        view execution, 261
        zoom, execution plan, 262
    design, 266
        column edit, 269
        create, stored procedure, 271
        creating a view, 270
        data table, view, 269
        dependencies graph, 265
        error message, 272
        foreign key creation, 268
        index creation, 267
        list, database instance, 264

page, tables, 266
    procedure execution, 272
    source and reference selection, 268
    stored procedures, 271
    tables, 263
    v_Documents, 264
    views, 270
  launch, 257
    admin summary, 259
    database dashboard, 257
    login screen, 258
    in Windows Azure portal, 258
SQL Database programming
  application deployment, 99–100
    azure-hosted, 100–101
    choosing, 101
    client libraries, 100
    on-premises, 100
    solution, Azure-hosted, 100
    windows communication foundation, 100
  connecting to DB, 101
    ADO.NET, 102
    Azure platform, 101–102
    clustered index, 106–107
    code replacement, 106
    command syntax, 110
    command, table creation, 112
    connection strings, 103
    data reader, 105
    dataset, 106
    executing SELECT command, 111
    GetConString method, 104, 107
    insert rows, sqlcmd, 113
    making ADO.NET connection, 103
    naming instance, 104
    new table, SSMS, 112
    ODBC, 107
    query result, sqlcmd, 111
    results, SSMS, 113
    shard, 102
    sharding, 102
    sqlcmd, 109
    SQLDataReader class, 105
    SQL Server Agent job, 109
    SSMS, 112
    task parallel library (TPL), 102
    through sqlcmd, 110
    WAMP, 104
  ODBC
    connection, 107
    connection string, 108
    form with data, 109
  practices, 119
    connection string, 120
    database instance, 120

    multiple active results sets, 120
    transient fault handling, 120–121
  transient fault handling
    adding blocks, 121
    ExecuteReaderWithRetry method, 123
    ReliableSqlConnection, 122
    retry policy constructors, 122
    SOA architecture, 123
    TFHAB, package manager, 121
    using TFHAB, 121
  WCF services
    Azure cloud services, 117
    client application, 117
    connecting model, 115
    creating data services, 114
    data model wizard, 114
    data services to solution, 115
    InitializeService method, 116
    projects in explorer, 119
    service references, 118
    solution explorer, 116
    WCFDataServiceWebApp, 118
    web application, 116
    web role project, 118
SQL reports
  architecture
    Azure services, 125–126
    gateways, 126
    nodes, 126
  cloud based, 142
  creation
    adding a report, 131
    adding data source, 131
    completed data source, 134
    connection properties, 133
    dataset, 135
    data source creation, 131
    design, 136
    design view, 136
    options, data source, 134
    practices and query, 134–135
    preview view, 137
    properties, data source, 132
    server project, 130
    SSDT, 130
  CTP, 125
  deployment, 137
    management portal, 138
    processes, 137
    solution property, 138
  instances, 125
  management portal
    execution log, 142
    ribbon, 141
    server tools, 141

SQL reports (*cont.*)
    pricing, 142
    provisioning, 128
        management portal, 129
        server dialog, 129
        Silverlight portal, 128
        Windows Azure portal, 128
    security
        Azure database, 139
        embed, 139
        managing users, 140
        roles, 139
        user creation, 140–141
    services and feature, 127
    SSRS, 125
    supports, 127
SQL Server Data Tools (SSDT), 130
SQL Server Management Studio (SSMS), 11, 249
SQL server reporting services, 125
Sync group, 149

T, U

Tabular Data Stream (TDS) protocol, 5
Transparent data encryption [TDE], 45
Triple data encryption standard (3DES), 49

V

Virtual machine (VM), 165

W, X, Y, Z

Windows Azure
    cloud services, 165
        affinity group, 167
        creation steps, 165
        final file, 168
        new service creation, 167
        system view, 166
        unique name, 166
        URL, 167
    project creation
        configuration, 176
        configure and deploy, 176–179
        connection string nodes, 174
        data source property, 174
        deployment model, 177
        environment configuring, 168
        GridView to SQL DB, 173
        local database, 178
        run and fetch data, 175
        scenario deployment, database, 178
        ServiceConfiguration.cscfg, 177
        settings, deploy and configure, 176
        Visual Studio, 169
SQL database, 275
    data types, 280–281
    invalid statement, 279
    NOT FOR REPLICATION, 279
    partial T-SQL support, 276
    statements, T-SQL, 275
    table syntax, 278
    T-SQL support, full, 275–279
    unsupported T-SQL statements, 280
    validity of statement, 277
Windows Azure Management Portal (WAMP), 8
Windows Azure Mobile Services (WAMS), 241
    authentication, 253
    data, 248
        browse, 248
        columns, 249
        CRUD (create, read, update and delete), 248
        execute, 248
        permissions, 249
        script, 251
    identity provider, 252
    initialization, 241, 243
        C# project directory, 246
        database instance, 244
        developing application, 245
        on navigation pane, 242
        REST services, 244
        services in portal, 244
        solution, 247
        support table, 246
        .xaml file, 247
OData services, 241
push notification, 251
reserved mode, 254
scale, 253
services tabs, 251
settings, 251

CPSIA information can be obtained at www.ICGtesting.com
Printed in the USA
LVOW020332131212

311438LV00023B/390/P